ELIZABETHAN ROGUES AND VAGABONDS

PLATE I

Harman's rogue, Nicholas Blunt *alias* Nicholas Gennings, as Upright Man and Counterfeit Crank (see p. 34).

(*From the Groundworke of Conny-catching*, 1592)

ELIZABETHAN ROGUES AND VAGABONDS

FRANK AYDELOTTE

LONDON AND NEW YORK

First published 1913 by
FRANK CASS AND COMPANY LIMITED

Published 2014 by Routledge
2 Park Square, Milton Park, Abingdon, Oxfordshire, OX14 4RN

711 Third Avenue, New York, NY 10017

First issued in paperback 2014

Routledge is an imprint of the Taylor & Francis Group, an informa business

Transferred to Digital Printing 2006

ISBN 978-0-714-61099-3 (hbk)
ISBN 978-1-138-01083-3 (pbk)

COVER DESIGN
BY DEREK WARD

Publisher's Note

The publisher has gone to great lengths to ensure the quality of this reprint but points out that some imperfections in the original may be apparent

PREFACE

So far as I know this is the first book to treat Elizabethan rogues and vagabonds from the point of view here taken, piecing together historical and literary material so as to make as complete a picture as possible of their life. They have received attention from writers on social history and on the poor laws; Professor F. W. Chandler has published a compendious account of the literature of the subject from the sixteenth century to the present, with preliminary sections devoted to Spanish, French, German, and Dutch works, but leaving untouched the historical aspect; and C. J. Ribton-Turner published in 1887 a *History of Vagrants and Vagrancy* covering all periods from the earliest times down to the present which touches the material I am using, but gives, as his scheme demanded, a very limited space to each period. One side of rogue lifc, their canting speech, already so fully treated by Henley and Farmer, has not been attempted in this book. For the rest I cannot pretend to have exhausted the material, either literary or historical, which relates to these rogues and vagabonds, but only hope to have made a little clearer the outlines of the life of this class which played no small part in the national affairs of Elizabethan England and fills no small place in its literature.

My thanks are due to the Librarian and Fellows of Magdalene College, Cambridge, to the authorities of the British Museum and the Public Record Office, and to Mr. F. Madan, Librarian of the Bodleian, for permission to reproduce various illustrations. My obligations to books are, so far as possible, indicated in the notes. I owe a debt of gratitude that cannot be so acknowledged to Sir Walter Raleigh and Professor C. H. Firth, of the University of Oxford, for help and advice at every stage of the work. To a large number of English scholars, among whom it is a pleasure to pay grateful tribute to the memory of Dr. Furnivall, my acknowledgements are also due for that generous help which makes England one great university for the student who is pursuing any historical or literary investigation. It is the presence in England of so large a body of scholars interested in research, and the ready hospitality with which they receive and assist any one who comes to them armed with the passport of similar interests which, added to the great resources of Oxford University, makes the Rhodes Scholarship such an unusual opportunity for the graduate student. To the memory of Cecil John Rhodes and to the men who so generously administer his bequest this book is gratefully dedicated.

BRASENOSE COLLEGE, OXFORD.
January, 1913.

CONTENTS

PAGE

INTRODUCTION 1

CHAPTER I

ORIGINS.

Size of the vagabond class 3
Enclosures and sheep-farming 5
The change from the mediaeval to the modern system of land tenure 7
The sixteenth-century literature of economic protest . . . 10
The breaking up of the bands of feudal retainers 14
The dissolution of the monasteries 15
The question of gipsy origin 17

CHAPTER II

THE ART OF BEGGING.

Traditional methods 21
Prevalence of indiscriminate charity 22
Licences to beg 23
Harman's twenty-four orders of vagabonds 27
Rufflers and upright men 28
Hookers or anglers 30
Rogues 31
Counterfeit cranks 33
Dommerers, palliards, and Abraham men 35
Priggers of prancers 39
Counterfeiters of licences 40
Pedlars and tinkers 42
Minstrels 43
Jugglers 49
Movers of sedition and spreaders of false rumours 52
Popish spies 54

CHAPTER III

LAWS AGAINST VAGABONDS.

PAGE

Summary of legislative tendencies 56
1530–47: Legislation 58
1530–47: Enforcement of the laws 59
1547–72: Legislation 62
1547–72: Enforcement of the laws 63
1572–97: Legislation 68
1572–97: Enforcement of the laws 69
The poor laws of 1597 and 1601 72
Conditions at the end of the century 73

CHAPTER IV

THE ART OF CONNY-CATCHING.

The trustworthiness of the conny-catching pamphlets . . . 76
The tribe of gulls 78
The haunts of the conny-catchers 79
The conny-catcher's busy season 84
The conny-catching 'laws' 85
Conny-catching proper 86
Cheating law 89
Vincent's law 94
The nips and foists 94
Crossbiting law 97
Petty thieves and brokers 97
High law 98
The spirit of Elizabethan roguery 101

CHAPTER V

LAWS AGAINST CONNY-CATCHING.

Royal protection of 'unlawful games' 103
The patents of Thomas Cornwallis 105
Efforts to restrain the manufacture and sale of false dice . . 107
Patents for playing-cards 107
Laws against pickpockets 109
Cozening *versus* stealing in law 111

CHAPTER VI

THE ROGUE PAMPHLETS. PAGE

Influence of foreign rogue literature 114
Early trustworthy English rogue pamphlets 119
The *Manifest Detection* 120
Harman's *Caueat* 122
Greene's Conny-catching pamphlets 123
The fashion of exposing rogue life 126
The *Groundworke of Conny-catching* 127
The *Defence of Conny-catching* 128
Mihil Mumchance 129
Dekker's rogue pamphlets 129
Greenes Ghost and *Martin Mark-all* 133
Rid's *Art of Iugling* 136
Roguish lore in other books 136
The literary value of the rogue pamphlets 137

APPENDIX

A. DOCUMENTS

1. London orders of 1517 for restraining vagabonds and beggars (*Journal*, xi. 337) 140
2. Proclamation of Henry VIII against rogues and vagabonds, June 1530 (Bod. press-mark, Arch. F.C. 10, 2) 142
3. John Bayker's letter to Henry VIII accounting for the multitude of vagabonds in the realm (*S.P. Henry VIII*, 141 : 134–5) 145
4. Proclamation of Henry VIII against the stews, April 13, 1546 (*S.A. Proclamations*, ii. 164) 148
5. Rogues in Harman's list whose names are found in official records, 1571–89 150
6. Letter from the Privy Council to the London Aldermen ordering searches for vagabonds, June 20, 1569 (*Journal*, xix. 171b ff.) 152
7. Articles agreed upon by justices in Devon for suppressing rogues and vagabonds, November 5, 1569 (Bod. MS. Rawl. B. 285, 11 verso—12) 155
8. Letter from the Privy Council to Shrewsbury ordering watches and searches for rogues and masterless men, July 30, 1571 (Shrewsbury Corporation Muniments, Petitions to the Bailiffs, No. 2,621) 156

9. Characteristic certificates of the punishment of vagabonds: PAGE

A. Ewellme, Oxon., August 25, 1571 (*D.S.P.* Eliz., lxxx. 45) . 158

B. Eccleshall, Stafford, August and September, 1571 (*D.S.P.* Eliz., lxxxi. 25, 1) 159

C. Several hundreds in Cambridgeshire, August and September, 1571 (*D.S.P.* Eliz., lxxxiii. 36, v) 161

10. Table of searches, 1571–2 162

11. Order for search for false dice in London, 1598 (*Repertory* 24, fo. 349 ff.) 162

12. Letter about corrupt brokers in London, December 1, 1601 (*Remembrancia*, ii. 213) 164

13. A licence to keep a gaming-house in the time of James I (Petty Bag, Cert. Var., Bundle i) 165

14. Hext's letter, 1596 (British Museum, MS. Lansdowne, 81, Nos. 62 and 64) 167

B. PLAGIARISM IN ELIZABETHAN PAMPHLETS

Manifest Detection, sig. B_8 verso—C_1 verso 175

Mihil Mumchance, sig. B_4 verso, ff. 175

Dekker, *Belman of London*, 1608, sig. E_3 verso 176

Rid, *Art of Iugling*, 1612, sig. C_4 177

INDEX 179

LIST OF ILLUSTRATIONS

PAGE

Plate I. Nicolas Gennings, alias Blunt, as Upright Man and Counterfeit Crank. This cut appeared originally in Harman's *Caueat*, 1566, but is here reproduced from the Bodleian edition of *The Groundworke of Conny-catching*, 1592 . . . *Frontispiece*

Plate II. A printed proctor's licence. From the British Museum, press mark, C. 41. h. 1: it is dated in the B. M. catalogue 1560 . . . . *Face* 25

Plate III. A forged passport with which a vagabond travelled the length of England in 1596, until he was finally apprehended and his deceit exposed by Justice Hext in Somerset. From MS. Lansdowne 81, No. 64, in the British Museum. See Appendix A, 14, pp. 171 and 173–4, for Hext's account and a transcription of the passport . . . . *Between pp.* 40 *and* 41

Plate IV. Two of Rembrandt's beggars, etched 1630. (See note to Fig. 1.) From the British Museum collection, Case I (M. 37, I) *Face* 55

Plate V. Dr. Simon Forman's cure for a brain-sick gallant. From a print by Martin Droeshout, British Museum collection, 1612, No. 82 . . . . *Face* 79

Plate VI. Callot's 'Le Brelan, ou l'Enfant prodigue trompé par une troupe de filous'—a conny-catching trick. Etched at Nancy, 1627. (See note to Fig. 1.) From the British Museum collection, v. 32 (Meaume, p. 321, No. 666) . . . . *Face* 89

Fig. 1. One of Callot's beggars corresponding to Harman's Upright Man. According to Meaume the series from which this illustration and Fig. 4 are reproduced were etched at Nancy in 1622. From the British Museum collection, v. 44 (Meaume, p. 329, No. 685). The excuse for using these etchings from Callot and the one from Rembrandt (Plate IV) is that, while not English, they illustrate contemporary and very similar rogue life with so much more art and truth than any English pictures of the time that they contribute materially to our idea of what English rogues were like 29

Fig. 2. Harman's Counterfeit Crank, Nicolas Gennings, in the pillory. From the Bodleian edition of Harman's *Caueat*, 1567 . 35

Fig. 3. An Abraham Man or Tom o' Bedlam. From the *Roxburghe Ballads* in the British Museum, i. 352. (Early 17th century) . . 36

PAGE

Fig. 4. One of Callot's beggars corresponding to Harman's Palliard or Clapperdudgeon. (See note to Fig. 1.) From the British Museum collection, v. 45 (Meaume, p. 332, No. 697) 37

Fig. 5. A pedlar. From a ballad in the Pepysian collection, Magdalene College, Cambridge, iv. 298. (This woodcut and the two following are late 17th century.) 43

Fig. 6. A minstrel. From the *Roxburghe Ballads* in the British Museum, i. 349 44

Fig. 7. A minstrel in the stocks. From the *Roxburghe Ballads* in the British Museum, i. 263. (The couplet, by Dr. John Bull, is quoted by Ritson, *Ancient Songs and Ballads*, ed. Hazlitt, 1871, xiv, note.) 45

Fig. 8. A juggler's trick. From Reginald Scot's *Discouerie of Witchcraft*, 1584, in the British Museum, p. 353 51

Fig. 9. Two pretended fortune-tellers in the pillory. From the title-page of Robert Burton's copy of *The seuerall Notorious and lewd Cousnages of Iohn West and Alice West*, 1613, in the Bodleian . 59

Fig. 10. Whipping vagabonds at the cart's tail. From the title-page of Harman's *Caueat*, 1567, in the Bodleian 65

Fig. 11. A hanging. From a ballad in the Pepysian collection, Magdalene College, Cambridge, ii. 153. (This woodcut and the following are early 17th century.) 71

Fig. 12. A tavern scene. From a ballad in the Pepysian collection, Magdalene College, Cambridge, ii. 89 80

Fig. 13. Conny-catching law. From the title-page of Greene's *Notable Discouery of Coosnage*, 1591, in the British Museum . 87

Fig. 14. The Black Art. From the title-page of Greene's *Second and Last Part of Conny-catching*, 1592, in the Bodleian . . . 98

Fig. 15. A man in the pillory with a paper over his head describing his offence. From a ballad in the Pepysian collection, Magdalene College, Cambridge, ii. 236. (Late 17th century.) The same cut occurs on one of the Bagford Ballads in the British Museum with the words on the paper altered to 'For a seditious libel' . . 112

INTRODUCTION

THE essay which follows has grown out of a study of a number of Elizabethan pamphlets dealing with rogues and vagabonds, the most important of which are the Conny-catching series of Robert Greene and the *Caueat for Commen Cursetors* of Thomas Harman. 'Conny-catching' was an Elizabethan slang word for a particular method of cheating at cards, but it came to be used in a general sense for all kinds of tricks by which rogues and sharpers beguiled simple people of their money. Greene passed a large part of his life among the worst company to be found in London. During the two years before his death, moved, as he professed, by repentance, he published the series of Conny-catching pamphlets, exposing the tricks of this wicked crew of sharpers in order that innocent folk might read and take warning. The books are vivid and well written, and they picture an elaborately organized profession of roguery with a language of its own and a large number of well-defined methods and traditions. There was a live *esprit de corps* among the thieves, and a pride in clever and dexterous work which made their profession more of an art than a trade. All this Greene explains in detail. The first question that any reader would ask himself after finishing these very entertaining descriptions of the art of Conny-catching is, How much foundation had they in fact?

Thomas Harman's *Caueat for Commen Cursetors*, which was published about twenty-five years before Greene's pamphlets, describes the habits and tricks of a class of rogues who were much lower in the social scale than Greene's Bohemian friends. These were the vagrants and masterless men who roamed from place to place like modern tramps and gipsies, begging and stealing by turns, and, in the absence of regulation, living a merry life. These vagabonds had little in common with the conny-catchers; they were dirty, lousy beggars who throve best in the country villages and towns, while the conny-catchers were shrewd, well-dressed sharpers who stuck pretty closely to London. Harman sets forth the life of these wandering beggars minutely. According to him their mystery was likewise well organized. There was a ceremony by which a man was 'stalled to the roge' at the end of his apprenticeship; there were various ranks or degrees; and the beggars also had a cant language, in some respects different from that of conny-catching, in some respects the same. Harman's *Caueat* is much more convincing on its face than the works of Greene. However, in this case as in the other, the reader immediately asks, What confirmation can be found in the history of the times? To describe this rogue life and to present the historical evidence concerning it is the first task which this essay undertakes.

The works of Greene and Harman do not stand alone. Among the pamphlets preserved from the reigns of Elizabeth and James I there are a large number dealing with rogues and vagabonds which follow the fashion of 'muck-raking' started by Greene's exposures. The demand for rogue pamphlets was supplied by hack-writers in the most unscrupulous ways, so that it speedily becomes necessary to separate the literature of the subject into different classes: that which was the result of real observation, that which was purely fictitious, and that which was calmly stolen. This last is by far the largest in amount. The ephemeral nature of pamphlet literature made cribbing easy and safe, and a study of these books throws much light on the methods of Elizabethan pamphleteers. To unravel this literary tangle, and in so doing to show how intimate the connexion often was between author and rogue is the second task attempted in the following pages.

CHAPTER I

ORIGINS

BEGGING and vagabondage in England did not begin in the sixteenth century. Doubtless there were rogues in every age, and there are records which indicate that in the fourteenth century especially they formed a numerous and ingenious class. M. Jusserand's *English Wayfaring Life* gives an excellent account of them and of the tricks by which they gained their dishonest living. Nevertheless there is abundant evidence that in the sixteenth century the numbers of rogues and vagabonds were larger in proportion to the population than they have ever been before or since, and the history of the times shows why this should be true. It will add meaning to our study of their customs to consider first the historical facts which explain the existence of the rogues themselves.

There are no figures that can be relied upon for the actual numbers of these vagabonds any more than for the population of London or of England in the sixteenth century. One finds mention of them everywhere in contemporary literature, in pamphlets, plays, poems, sermons, and books of travel. In all sorts of historical records likewise the vagabonds fill a large space. The Acts of the Privy Council mention them continually, the Domestic State Papers contain hundreds of documents concerning them, there are dozens of Royal Proclamations against them, and the archives of London and of many of the provincial towns contain a mass of material—ordinances, reports of punishments, and measures of relief—which offers striking witness to the numbers of vagrants all over England. Perhaps the most significant evidence of all is that contained in the Statutes of the Realm in the record of the long series of experiments and advances by which the

English Parliament finally worked out the remarkable poor law of Elizabeth.

There are several contemporary estimates of the number of vagabonds in different places at different times which may be given for what they are worth. In 1517 the Aldermen of the city of London made a list of deserving beggars, ward by ward throughout the city, for the purpose of providing tin badges allowing the wearers to ask alms in the streets. This census placed the total number in the city at 1,000.[1]

A second estimate concerns the year 1569. In this year the Privy Council inaugurated over the whole of England a system of 'privy watches and searches' for vagabonds. These searches were held irregularly for the next four years and occasionally throughout the remainder of Elizabeth's reign. The constables of each parish were required to apprehend and punish all vagabonds and masterless men, to send the vagrants the most direct way home 'or where they last dwelt for the space of two years', and to return to the Privy Council certificates containing the names of those so punished. In the British Museum is preserved a contemporary document which states that in the watches and searches of this year (1569) were apprehended 13,000 rogues and masterless men.[2]

There are plenty of figures in Harrison's *Description of England* published in 1577. 'It is not yet full three-score yeares since this trade began:' he says in one place, 'but how it hath prospered since that time, it is easie to iudge, for they are now supposed of one sex and another, to amount vnto aboue 10,000 persons; as I haue heard reported'. A little farther on he asserts that 'there is not one yeare commonlie, wherein three hundred or foure hundred of them are not deuoured and eaten vp by the gallowes in one place and other'.[3]

A fourth estimate, made by the Lord Mayor of London, Sir John Spenser, in 1594, places the number of begging poor in the city alone at 12,000.[4]

[1] See Appendix A, 1.

[2] Cotton MS. Titus B II, fo. 471. (Printed in Strype, *Annals*, vol. i, chap. lv.) For a fuller account of these searches and the returns see Chapter III below.

[3] Harrison, *Description of England* (N. Sh. Soc.), Bk. ii, pp. 218 and 231.

[4] *Remembrancia*, ii. 74. (Analytical Index, p. 357.)

It is useless to make arithmetical commentary on these figures. Possibly some credence may be given those for 1517, inasmuch as they seem to be the result of actual count. The others are, so far as one can see, mere guesses. Harrison's figures are just such historical gossip as his oft-quoted statement that 72,000 'great theeves, pettie theeves, and roges' were hanged in the reign of Henry VIII. This statement Harrison took from Cardan, the Italian physician and astrologer, who in 1552 predicted a long and happy life to Edward VI. Harrison does not get it quite right; Cardan says, as a matter of fact, that the 72,000 perished in the last two years of Henry VIII's reign. The Bishop of Lisieux told him so at Besançon. Where the Bishop got his information does not appear.[1] The other estimates are doubtless of much the same character; one thing, however, they do show: that in the eyes of contemporaries the vagrants were a large and important class.

The history of the economic changes in England from 1350 to 1550 contains clear and abundant explanation of the size of this vagabond class. Elizabethan rogues and beggars were a by-product of an economic progress, of the change from the mediaeval to the modern system of holding land and paying agricultural labour, which took place during the fourteenth and fifteenth centuries. The details of this change may best be understood by examining the social conditions of the first half of the sixteenth century, when the evils which produced vagabondage were most keenly felt. The majority of contemporary writers on economic questions attribute poverty and vagabondage to the hard times caused by enclosures and sheep-farming, with the consequent eviction of poor tenants who had practised tillage, and to the destruction of the great bands of retainers, which had been gradually taking place since the beginning of Henry VII's reign. Enclosures were the most important cause: they were the special grievance of the poor, and the sufferers found many writers to voice their complaint.

[1] Harrison (N. Sh. Soc.), Bk. ii, p. 231; H. Cardani *Opera*, 1563, v. 508 (*Liber duodecim geniturarum*). Froude has a note exposing Harrison's figures, *Hist. of Eng.* (1858), iii. 407 ff.

. . . 'Your shepe that were wont to be so meke and tame, and so smal eaters', says one speaker in the *Utopia*, 'now, as I heare saye, be become so great devowerers and so wylde, that they eate up, and swallow downe the very men them selfes. They consume, destroye, and devoure whole fieldes, howses, and cities. For looke in what partes of the realme doth growe the fynest and therefore dearest woll, there noblemen and gentlemen, yea and certeyn abbottes, holy men no doubt, not contenting them selfes with the yearely revenues and profytes, that were wont to grow to theyr forefathers and predecessours of their landes, nor beynge content that they live in rest and pleasure nothinge profiting, yea much noyinge the weale publique, leave no ground for tillage, thei inclose al into pastures; thei throw doune houses; thei pluck downe townes, and leave nothing standynge, but only the churche to be made a shepehowse. And as thoughe you loste no small quantity of grounde by forestes, chases, laundes and parkes, those goode holy men turne all dwellinge places and all glebeland into desolation and wildernes. Therefore that on covetous and unsatiable cormaraunte and very plage of his natyve contrey maye compasse aboute and inclose many thousand akers of grounde together within one pale or hedge, the husbandmen be thrust owte of their owne, or els either by coveyne and fraude, or by violent oppression they be put besydes it, or by wronges and injuries thei be so weried, that they be compelled to sell all: by one meanes therefore or by other, either by hooke or crooke they muste needes depart awaye, poore, selye, wretched soules, men, women, husbands, wives, fatherlesse children, widowes, wofull mothers, with their yonge babes, and their whole houshold smal in substance and muche in numbre, as husbandrye requireth manye hands. Awaye thei trudge, I say, out of their knowen and accustomed houses, fyndynge no place to reste in. All theire housholdestuffe, which is verye litle woorthe, thoughe it myght well abide the sale: yet beeynge sodainely thruste oute, they be constrayned to sell it for a thing of nought. And when they have wandered abrode tyll that be spent, what can they then els doo but steale, and then justly pardy be hanged, or els go about a beggyng. And yet then also they be caste in prison as vagaboundes, because they go aboute and worke not: whom no man wyl set a worke, though thei never so willyngly profre themselves thereto'.[1]

The excuse for this long quotation lies in the fact that it is an exact and authoritative statement of this particular grievance.

[1] *Utopia*, ed. Lumby, pp. 32–3.

But in order to decide finally on the soundness of the indictment it is necessary to examine a little more closely into conditions and to look at the question from both sides. During the century which was probably required for the country to recover from the scarcity of labour following the Black Death, the English wool-growing industry, which demanded very few labourers as compared with tillage, had become more and more important.[1] There was an excellent market for wool in Flanders, and, during the latter half of the fifteenth century, there grew up a market rivalling this in the cloth-weaving towns of England, so that by the year 1500 sheep-raising had come to be far more profitable than tillage. Enclosures for the purpose of sheep-raising at first merely compensated for the dearth of labourers without causing hardship, but, in the reigns of Henry VII and Henry VIII, as the industry became more profitable, landlords and more substantial copyholders gradually began to enclose commons and to evict such tenants as they could, turning land which had formerly been under tillage and had furnished work for many plowmen and reapers to the more profitable pasture, which demanded only a few shepherds. The result was that while the classes which owned the land or had capital enough to rent it and stock it with sheep grew richer and richer, the poorer classes, helpless and inefficient under the new industrial conditions and without possession of the land, were driven from their homes to beg or steal.

The conditions which prevailed in 1550 were based on a new idea of ownership of land, individual rather than communal.[2] In the Middle Ages the tenants were such in name rather than in fact. Custom gave even the unfree villein certain rights which we associate with ownership. By custom he left his holding to his heir and he was not subject to eviction so long as he kept up his dues and performed his stipulated services.[3]

[1] Cp. Seebohm, Articles on Black Death, *Fortnightly Review*, vol. ii, pp. 149 and 268.

[2] Cheyney, *Social Changes in England in the Sixteenth Century*, pp. 53–4.

[3] Trevelyan, *Age of Wycliffe*, 1909, 184. This is a loose statement of the fact but substantially true. Vinogradoff explains the difference between

The first step in the emancipation of the villein was the commutation of feudal services for a money payment, which payment amounted to a rent for his holding. The lord in turn paid for the labour required to cultivate the demesne land.[1] This process worked better for both sides than the old and complicated system of feudal services. For one thing, it was simpler and required less administration on the part of the lord; on the other hand, it ministered to the growing desire of the serf for independence. This commutation of feudal service went on steadily during the first half of the fourteenth century, and much more rapidly after the Black Death, in spite of many attempts on the part of the landlords to return to the old system. The serfs had one resource when they could not get what they wanted, namely, to run away, and it is clear that this is what large numbers of them did.[2]

During the second half of the fourteenth century the advantages of commuted services were all on the side of the serfs. An open labour market meant prosperity for every man who was free to sell his labour wherever he liked. The peasants understood this, and all over England they made a determined and usually successful effort to get the market value of their labour. Thus it was that for a time the peasants seemed to be victorious in their fight for freedom and for improvement in their economic condition. But in one respect their position had become worse, although the evil effects were not yet felt. In their struggle to better their condition the peasants had more and more severed their con-

theory and practice in the complicated subject of villein tenure. Theoretically at the death of a serf his holding and chattels reverted to the lord and were then by custom bestowed upon the villein's heirs upon payment of *heriot* and *relief*. But this custom was binding and the whole process amounted to the right of inheritance subject to a certain tax.—Cp. Vinogradoff, *Villainage in England*, 1892, Essay I, chap. v, pp. 159 ff.

[1] Trevelyan, *Age of Wycliffe*, pp. 185 ff.

[2] Cp. Vinogradoff, p. 158. After the Black Death one finds frequently in the *Rolls of Parliament* complaints from the landlords that when they try to enforce the Statutes of Labourers against their serfs this is the result: 'que si tost come lours Mestres les chalengent de mal service ou les voillent paier pur lour dite service solome la forme des ditz Estatutz, ils fuont & descurront sodeynement hors de lours services, & hors de lours pays propre, de Countee en Counte, de Hundred en Hundred, de Ville en Ville, en estranges lieux desconuz a lours dites Mestres.'—*Rolls of Parliament*, ii. 340 (1376).

nexion with the soil, which meant the loss of certain rights as well as the escape from burdens. The lord came to be thought of as sole owner of the land and to have the right to do with it what he pleased—a notion inconsistent with the mediaeval theory of tenure. The serf threw away his rights by flight and revolt at a time when they were less precious to him than freedom. In this way the peasants led in the change from mediaeval to modern economic conditions; their descendants were destined to suffer bitterly from the results.

In the fifteenth century sheep-farming increased steadily, and, as we have seen, proved to be extremely profitable. It required fewer labourers than agriculture, it increased the relative price of land, and offered to strong and unscrupulous landlords a constant temptation to enclose common wastes and pastures. All these elements operated to the disadvantage of the labourers, and as the peasantry increased in numbers their economic condition grew worse. Doubtless the wars and the enormous bands of retainers kept by nobles in the fifteenth century tended to some extent to offset these disadvantages. But the peace of the Tudor period and the gradual decay of the bands of retainers took away this alleviation and allowed the natural forces to work out unchecked. Thus it was that the evolution of the modern system by which land is held and agricultural labour paid left large numbers of the peasantry of England at the beginning of the sixteenth century divorced from the soil and able only with the greatest difficulty to find a living.

The influence of the landlords had at first been directly against this change. The Statutes of Labourers in the fourteenth and fifteenth centuries were nothing more than an attempt to preserve the older conditions. Now in the sixteenth century the landholders began tardily to assert their right to the market price of land, as the serfs had asserted theirs to the market price of labour. The result was that thousands of the peasants were compelled to join the tattered regiments of rogues and vagabonds who pestered the land with their petty thieving and endangered the peace of the realm with their restless and seditious resentment against the persons whom they considered responsible for their poverty.

The wrongs of the peasants found indignant expression in the literature of the middle of the sixteenth century. Fierce and eager men like Robert Crowley, Henry Brinklow, and Simon Fish attacked the problem of what could be done to make times good again for the poor. Their remedies do not seem sound to us, but their works reflect vividly the social disease of the age—the sufferings of the poor and the over-prosperity of the rich—and for that reason they are worth a brief examination.

Robert Crowley was the author of some of the most forcible of these protests. He was a B.A. of Oxford and lived in London, where he combined the vocations of printer, author, and preacher. He printed for the first time the *Vision of William Concerning Piers the Plowman*, and he championed the cause of the poor in the sixteenth century as the author of that poem did in the fourteenth. In a tract called *Informacion and Peticion Agaynst the Oppressours of the Pore Commons of this Realme*, addressed to a parliament of Edward VI, he gives a vivid picture of the poverty and disorder resulting from the landlords' 'more then Turkyshe tyranie'. Men who had been honest householders were driven from home and became dependent upon others not so honest; their sons were doomed to the meanest labour, to beg or to steal; their daughters to 'ungrate servitude', to marry into miserable poverty, or to become sisters of the Bank, living the vile life of the stews, and dying penniless and full of diseases in the streets.[1] All this came, according to him, from

[1] 'What a sea of mischifes hath floued out of thys more then Turkyshe tyranie! What honeste housholders haue ben made folowers of other not so honest mens tables! What honeste matrones haue ben brought to the needy rocke and cardes! What menchyldrene of good hope in the liberall sciences, and other honeste qualities (wherof this realme hath great lacke), haue ben compelled to fal, some to handycrafts, and some to daye labour, to sustayne theyr parents decrepet age and miserable pouertie! What frowarde and stoubourn children haue herby shaken of the yoke of godly chastisement, rennying hedlonge into all kyndes of wickednes, and finaly garnyshed galowe trees! What modeste, chaste,

the cruel landlords who, eager to make the utmost penny from their lands in fines and rents and not willing to give the poor a chance for even a starving existence, enclosed all, evicted their tenants, and converted their fields to pasture. Crowley is only one of many preachers against enclosures.

The contemporary pamphlets contain bitter complaints against the rent-raisings which compelled many smaller farmers to give up their tenures; these were looked upon by the poorer classes and by most writers on social questions as acts of high-handed tyranny and oppression on the part of the owners of the land. Perhaps the best illustration of the popular attitude toward landlords is to be found in a letter in the Public Record Office from a poor artificer, John Bayker, addressed to King Henry VIII, designed to explain the cause of the increasing number of vagabonds in the realm. Bayker describes in detail, with the tone of an eyewitness, the process of evicting a poor tenant by means of increased rents and fines. His theorizing as to the rights and wrongs of the question is open to dispute, but on the manner of such evictions he is to be taken as authority. The tenant is compelled to sell his goods to pay an excessive fine for a decayed house which never had a fine before. This impoverishes him so much that he cannot afford to repair the house and, after being twice reproved in the manor court for not doing so, he is finally driven out. By this time the house is so decayed that nobody wants it; instead of repairing it the lord lets it fall down, knowing that he can get as much from the

and womanly virgins haue, for lacke of dourie, ben compelled, either to passe ouer the days of theyr youth in vngrate seruitude, or else to marye to perpetuall miserable pouertie! What immodest and wanton gyrles haue hereby ben made sisters of the Banck (the stumbling stock of all frayle youth) and finaly, moste miserable creatures, lyeinge and dieynge in the stretes ful of all plages and penurie!'—Crowley, *Informacion and Peticion* (E.E.T.S.), p. 166.

The same thing is often to be found in the sermons of the best preachers of the time. 'Now the Robberies, Extortions, and open Oppressions of covetous Cormorants have no End nor Limits, no Banks to keep in their Vileness. As for turning poor Men out of their Holds, they take it for no Offence, but say, their Land is their own. And so they turn them out of their Shrowds like Mice. Thousands in *England* thro' such, beg now from Door to Door, who have kept honest Houses.'—Bern. Gilpin's Sermon. Quoted in Strype, *Ecclesiastical Memorials*, 1721, vol. ii, p. 441.

land by sheep-farming as the whole tenement formerly brought.[1]

We are told by some writers that the expiration of every lease furnished occasion for enhancing the rent from the old customary rate to what the land was worth under new conditions. Many of the receivers of land formerly belonging to monasteries persuaded their tenants that the change of proprietorship made new leases necessary, for which they exacted increased fines and higher rent.

> 'But now these extorsioners haue so improued theyr landes that they make of xl. s. fyne xl. pounde, and of v. nobles rent v. pound, yea, not suffised with this oppression within theyr owne inheritaunce, they buy at your Highnes hand such abbay landes as you appoint to be sold. And, when they stand ones ful seased therin, they make vs, your pore commons, so in dout of their threatynges, that we dare do none other but bring into their courtes our copies taken of the couentes of the late dissolued monastaries, and confirmed by youre Hygh Court of Parliament, thei make vs beleue that, by the vertue of your Highnes sale, all our former writynges are voyde and of none effect. And that if we wil not take new leases of them, we must then furthwith avoid the groundes, as hauyng therin none entrest.'[2]

John Bayker and other authors of complaints and supplications ascribed the rise in rents to the covetousness of the landlords. But the fact that tenants were found proves that to some men the farms were worth the increased price. Other causes operated to give the land a greater money value. Most important among these were the debasing of the coinage, the increased production of the soil under enclosures, and the substitution of competitive for customary rents.[3] The effect of debased coinage on prices needs no comment, and the more level-headed thinkers of the time understood it.[4] Enclosed land was worth more for any purpose than land

1 See Appendix A, 3, for a transcription of this letter.

2 *Supplication of the Poore Commons* (E.E.T.S.), p. 80. For exactly the same grievance see *Complaynt of Roderyck Mors* (E.E.T.S), p. 9.

3 Cheyney, *Social Changes in England in the Sixteenth Century*, pp. 45–54.

4 Cp. *Discourse of the Common Weal* (Lamond's edition), pp. 69–88.

unenclosed. Fitzherbert, in a chapter in his *Boke of surueyeng* on ‘Howe to make a townshippe that is worthe twentie marke a yere worthe .xx. li. a yere’, shows plainly that enclosures make the land more profitable for tillage as well as for pasture. He is not the only writer of the time to maintain it.[1] If, then, enclosures had increased the average productive power of the soil it seems reasonable that rents should increase. With the decay of the old feudal tenures and the development of the capitalized industry of sheep-farming the old system of customary rents was broken down. The modern investor took the place of the feudal tenant. In the early part of the sixteenth century there was a clearly defined tendency on the part of wealthy merchants to invest their surplus funds in land. It is complained of as one of the grievances of the poor; the ensuing competition was considered unfair. The merchants were accused of having lost the old English spirit of adventure and to have descended to an unworthy race for land in order to make their sons gentlemen.

Lett marchant men goe sayle,
for that ys ther trwe waylle;
for of one .C. ye haue not ten
that now be marchantes ventring men,
that occupi grett in-awnderes
forther then into flanderes,—
flawnderes or in-to france—
for fere of some myschance,
but lyeth at home, and standes
by morgage and purchasse of landes
Owtt of all gentyll menes Handes,
wiche showld serve alwaye your grace
with horse and men in chasse:
wiche ys a grett dewowre
vnto youre regall pawre.[2]

[1] The same opinion is expressed in the *Discourse of the Common Weal*, pp. 48–52.

[2] *Vox Populi, Vox Dei* (Ballad Society), ll. 282–96. Cp. also Crowley, *Way to Wealth* (E.E.T.S.), pp. 132–3; and *The Last Trump*, section headed ‘The Merchants’ Lesson’ (E.E.T.S.), pp. 86–90.

Edward VI’s *Discourse about the Reformation of Many Abuses* (reprinted in Burnet’s *History of the Reformation*, v. 96 ff.) contains the following sentence in regard to this matter: ‘The merchants adventure not to bring in strange commodities, but loiter at home, send forth small hoyes

These mid-century writers on economic questions show us clearly enough that the time was out of joint, but their attempts to fix the blame on either the rent-raising landlords or the farming merchants are unconvincing. Interesting and moving as they are, the contemporary complaints fail to point out conclusively who was at fault, or to suggest any better remedy than a return to the mediaeval economic system. The great fault of all the moralists of the time, says Cunningham, is that they could not point out the duty of employers.[1] The *Discourse of the Common Weal*—perhaps the soundest of all the economic writings of the sixteenth century—admits that good might come from enclosures if each man had his share of the land. Husbandmen who had laid down the plough and cultivated pasture had grown rich, and were the land not intermingled all would enclose.[2] Substantial copyholders enclosed their farms, evicted smaller tenants, stocked their fields with sheep, and prospered. Even the old methods of tillage would have gained a man a living had he had possession of the soil. It was the poor labourers without land of their own and without capital necessary for sheep-raising who suffered.

The bands of feudal retainers were another common source of vagabondage. They had been a lawless element in the country during the period of their masters' power. During the Wars of the Roses the presence of a feudal army for a long time in one place impoverished the countryside for years to come. In time of peace many of the retainers seem to have been little more than ordinary marauders, often unjustly protected by their lords. From 1485 to 1550 we hear more and more of this class of thieves. In 1495 a statute

with two or three mariners, occupy exchange of money, buy and sell victual, steal out bullion, corn, victual, wood and such like things, out of the realm and sell their ware unreasonably.' There was a widespread feeling that each man should stick to his own occupation and let the poor labourers have the land.

Cp. also, in this connexion, Cunningham, *Growth of English Industry and Commerce*, 1905, vol. i, pp. 551 ff.

[1] *Growth of English Industry and Commerce*, 1905, vol. i, p. 557.

[2] *Discourse of the Common Weal* (Lamond's edition), p. 56.

was made against retainers who committed riots and depredations and then withdrew themselves into hiding 'by the agrement covyne and counsell of their seid Maisters'. The *Complaynt of Roderyck Mors* describes a similar state of affairs as late as 1544. There are many retainers, it asserts, who have no wages and must steal for their living. Indeed, many of them are glad to serve for nothing and even to provide their own liveries in order to conceal and protect their thefts.[1]

As these fellows were gradually dismissed they became excellent vagabonds. There were few other opportunities for them to earn a living, and this trade they had already learned. In the words of the ballad of *Now-a-Dayes*:

Temporall lordes be almost gone,
Howsholdes kepe thei few or none,
Which causeth many a goodly mane
  ffor to begg his bredd:
Iff he stele ffor necessite,
ther ys none other remedye
But the law will shortlye
  Hange him all save the hedd.

If the origin of the vagabond class is to be looked for chiefly in enclosures and in the breaking up of the bands of feudal retainers, the monasteries exerted a less important

[1] 'Also ther is another thing worthy to be loked vpon, which is this:—Many noble men and gentylmen retayne seruantys, and neuer gyue them peny wages, and scant a cote; for some be fayne to pay for their owne cotys, and spend all that thei haue of their owne and of other mennys also, hopyng vpon some reward; and whan he seyth that all is spent, than he wold depart and dare not. And gay he must goo lyke his felows; and now his fryndes fayle hym, what remedy? Forsoth shortly euyn to wat[c]h for a bowget.

'Another sort there is, and thei be lyght ryding men all ready; and thei wil lyue lyke gentylmen. And for his buclar or shyld, he wil seke to be retayning to some nobleman or gentylman that bearyth rule in the court or contry, though he pay for his own lyuery. And the noblemen and gentylmen, which shold be the ponysshers of theft, be the chefe maynteyners of robry; bi this meanys often thei robbe and be not taken; but in case he be taken, eyther he shal haue fauor for his masters sake, or els bragg it owt with a carde of .x; ye euyn face it owt, that neyther the playntyue nor the xij men dare cast a thefe. Or if all this wyll not helpe, than procure thei the kinges pardon.'—*Complaynt of Roderyck Mors* (E.E.T.S.), pp. 44-5.

but not insignificant influence in the same direction. Both before and after their dissolution they increased the beggar class. In their prime they gave a great deal in charity, but without much discrimination between worthy and unworthy: whoever came to the door received an alms. They had many bequests providing that so much should be 'given to the poor', and these bequests were always respected by law. The earliest poor laws of Henry VIII's reign prohibit common alms, but invariably make a proviso allowing alms from monasteries.[1] Their charity was one of the most frequently urged excuses for their existence. They relieved an enormous amount of distress, but their indiscriminate giving must have fostered many a sturdy vagrant and thief. When the monasteries were dissolved this aid ceased abruptly and there was nothing to take its place. The new clergy were notoriously uncharitable; and had they been never so kind they lacked the funds which the monks had had to give away.[2] Consequently the deserving and undeserving poor who had depended upon doles from the monasteries were driven elsewhere for food, and the number of vagabonds and beggars was increased. In addition to this, Henry VIII, when he seized the Church lands, made no adequate provision for the homeless monks. As a class they were not very intelligent, and many of them were soon reduced to begging. Thus they swelled still further, after the dissolution of the monasteries, the ranks which they had helped to maintain before.

A great many monks and priests who did not have to beg roamed up and down the country as vagabonds for the purpose of enlisting the people on their side in the conflict between Protestantism and Catholicism. Burnet thought that the severe branding statute of Edward VI's reign was directed principally against these wandering monks [3]; there were many

[1] Such provisions are included in both the 22 Henry VIII, c. 12 (1530–1), and in the 27 Henry VIII, c. 25 (1535–6).

[2] Cp. Crowley, *Informacion and Peticion*, opening paragraphs; *Supplication of the Poore Commons* (E.E.T.S), pp. 79 and 84–5.

[3] *History of Reformation*, ed. Pocock, 1865, vol. ii, p. 100. Certain clauses of the statute do treat vagabond priests with unexampled severity, but Burnet overstates the case in saying that the law was directed principally against them.

proclamations against Popish vagabonds accused of spreading discontent and sedition in regard to religion and government; and the Privy Council carried on a never-ending secret campaign against them, in which the machinations of the Papists were opposed by all kinds of spying, deceit, and torture.

The causes which have been outlined above do not account for all the vagabonds, but they explain the larger part of the class, which included men of all degrees. There were many wilde rogues', descendants of the generations of fifteenth-century vagabonds, and there was the multitude who went about on the real or pretended business of catering to the wants of the country people or providing them with amusement.

Far from being either an impotent or a harmless class, the vagabonds of the sixteenth century represented much of the solid strength of mediaeval England. Many of them came from good stock, but in the economic scheme of modern England they found no useful place. They had brains to plan villany and audacity to execute it. Their ranks contained political, religious, and social malcontents and agitators. Hence it was that they were a danger as well as a pest in the England of Elizabeth. The vagabonds were menace enough to cause the law-makers, from Henry VII onwards, to give their best thought to a remedy, both by framing statutes and providing for their execution, until the problem was finally solved, as far as legislation could solve it, by the admirable poor laws of 1572, 1597, and 1601.

There remains to be discussed in this chapter the question of how far the sixteenth-century vagabonds were of gipsy origin. The gipsies came to England as early as the beginning of the sixteenth century, and several writers on them have assumed that the begging tricks and canting language of the English rogues were also common to them. The life led by the wandering vagabonds was similar in many respects to that of the gipsies, and there is much evidence that they were closely associated in the popular mind. Almost every statute against rogues and vagabonds includes 'Egyptians' as well. There are several statutes against English vagabonds disguising themselves as gipsies or wandering in company with them, which indicates that there were some relations between the two races. English vagabonds soon began to practise the fortune-telling which made the gipsies so welcome to the country people everywhere. Some Romany scholars claim that the popular Morris dance, about which so much is heard in Elizabethan literature, was brought by the gipsies from Spain: the name means Moorish. One sentence in Dekker's description of the gipsies offers a slight confirmation of this theory:

'Their apparell is od, and phantasticke, tho it be neuer so full of rents: the men weare scarfes of Callico, or any other base stuffe hauing their bodies like Morris dancers, with bells, and vther toyes, to intice the countrey people to flocke about them, and to wounder at their fooleries or rather rancke knaueryes.' [1]

Wearing bells about the knees was a distinctive feature of the Morris dance, and since the gipsies were a conservative race, little given to borrowing customs from the nations among whom they lived, it seems an open question whether they were not the originators of this dress, instead of being, as Dekker believed, the imitators. Modern gipsies, according to the vocabularies of Borrow and of Smart and Crofton, use a few words belonging to the cant language of the sixteenth-century rogues, and, no matter from which they were borrowed, there must have been some intercourse between the two races.

Although the facts given in the preceding paragraph indicate that there was some connexion between the gipsies and the English rogues, they do not prove that these relations were very intimate, and there is ample evidence that the two races were not identical. The rogues' cant given by Harman is entirely distinct from Romany, the gipsy language; the connexion noted above is confined to a very few words.[2]

[1] Dekker, *Lanthorne and Candle-light*, 1608, sig. G_3 (Temple edition, pp. 237-8).

[2] Borrow, in *Zincali*, insists strongly on the difference between robber's cant and the gipsy language. The number of words common to the two is fewer than one would expect.

Contemporary writers who described rogue life at first hand or copied from the early reliable descriptions always made a clear distinction. It is true that Ben Jonson in the *Masque of the Metamorphosed Gypsies*, working entirely at second hand, completely confuses the two classes, but Harman separates them sharply; speaking of the English rogues in his dedicatory epistle, he says:

'I hope their synne is now at the hyghest; and that as short and as spedy a redresse wylbe for these, as hath bene of late yeres for the wretched, wily, wandering vagabonds calling and naming them selues Egiptians, depely dissembling and long hyding and couering their depe, decetfull practises,—feding the rude common people, wholy addicted and geuen to nouelties, toyes, and new inuentions,—delyting them with the strangenes of the attyre of their heades, and practising paulmistrie to such as would know their fortunes: And, to be short, all theues and hores (as I may well wryt),—as some haue had true experience, a number can well wytnes, and a great sorte hath well felte it. And now (thankes bée to god), throughe wholsome lawes, and the due execution thereof, all be dispersed, banished, and the memory of them cleane extynguished; that when they bée once named here after, our Chyldren wyll muche meruell what kynd of people they were: and so, I trust, shal shortly happen of these.'

Dekker, in his chapter on 'Moone-men', as he called the gipsies, does the same: 'Looke what difference there is betwéene a ciuell cittizen of Dublin and a wild Irish Kerne, so much difference there is betwéene one of these counterfeit Egiptians and a true English Begger.'[1] A letter from a Somersetshire justice, Edward Hext, written in 1596, makes the distinction no less clearly.[2]

On one very interesting point Awdeley seems to have confused the two. He includes last of all in his *Fraternitye of Vacabondes* one kind of rogue called a Patrico—a sort of hedge-priest—who performed marriages which should hold until death did part the married couple. This meant that whenever they were tired of living together they could be

[1] *Lanthorne and Candle-light*, 1608, sig. G_2 verso—G_3 (Temple edition, p. 236).
[2] Cp. Appendix A, 14.

divorced over the body of any dead animal they found in the road, by shaking hands and parting, the husband on one side of it, the wife on the other. Simson, who published a *History of the Gypsies* in 1865, claimed that a similar form of divorce was practised by them in Scotland at the time he wrote, with only the difference that instead of looking for a dead animal in the road, the husband killed his best horse and over its body parted from his wife. This may be only a semi-humorous rogue custom borrowed by the gipsies, and still surviving, but Simson attempts to identify it with a Hindu ceremony for divorce of great antiquity. The evidence he adduces, though not convincing, has a great deal of interest.[1] The hypothesis that the custom belonged to the gipsies rather than to English rogues is still further confirmed by the fact that Harman denies that any such custom existed among the rogues and that there was any such name as Patrico, while Borrow, on the other hand, gives Patrico as a gipsy word. Awdeley's description of the Patrico is probably a bit of gipsy lore which he picked up somewhere and included in his pamphlet on vagabonds. But the gipsies and the English rogues were two different classes. The gipsies are an exclusive people, not likely to admit outsiders into their fellowship, and probably did so in the sixteenth century only to a very limited extent. The history of their life in England and the measures employed against them is quite distinct from the history of English vagabond life, and far less important.

[1] Walter Simson, *History of the Gipsies*, 1865, pp. 266–80.

CHAPTER II

THE ART OF BEGGING

Jog on, jog on, the foot-path way,
  And merrily hent the stile-a;
A merry heart goes all the day,
  Your sad tires in a mile-a.

Winter's Tale, Act IV, sc. 3.

FROM the last chapter it should be clear that social conditions in the reigns of Henry VIII, Edward VI, Mary, and Elizabeth forced thousands of small farmers, labourers, and old-time dependants upon nobles to become vagabonds. The problem that confronted these poor homeless rogues was how to get a living without land and, if possible, without labour. In order to find out how they did this we must study the contemporary literature describing their lives and tricks, supporting this account, where we can, by the evidence of historical records, which, interesting in themselves, become doubly so with this voluminous literature of rogue pamphlets for commentary.

This problem of how to live well on nothing a year was not one which confronted English vagabonds for the first time in the sixteenth century. Many solutions, sanctioned by long tradition and even by the practices of holy men, had come down from the Middle Ages. The friars had successfully solved the problem and had made begging a fine art. Vagabond gamesters, bearwards, fortune-tellers, jugglers, and pedlars existed in the fourteenth century as well as in the sixteenth.[1] Vagabond players certainly existed in England in the fifteenth century. As Mr. A. W. Pollard has pointed out in his Introduction to the E.E.T.S. edition of the *Macro Plays*,

[1] Reference has already been made to M. Jusserand's excellent and entertaining account of them in *English Wayfaring Life in the Middle Ages.*

the morality *Mankynd* shows plainly that it was presented by a band of strolling actors of a very low class. All the fun of the play is rough knock-about farce among the devils and vices who constitute most of the characters. Before the entrance of the principal devil, Tityvullus, the others take up a collection among the audience:

> We xall gather mony onto
> Ellys ther xall no man hym se,

says one rogue. A second makes a plea for large contributions —no groats nor pennies but red royals:

> He louyth no grotis, nor pens or to-pens:
> Gyf ws rede reyallays if ye wyll se hys abhomynabull presens.

to which the other hastily puts in the qualification: 'Ye that mow not pay the ton, pay the tother.' The whole play reflects the character of the actors who played it: there is only one virtuous character, and he is burlesqued half the time; Tityvullus and his evil crew rule the stage, making all manner of coarse fun of the over-righteous Mercy and the 'flexibull' Mankynd.

All these classes of fourteenth- and fifteenth-century vagabonds were represented in the sixteenth century, but by this time rogue life had become more complex and varied. Elizabethan wanderers who could not find work or did not wish to, invented and practised a large variety of devices for extorting money from all mankind—vagabond vocations which were in reality only skilful methods of begging or stealing.

The problem of getting a living without work was simplified for these vagabonds by the fact that there was everywhere a large amount of indiscriminate charity: at the monasteries before their dissolution, and all through the century at weddings and other such feasts, and daily at the houses of foolish, soft-hearted persons. Thomas Harman dedicated his book to one of these last, the Lady Elizabeth, Countess of Shrewsbury, because she habitually gave alms, not only to the poor of her own parish, but to all who came to her gates, and he wished her to understand 'the abhominable, wycked, and detestable behauor of all these rowsey, ragged rabblement of rakehelles, that—vnder the pretence of great misery, dyseases, and other innumerable calamities whiche they fayne—through great hipocrisie do wyn and gayne great almes in all places where they wyly wander, to the vtter deludinge of the good geuers, deceauinge and impouerishing of all such poore housholders, both sicke and sore, as nether can or maye walke abroad for reliefe and comforte'.[1]

Life was further made easy for the rogues by the fact that the authorities granted to a wide variety of what were considered deserving poor licences allowing them to wander and to ask alms on the streets and highways. A licence, properly signed and sealed, instantly transformed any lawless vagrant into a law-abiding citizen whom all persons were expected to aid.[2] The number of these licences regularly issued was enormous. Often they were signed by very important men—justices, noblemen, or bishops—and they apparently inspired great respect among simple people, especially, one may imagine, among those who did not know how to read. They were, as we shall see later, counterfeited by undeserving rogues on every hand. It is impossible to form any idea of the wide opportunity for such frauds unless the reader first considers the number and variety of legitimate licences in use.

Licences to beg for the ransoms of Christians captured by the Turks were common long before and long after the reign of Elizabeth. Several of the time of Henry VIII are preserved in the British Museum.[3] A famous case in Elizabeth's reign was that of Lucas Argenter, who was granted a licence in 1581 to beg for money to ransom his wife and children held in bondage in Turkey.[4] There were many of the same kind; so common were they that a regular weekly collection was taken for them at St. Paul's.

Licences to beg on account of losses by fire and at sea were also common. A writing under seal for Thomas Moone of

[1] Harman, *Caueat* (N. Sh. Soc.), pp. 19–20.
[2] In Appendix A, 2 will be found the form of licence prescribed in 1530.
[3] Cp. *Fragmenta Antiqua*, Press-mark c. 18. e. 2 (8 and 49).
[4] *Remembrancia*, i. 290, fo. 136. See also i. 404, iv. 106, and heading 'Captives' in printed calendar, for other instances.

London and wife whose house was burnt is mentioned in the records of the London Court of Aldermen, November 28, 1536.[1] Strype alludes to a number of them of the time of Edward VI.[2] Elizabeth granted one to Thomas Norman of Barnstaple (co. Devon) about 1575, who had suffered losses at sea and afterwards fallen sick. He or his deputies were allowed by it to beg through Devon and Cornwall for his relief.[3] These permits were looked at with something of the same attitude that we have to an insurance policy—a means of compensating one individual for extraordinary calamity by a small sacrifice from many.

Scholars from the Universities with licences from the Vice-Chancellor to beg were still found in the reign of Elizabeth. The Register of the University of Oxford[4] gives a list of fifteen licences granted between 1551 and 1572. They were usually given to students in pairs and for the period of one vacation, the scholars giving security for the return of the licence.

Lepers and helpless poor were licensed to beg by proxy. The person who acted as agent to go about and receive the alms was called a Proctor. Many hospitals were supported in this way. The Proctors were notorious rogues, and instead of being content with their legitimate share of the collections, were commonly supposed to keep almost all they received. Begging Proctors had been known since the Middle Ages. Before the break with the Papacy, gifts to them had commonly been rewarded by indulgences and pardons. These incentives to liberality were stopped after the Reformation (though there is evidence in such a licence as that quoted below that they were used *sub rosa*), but the licences were still issued. There is in the British Museum[5] a form of a 'protection of beggerie'

[1] *Repertory*, ix, fo. 226b.

[2] *Ecclesiastical Memorials* (1721), II. ii, p. 516.

[3] P.R.O. Warrant Book, i. 17. Among the broadsides in the Library of the Society of Antiquaries of London is one of the same sort granted by John Aylmer, Bishop of London, September 15, 1586, to Thomas Butler, who was injured while manufacturing gunpowder.—Lemon's *Catalogue*, No. 82.

[4] Edited by the Rev. Andrew Clark, O.H.S., vol. ii, pt. ii, pp. 1–5.

[5] Harleian MS. 364, fo. 22. It is preserved in a collection of papers evidently intended, according to the catalogue, to be used as models in making out similar documents.

PLATE II

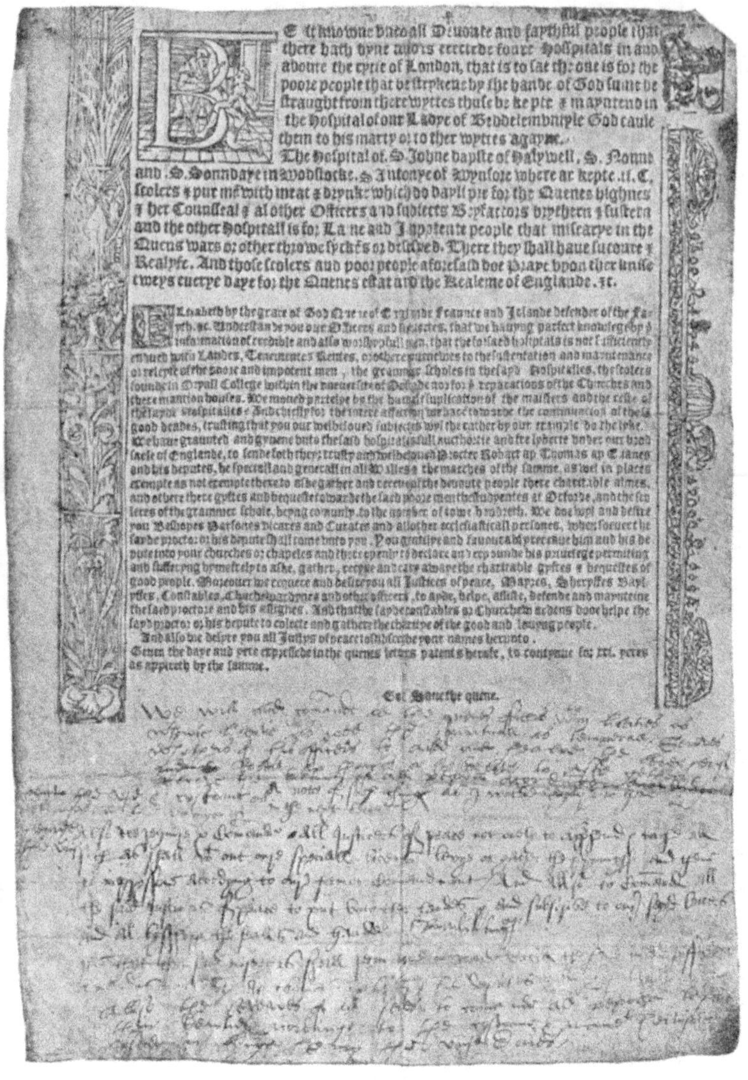

Be it knowne unto all Devoute and faythful people that there hath byne afore erected foure Hospitals in and aboute the cytie of London, that is to sae the one is for the poore people that be strycken by the hande of God [illegible] be straught from there wyttes thuse be kepte & mayntend in the Hospital of our Ladye of Beddelem untyle God cause them to his marcy or to ther wyttes agayne.

The Hospital of. S. Johne bapiste of Halywell, S. [illegible] and S. Sonndaye in Wodstocke. S. Antonye of Wyndsore where ar kepte .ii. C. scolers & pur men with meat & drynke which do dayli pre for the Quenes highnes & her Counseal & al other Officers and subiects Benefactors brythern & sisters and the other Hospitall is for Lame and Impotente people that miscarye in the Quens wars or other throwe syckes or desesed. There they shall haue sucoure & Realyfe. And those scolers and poor people aforesaid doe praye upon ther knise tweys everye daye for the Quenes estat and the Realeme of Englande. &c.

Elizabeth by the grace of God Quene of Englande Fraunce and Irelande defender of the Fayth. &c. Understande you our Officers and subiectes, that we hauyng parfect knowlege by the information of credible and also worshypfull men, that the forsaed hospitals is not sufficiently endued with Landes, Tenementes Rentes, or othere [illegible] to the sustentation and maintenance or releyfe of the poore and impotent men, the grammer scholes in the sayd hospitalles, the scolers founde in [illegible] College within the universite of Oxforde nor for the reparations of the Churches and there mansion houses. We moved partelye by the humble supplication of the maisters and the reste of the sayde hospitalles: And chiefly for the [illegible] affection we have towarde the continuation of these good deades, trusting that you our welbeloued subiectes wyl the rather by our example do the lyke. We have graunted and gyvene unto the said hospitales full authoritie and fre lybertie under our brod seale of Englande, to sende forth ther trusty and welbeloued Procter Robart ap Thomas ap Evanes and his deputes, he specially and generally in all Walles & the marches of the samme, as wel in places exempte as not exempte thereto as gather and receyve of the devoute people there charitable almes, and othere there gyftes and bequestes towarde the said poore men the studentes at Oxforde, and the scolers of the grammer schole, beyng comunly to the number of towe hundreth. We doe wyl and desire you Bishopes Parsones Vicares and Curates and all other ecclesiasticall persones, whensoever the sayde procter or his depute shall come unto you. You gentilye and favourablye receave him and his depute into your churches or chapeles and there openly to declare and expounde his priuilege permitting and sufferyng hym [illegible] to aske, gather, receyve and cary awaye the charitable gyftes & bequestes of good people. Moreover we requere and desire you all Justices of peace, Mayres, Sheryffes Baylyffes, Constables, Churchewardynes and other officers, to ayde, helpe, assiste, defende and mayntaine the said proctore and his assignes. And that the sayde constables or Churchewardens doe helpe the sayd proctor or his depute to colecte and gather the charitye of the good and lovyng people.

And also we desyre you all Justys of peace to subscribe your names hereunto.

Geven the daye and yere expressede in the quenes letters patents herafe, to contynue for .xx. yeres as appereth by the samme.

God Save the quene.

A Proctor's licence.

(*B. M. Press-mark c.* 41. *h.* 1.)

given by Henry VIII and Wolsey in 1544 commanding all prelates and other ecclesiasticall persones to allow the Proctor and his deputy to repair to their churches to ask and fetch the alms of all charitable people, 'provided alwaies that the said William B. nor his said deputie do not in eny wise declare shew or sett forth eny pardones or indulgences graunted by the Busshope of Rome or by coloure and vertue of the same aske gather receyve or take enye money almose or other deuocion of oure said Subjects.' Strype notes half a dozen licences for Proctors granted under Edward VI,[1] and there is in the British Museum a printed broadside certifying that permission has been granted by Elizabeth to Robert ap Thomas ap Evanes to beg throughout Wales for the hospitals of Our Lady of Bethlehem, Saint John the Baptist of Holywell, Saint Nonne and Saint Sonndaye in Woodstock, and Saint Anthony of Windsor, for the relief of all the insane, sick and lame persons, poor children, and scholars in Oriel College in Oxford, cared for by those institutions. Apparently when such a patent was granted a number of licences were printed off for the use of the Proctor and his deputies, to show that they were not impostors (compare Harman on printed licences, p. 41 below). This document is folded, worn, and dirty, evidently by being so carried about.[2] Proctors begged sometimes for other things than hospitals; for example, to renew the furniture of a church when it had been destroyed by ruffians,[3] or for funds to repair a bridge.[4]

Besides all these there was a still larger number of what might be called ordinary licences issued to deserving poor: the earliest form of poor relief had been to separate the deserving from the undeserving and to give the former a signed and sealed permit to beg for aid from all persons they met.[5] Other very common licences were the passports given

[1] *Ecclesiastical Memorials*, II. ii, p. 516.

[2] 'Queen Elizabeth's Letters Patent for Wales.' B.M., Press-mark c. 41. h. 1. Here reproduced as Plate II.

[3] For such a licence for the church at Rickmansworth see *Fragmenta Antiqua*, B.M., Press-mark c. 18. e. 2 (96).

[4] *Records of the Borough of Nottingham*, ii. 264-7.

[5] See London Orders of 1517 in Appendix A, 1; also 22 Henry VIII, c. 12 (1530-1).

to rogues who were sent homeward after being whipped (the law was not quite clear as to whether or not they had a right to beg, but in practice they seem to have exercised it),[1] and licences from justices allowing bearwards, tinkers, pedlars, jugglers, fencers, minstrels and the like to wander. Licences of this nature, which could be granted by any justice of the peace, are noticed rarely in the records, except for such an entry as that in the Repertory of the London Court of Aldermen, May 22, 1551, ordering the Chamberlain of the city to provide 600 'bylls' for impotent beggars to beg, and 200 bills of passports for vagabonds whipped in the city and sent home.[2] The passport was as much a part of the ordinary beggar's equipment as ragged clothing or a dog; when Francesco sends a beggar-woman with a letter to his sweetheart in Greene's euphuistic romance, *Neuer too late* (1590), this is the device he hits on at once:

> 'The begger desirous to do the Gentleman anie pleasure, said shee was readie to take anie paines that might redound to his content. Whereupon he replied thus; Then mother, thou shalt goe to yonder Abbey which is her fathers house . . . then, oh then mother, looke about if thou séest Diana masking in the shape of a Virgin, etc. . . . she is my loue, faire *Isabel*: . . . to her from me shalt thou carrie a letter, foulded vp euerie way like thy pasport, with a greasie backside, and a great seale.'[3]

But in the reign of Elizabeth there were too many beggars and vagabonds to exist even on such elaborate charity as was provided without the use of some cleverness on their part to make the alms flow, and some trickery to eke them out. For a description of their methods and tricks there is no authority so good as Thomas Harman's pamphlet, the *Caueat for Commen Cursetors*. The first impression one gets from Harman's book is that of the close-knit good fellowship among the rogues. They helped each other in their common pursuit of preying

[1] See Dalton, *Countrey Iustice* (1618), pp. 99 ff., which shows the state of confusion on this subject.

[2] *Repertory*, xii, pt. i, fo. 233.

[3] Greene, *Neuer too late* (1590), sig. D_2 and verso (Grosart's edition, viii. 38–9).

upon the public. They often travelled in companies or assembled at some alehouse (bowsing ken) for merry meetings. They spoke together in a cant language as do rogues of all periods. There were orders or ranks depending partly on experience, partly on methods of stealing or begging, and partly, it seems, on physical strength. These orders were described by fantastic cant names which Harman gives, and which we shall use as a basis for a detailed account of rogue customs. The twenty-four orders are as follows:

Rufflers, sturdy vagabonds who begged from the strong and robbed the weak.

Upright Men, vagabonds who were strong enough to be chiefs or magistrates among their fellows.

Hookers or Anglers, thieves who stole clothing and other light articles by pulling them through an open window with a hooked stick.

Rogues, ordinary vagabonds, weaker than the Upright Men.

Wild Rogues, rogues born on the road, of vagabond parents.

Priggers of Prancers, horse thieves.

Palliards, beggars who excited compassion by means of artificial sores made by binding some corrosive to the flesh.

Fraters, sham proctors, who pretended to be begging for hospitals and lazar houses.

Abraham Men, pretended mad men.

Whip-jacks, vagabonds who pretended to be shipwrecked sailors.

Counterfeit Cranks, beggars pretending the falling sickness.

Dommerers, sham deaf mutes.

Tinkers and Pedlars, who ordinarily used their trades as a cloak for thieving.

Jarckmen, makers of false licences.[1]

Patricoes, hedge-priests.[1]

Demanders for Glimmer, men or women begging for pretended losses by fire.

Bawdy baskets, female pedlars.

Autem Morts, women who had been married in church.

Walking Morts, unmarried whores.

Doxies, female companions of common rogues.

Dells, young girls not yet broken in by the Upright Men.

Kynchin Morts, female children.

Kynchin Coes, male children.

[1] Harman mentions these two classes, described in Awdeley's *Fraternitye of Vacabondes*, only to say that they do not exist.

These terms were not the invention of Thomas Harman. They agree substantially with the names given in Awdeley's tract, *The Fraternitye of Vacabondes*, published six years before, and they appear everywhere in Elizabethan literature where there is reference to rogues and vagabonds. Harman's explanation of their tricks and ruses is likewise well supported by outside evidence, various bits of which will be found with the descriptions of the several classes following.

According to Harman's description the Rufflers and the Upright Men seem to have been much alike.[1] They were old, strong, and experienced vagabonds—old soldiers, Harman says, or serving-men and labourers who had been forced out of employment or who had deserted an honest occupation for the free idle life on the road. They were strong fellows and ruled the roast. Often they got their living by bullying the weaker beggars. The Upright Men were self-constituted chiefs or magistrates, as might be expected. They had their choice of the women in any gang, and to them belonged the right to initiate new beggars. The ceremony of initiation seems to have consisted merely of making the neophyte buy drink for the gang and then compelling him to submit to having his part of the 'bene bowse' poured over his head by way of anointment to his high office. Harman's account is as follows:

'And if he (the Upright Man) mete any begger, whether he be sturdye or impotent, he wyll demaund of him, whether euer he was stalled to the roge or no. If he saye he was, he wyll know of whom, and his name that stalled hym. And if he be not learnedly able to shewe him the whole circumstaunce thereof, he wyll spoyle him of his money, either of his best garment, if it be worth any money, and haue him to the bowsing ken, Which is to some typpling house next adioyninge; and laieth their to gage the best thing that he hath for twenty pence or two shyllinges: this man obeyeth for feare of beating. Then doth this vpright man call for a gage of bowse, whiche is a quarte pot of drinke, and powres the same vpon his peld pate, adding these words:—" I. G. P. do stalle thée W. T. to the Roge, and that from hence forth it shall be lawefull for the to Cant"—that is, to aske or begge—" for thy liuing in al

[1] Harman, *Caueat* (N. Sh. Soc.), pp. 29, 31.

FIG. 1. One of Callot's beggars corresponding to Harman's Upright Man.
(From the British Museum Collection.)

places." Here you se that the vpright man is of great auctorite. For all sortes of beggers are obedient to his hests, and surmounteth all others in pylfring and stealinge.'[1]

Beaumont and Fletcher's *Beggars Bush*, which is full of rogue cant and vagabond lore, has this initiation somewhat elaborated. Hubert has been accepted as a member of the band of rogues.

> *Clause:* . . . welcom him, all.
> *Higgen:* Stand off, stand off: I'll do it,
> We bid ye welcom three ways; first for your person,
> Which is a promising person, next for your quality,
> Which is a decent, and a gentle quality,
> Last for the frequent means you have to feed us,
> You can steal 'tis to be presumed.
> *Hubert:* Yes, venison, and if you want—
> *Higgen:* 'Tis well: you understand right,
> And shall practise daily: you can drink too?
> *Hubert:* Soundly.
> *Higgen:* And ye dare know a woman from a weathercock?
> *Hubert:* If I handle her.
> *Gerrard:* Now swear him.
> *Higgen:* I crown thy nab with a gage of ben bouse,
> And stall thee by the salmon into the clows,
> To mand on the pad, and strike all the cheats;
> To Mill from the Ruffmans, commision and slates
> Twang dells i' the stiromel, and let the Quire Cuffin:
> And Harman Beck strine, and trine to the Ruffin.
> *Gerrard:* Now interpret this unto him.
> *Higgen:* I pour on thy pate a pot of good ale,
> And by the Rogues [oth] a Rogue thee instal:
> To beg on the way, to rob all thou meets;
> To steal from the hedge, both the shirt and the sheets:
> And lye with thy wench in the straw till she twang
> Let the Constable, Justice, and Devil go hang. . . .
> You are welcom, Brother
> *All:* Welcom, welcom, welcom . . .[2]

One of the queerest facts in connexion with the practices of Elizabethan sneak-thieves is that they were willing to risk their lives for all kinds of bulky articles of only trifling value. A bed-covering valued at two shillings and a pair of sheets at

[1] Harman, *Caueat* (N. Sh. Soc.), p. 34.
[2] Beaumont and Fletcher, *Beggars Bush*, Act III, sc. 3.

three were considered worth while. Witness the following extract from the Middlesex Sessions' Rolls:

'2 October, 1 Elizabeth.—True bill that at Cowley, co. Midd on the said day, Alexander Raynford late of Rypley co. Kent yoman stole "vnum coopertorium vocat' a bed kyveringe" worth two shillings, and a pair of flaxen shetes worth three shillings and four pence, of the goods and chattels of Roger Burton of Harlington.'

Greene describes an elaborate trick, which if it worked, enabled the thief to get away with a sheet and a pair of pillow-cases.[1] Harman's chapter on Hookers or Anglers explains the common method of stealing such articles. These rogues carried long staves with a hole in the end, into which they inserted an iron hook to pull pieces of clothing and other light articles out through an open window when occasion offered. 'I was credebly informed', says Harman, 'that a hoker came to a farmers house in the ded of the night, and putting back a drawe window of a low chamber, the bed standing hard by the sayd wyndow, in which laye three parsones (a man and two bygge boyes), this hoker with his staffe plucked of their garments which lay vpon them to kepe them warme, with the couerlet and shete, and lefte them lying a slepe naked sauing there shertes, and had a way all clene, and neuer could vnderstande where it became.'[2]

This custom of angling for booty is widely described. Greene and his pamphleteering followers call it *Courbing Law*, and one entertaining but unquotable story about it was widely copied.[3]

The Rogue, in canting language, was a fellow 'niether so stoute or hardy as the vpright man' who, in begging, used the commonest of all devices—the pretence of being weak or lame or sick.[4] When Autolycus falls fainting before the clown he follows the book exactly. The clown is on his way to market and is conning over the list of dainties he must buy for the

[1] Greene, *Thirde and Last Part of Conny-catching* (Grosart), x. 167–9.
[2] Harman, *Caueat* (N. Sh. Soc.), p. 36.
[3] For this see Greene, *Blacke Bookes Messenger*, 1592 (Grosart), vol. xi, p. 32; *Greenes Ghost Haunting Conie-catchers*, by S. R., attributed to Samuel Rowlands (Hunterian Club), p. 28.
[4] Harman, *Caueat* (N. Sh. Soc.), pp. 36–41.

sheep-shearing; Autolycus meets him and falls down as if in agony.

Clo. . . . I must have saffron to color the warden pies; mace; dates?—none, that's out of my note; nutmegs, seven; a race or two of ginger, but that I may beg; four pound of prunes, and as many of raisins o' the sun.

Aut. O that ever I was born! (*Grovelling on the ground.*)

Clo. I' the name of me—

Aut. O, help me, help me! pluck but off these rags; and then, death, death!

Clo. Alack, poor soul! thou hast need of more rags to lay on thee, rather than have these off.

Aut. O sir, the loathsomeness of them offends me more than the stripes I have received, which are mighty ones and millions.

Clo. Alas, poor man! a million of beating may come to a great matter.

Aut. I am robbed, sir, and beaten; my money and apparel ta'en from me, and these detestable things put upon me.

Clo. What, by a horseman, or a footman?

Aut. A footman, sweet sir, a footman.

Clo. Indeed, he should be a footman by the garments he has left with thee: if this be a horseman's coat, it hath seen very hot service. Lend me thy hand, I'll help thee: come, lend me thy hand.

Aut. O, good sir, tenderly, O!

Clo. Alas, poor soul!

Aut. O, good sir, softly, good sir! I fear, sir, my shoulder-blade is out.

Clo. How now! canst stand?

Aut. (*Picking his pocket*) Softly, dear sir; good sir, softly. You ha' done me a charitable office.

Clo. Dost lack any money? I have a little money for thee.

Aut. No, good sweet sir; no, I beseech you, sir: I have a kinsman not past three quarters of a mile hence, unto whom I was going; I shall there have money, or any thing I want: offer me no money, I pray you; that kills my heart.[1]

Autolycus has all the traditional rogue tricks and more besides. He is compounded of many simples and mellowed by a touch of poetry which magically transforms the realism of the picture into something still more real. He has been a serving-man—a servant of the prince and for his vices whipped out of court. 'He hath ben since an ape-bearer; then a process

[1] *Winter's Tale* (Globe edition), Act IV, sc. 3.

server, a bailiff; then he compassed a motion of the Prodigal Son, and married a tinker's wife . . . and having flown over many knavish professions, he settled only in rogue.' He is pedlar, balladmonger, and pickpocket, as occasion demands, and withal has the care-free spirit of the real vagabond as he trudges gaily on his knavish road.

A Wild Rogue was a vagabond born on the road. 'I once rebuking a wyld roge because he went idelly about,' writes Harman, 'he shewed me that he was a begger by enheritance —his Grandfather was a begger, his father was one, and he must nedes be one by good reason!'[1] These Kynchin Morts or Kynchin Coes, as the children of vagabond parents were called, lived a pitiful life. They were valuable in the begging trade as a means of exciting sympathy. As they grew up they had the habit of wandering so firmly fixed that it was difficult to cure them. A letter of 1585 preserved in the Leicester Borough Records describes a vagrant boy ten years old who was found almost devoured with lice and suffering from many sores. The kind family who took him in cured his sores and kept him four or five months. But his vagabond habits were already too strong; he fell to wandering again, and was sent to the authorities of Leicester, which he said was his home, to be dealt with.[2]

The Counterfeit Cranks were something like the Rogues: they pretended to have the mysterious falling-sickness, the palsy, or some other terrible disease.[3] Harman says that he found one, Nicholas Gennings *alias* Nicholas Blunt, in London while his book was going through its first impression, and set the printer's boy to watch him. The vagabond begged all day in the streets, only retiring at noon to renew the blood on his face and the mud on his clothing, and left about dusk for his home across the river. Harman and the printer followed him to his dwelling, where they had him arrested and despoiled of his gains, which amounted to 14*s.* 3½*d.*—not a bad day's work at a time when an ordinary labourer earned 6*d.* a day

[1] Harman, *Caueat* (N. Sh. Soc.), p. 42.
[2] Referred to in *Records of the Borough of Leicester*, vol. iii, p. 222, No. cclxiii.
[3] Harman, *Caueat* (N. Sh. Soc.), pp. 51–6.

in the fields. Gennings was an Upright Man as well as a Counterfeit Crank. Harman's book has a rude woodcut, which is reproduced as the Frontispiece to this volume, showing him in each rôle. On one side of the picture he is clothed in filthy rags, his head bound up and his face bloody; and on the other he is neatly dressed, walks erect, and carries a stout cudgel to maintain his authority over other rogues and perhaps to enforce charity.

Such a Counterfeit Crank was tried twice by the London Court of Aldermen in 1547–8. The first time his pretended disease fooled the court, and he received no severer punishment than to be ordered to leave the city. The first entry in the Aldermen's records is as follows:

'Robt Shakysberie being butt a boy and dyseased with the palsey or some other dysease wherwith his bodie shakethe verie sore shall lykewyse furthwith departe out of ye cytie vppon payne of whypping if he make defaute.'[1]

It was only when he was caught playing the same trick a few months later that his deceit was discovered and he was ordered to be whipped at a cart's tail.

'*Item* it is agreyd that Robt Shakysbery who falsely counterfeytheth the dysease of the palsey and here loytereth and contynueth begging contrary to the order here taken 15 December vlt shall according to the same order be whypped tomorowe thurrouth the markett places of the cytie att a carts [tail] and be then expelled out of the same cytie.'[2]

There is in the records of this court the confession of a Counterfeit Crank of a much earlier date (1517–18), who used exactly the same pretence.

'A vagabund dissembling with the Sekenes of the Fallyng evyll.

'Miles Rose dwellyng in the paryssh of Seynt Botulph without Aldrychgate confessyd that he diverse and many tymes dissembled the sekenes of the Fallynge evyll in diverse parysshe churches within the Cite and at the tymes of his

[1] *Repertories of the Court of Aldermen*, xi, fo. 364. Town Clerk's Office, Guildhall.

[2] *Repertory*, xi, fo. 394 b.

fallyng diverse persones of their good myndes hav putte vppon his fyngers jememes of sylver called Cramp Ryngs which he hath taken to hys owen vse besydes ijd at many tymes.'[1]

This is the fygure of the counterfet Cranke, that is spoken of in this boke of Roges, called Nycholas Blunt other wyse Nycholas Gennyngs. His tale is in the xvii. lefe of this booke, which doth showe vnto all that reades it, woundrous suttell and crafty deseit donne of & by him.

FIG. 2. Nicholas Gennings in the pillory.
(*From the Bodleian copy of Harman's Caueat.*)

The Dommerer, who pretended to have no tongue, the Palliard, or Clapperdudgeon, who corrupted his body with

[1] *Repertory*, iii, fo. 201, March 11, 1517–18. On cramp rings see Andrew Boorde, *Introduction of Knowledge* (E.E.T.S.), p. 121. For a Latin ceremony by which they were consecrated temp. Mary see Burnet, *History of the Reformation*, 1865, vol. v, p. 445.

horrible artificial sores made by binding some corrosive like spearwort, arsenic or ratsbane to the flesh, and the Abraham Man, who pretended to be mad, were all variations of the Rogue and Counterfeit Crank.[1] Edgar, in *King Lear*, is a veritable Abraham Man, and *Poor Tom* was a name they used before Shakespeare was born.[2]

Dekker's *O per se O*, 1612 (the first of the many seventeenth-century revisions of *Lanthorne and Candle-light*), has in one of

FIG. 3. An Abraham Man or Tom o' Bedlam.
(*From one of the Roxburghe Ballads.*)

the chapters added in this edition a section explaining how Clapperdudgeons make these artificial sores.

'How they make their great Soares,
called the great *Cleyme*.

'They take Crow-foote, Sperewort, and Salt, and bruising these together, they lay them vpon the place of the body which they desire to make sore: the skinne by this meanes being fretted, they first clappe a linnen cloath, till it stick

[1] Harman, *Caueat* (N. Sh. Soc.), pp. 44, 47, and 57.
[2] See Awdeley, *Fraternitye of Vacabondes* (N. Sh. Soc.), p. 3 (written about 1560-1).

faste, which plucked off, the raw flesh hath Rats-bane throwne vpon it, to make it looke vgly: and then cast ouer that a cloath, which is alwayes bloudy and filthy, which they doe so often, that in the end in this hurt they féele no paine, neyther desire they to haue it healed, but with their *Doxies* will trauell (for all their great *Cleymes*) from Fayre to Fayre, and from

FIG. 4. A Palliard or Clapperdudgeon, according to Callot.
(*From the British Museum Collection.*)

Market to Market, being able by their *Mawnding* to get fiue *Bordes* (that is, fiue shillings) in a wéeke, in money and Corne. Which money they hide vnder blew and gréene patches: so that sometimes they haue about them, sixe pound or seauen pound together.'[1]

[1] Dekker, *O per se O*, sig. N_2 verso. At sig. M_4 in the same pamphlet is an explanation of how counterfeit soldiers make their wounds by the use of unslaked lime, soap, and iron rust; if this is properly done, 'the arme appeares blacke, and the soare raw and reddish, but white about the edges like an old wound'.

Harman tells a good story (which reminds one instantly of the means by which Simpcox's lameness is cured in 2 *Henry VI*, Act II, sc. 1) of the way in which he and a surgeon friend of his made a pretended dumb man to speak. The story is worth quoting because it illustrates not only the practices of these vagabonds but also the methods by which Harman dealt with them.

'Hauing on a time occasion to ride to Dartforde, to speak with a priest there, who maketh all kinde of conserues very well, and vseth stilling of waters; And repayringe to his house, I founde a Dommerar at his doore, and the priest him selfe perusinge his lycence, vnder the seales and hands of certayne worshypfull men, had thought the same to be good and effectuall. I taking the same writing, and reading it ouer, and noting the seales, founde one of the seales like vnto a seale that I had aboute me, which seale I bought besides Charing crosse, that I was out of doubte it was none of those Gentlemens seales that had sub[s]cribed. And hauing vnderstanding before of their peuish practises, made me to conceaue that all was forged and nought. I made the more hast home; for well I wyst that he would and must of force passe through the parysh where I dwelt; for there was no other waye for hym. And comminge homewarde, I found them in the towne, accordinge to my expectation, where they were staid; for there was a Pallyarde associate with the Dommerar and partaker of his gaynes, whyche Pallyarde I sawe not at Dartford. The stayers of them was a gentleman called *Chayne*, and a seruant of my Lord Kéepers, cald *Wostestowe*, which was the chiefe causer of the staying of them, being a Surgien, and cunning in his science, had séene the lyke practises, and, as he sayde, hadde caused one to speake afore that was dome. It was my chaunce to come at the begynning of the matter. "Syr," (quoth this Surgien) "I am bold here to vtter some part of my cunning. I trust" (quoth he) "you shall se a myracle wrought anon. For I once" (quoth he) "made a dumme man to speake." Quoth I, "you are wel met, and somwhat you haue preuented me; for I had thought to haue done no lesse or they hadde passed this towne. For I well knowe their writing is fayned, and they depe dissemblers." The Surgien made hym gape, and we could sée but halfe a toung. I required the Surgien to put hys fynger in his mouth, and to pull out his toung, and so he dyd, not withstanding he held strongly a prety whyle; at the length he pluckt out the same, to the great admiration of many that stode by. Yet when we sawe his tounge, hée would neither speake nor yet could heare. Quoth I to the Surgien, "knit two of his fyngers to gether, and thrust a stycke betwene them, and rubbe the same vp and downe a lytle whyle, and for my lyfe hée speaketh by and by." "Sir," quoth this Surgien, "I praye you let me practise and other waye." I was well contented to sée the same. He had him into a house, and tyed a halter aboute the wrestes of his handes, and hoysed him vp ouer a beame, and there dyd let him hang a good while: at the length, for very paine he required for Gods sake to let him down. So he that was both deafe and dume coulde in short tyme both heare and speake. Then I tooke that money I could find in his pursse, and distributed the same to the poore people dwelling there, whiche was xv. pence halfepeny, being all that we coulde finde. That done, and this merry myracle madly made, I sent them with my seruaunt to the next Iusticer, where they preached on the Pyllery for want of a Pulpet, and were well whypped, and none dyd bewayle them.'[1]

The Priggers of Prancers[2] had a thriving trade in sixteenth-century England. The difficulty of communication and of search for stolen horses made them comparatively safe. A prigger if he went on horseback was called a 'Launce man', if on foot a 'Trayler'. The trailers had saddle, bridle, stirrups and spurs, which could be folded up and carried in a small innocent-looking bag, ready for use on a horse caught in the fields.[3] The thing which made horse-stealing so profitable was the ease with which the booty could be disposed of at any small country fair, a little distance from the scene of the theft. To make this more difficult, a law was passed in 1588–9 putting certain restrictions on buying and selling of horses. No sale of a horse was legal, unless the seller first proved by substantial witnesses, before the Toller (an official established for regulating such sales), that the horse belonged to him.[4] But this law was constantly evaded by the easy method of having two confederates, apparelled like honest citizens, swear that the thief was the owner of the horse.[5]

[1] Harman, *Caueat* (N. Sh. Soc), pp. 57–9. [2] Ibid., p. 42.
[3] Greene, *Second Part of Conny-catching* (Grosart), vol. x, pp. 75–9.
[4] 2 & 3 Philip & Mary, c. 7 establishes office of Toller. 31 Eliz. c. 12 provides that witnesses shall swear that seller of the horse is the owner.
[5] Greene, *Second Part of Conny-catching* (Grosart), vol. x, pp. 77–8.

Greene and Dekker describe many ingenious tricks for stealing horses. One of them, which seems somewhat over-elaborate, was this: four or five fellows dressed like serving-men of the better sort, dusty and dirty from travel, enter an inn, pretending to have just sent a footman into town with their horses. They stay several days, ordering freely of the best that the house affords, giving out that they are waiting for their master, about whose wealth and position they talk a great deal. After some time in comes another servant to say that their master commands them to meet him at a town ten or fifteen miles away for two days before he comes to the inn. On their master's credit they obtain horses and ride away, to sell the horses at 'some blinde drunken théeuish fayre' and divide up the money.[1] This is exactly the trick by which the three Germans in the *Merry Wives of Windsor* cozened the host of the Garter and 'all the hosts of Readins, of Maidenhead, of Colebrook, of horses and money'.[2]

From the early part of this chapter the reader will have some idea of the number and variety of legitimately licensed vagabonds and beggars. The opportunity for the use of false licences is obvious, and it was taken advantage of to the fullest extent. Harman gives cant names for several such beggars who were usually, he says, bearers of counterfeit licences or had obtained their permits under false pretences: Fraters, who went about with real or sham licences to beg for a hospital or lazar house; Demanders for Glimmer, who pretended to be authorized to beg for losses by fire; and Whip-jacks, who carried papers allowing them to ask relief for losses at sea, though perhaps 'their shipes were drowned in the playne of Salisbery'.[3] The forged passport here reproduced was used by a typical Whip-jack. Counterfeiters were examined frequently by the highest officers of the City and Kingdom. The London Aldermen punished two rogues for this offence in 1549, three in 1569, and three more in 1571.[4] The Privy

[1] Dekker, *Lanthorne and Candle-light*, chap. vii.
[2] *M.W.W.*, Act IV, sc. 5.
[3] Harman, *Caueat* (N. Sh. Soc.), pp. 45, 48, and 61.
[4] *Repertories*, xii, pt. i, fo. 38; xvi, fo. 449; xvii, fo. 234^b.

Plate III

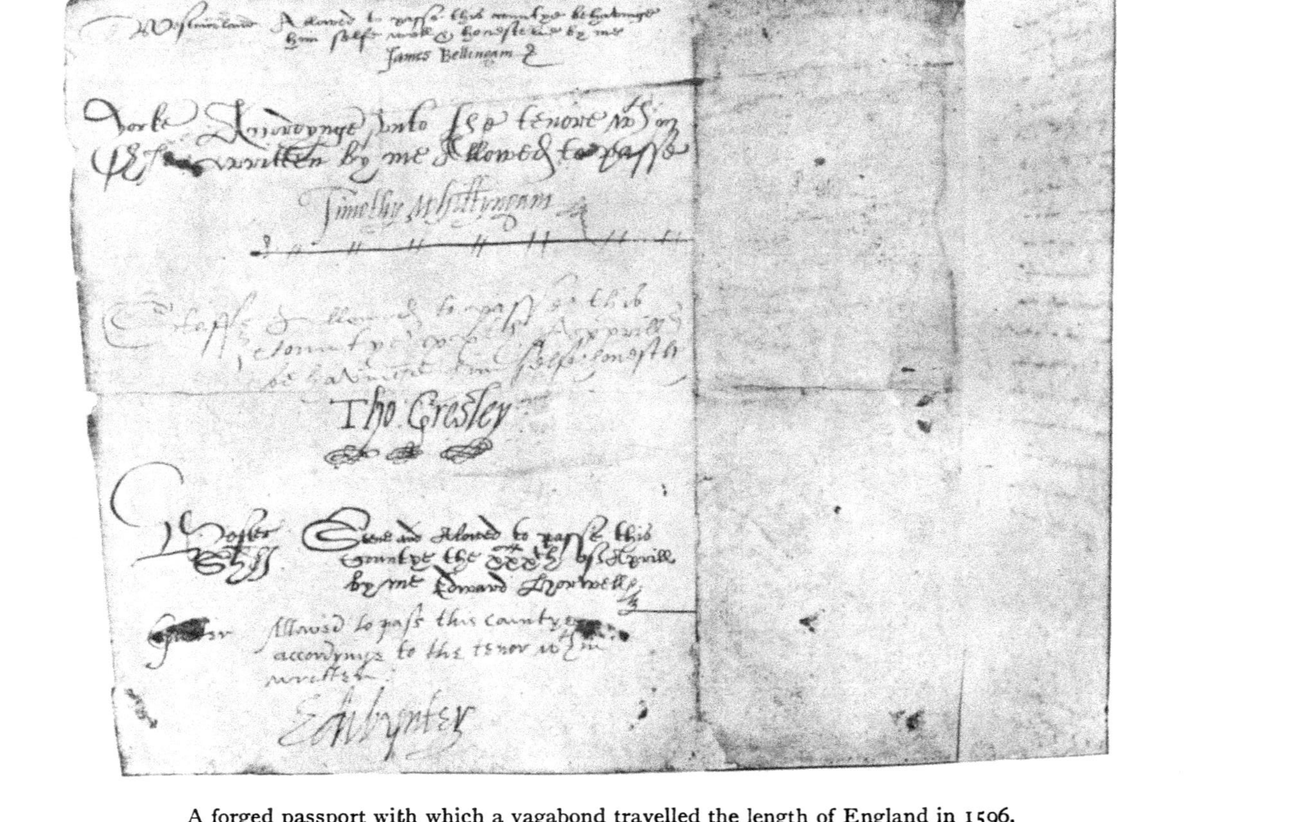

Westmerland Allowed to passe this countye behavinge him selfe well & honestlie by me
James Bellingam

Timothy Whittingam

Tho. Gresley

Allowed to pass this countye accordinge to the tenor within written

A forged passport with which a vagabond travelled the length of England in 1596.
(See Appendix A, 14, for transcription.)

(*From the British Museum*, *MS. Lans.* 81, *No.* 64.)

Council examined some fellows who had counterfeited the seal of the Admiralty in 1551,[1] and warned the London Aldermen in 1569 to write their passports for rogues so discreetly as to make imitation difficult.[2] Harman mentions taking false licences away from rogues several times, and warns his readers to trust no Proctor's licence unless it bears the Great Seal or is printed, 'For the Printers will sée and wel vnderstand before it come in presse that same is lawfull.'[3] Awdeley says there was one class of vagabonds called Jarckmen,[4] whose business it was to counterfeit licences and seals; Harman denies their existence,[5] and says very plausibly that the rogues had no difficulty in buying false licences in any town. In *O per se O* we have some further account of the way in which false licences are made and how to tell them from true ones. According to this pamphlet the counterfeit seals are carved on the end of a stick, and are usually a poor imitation of the head of a dog or a horse or a unicorn. They can be told from a genuine seal by the fact that there is no circle around the figure and by the rough way in which they are made. It says also that the false licence is likely to have the words 'For *Salomon* saith; Who giueth the poore, lendeth the Lord, etc.', and that the bearer is sure to have at least one hundred miles to go to his home.[6]

The closing paragraph of a proclamation against false pursuivants in 1596 indicates that counterfeit licences were then very common.

'Moreouer where there are another sort of vagabond persons that either themselues doe make, or cause counterfeite Pasports to be made, and licenses to begge and gather Almes, pretending that they haue beene hurt and maymed in her Maiesties seruice, or receiued some other great losse or hinderance by casualty, and vnto those licenses doe counterfeit the hands and seales of the said Lords, and others of her Maiesties priuy Counsell, or of some of them, or of some Justices of the Peace,

1 *Acts of the Privy Council*, October 16, 1551.
2 *Journals of the Common Council of the City of London*, xix, fo. 171 b (quoted in Appendix A, 6).
3 Harman, *Caueat* (N. Sh. Soc.), p. 45. Cp. p. 25 above.
4 *Fraternitye of Vacabondes* (N. Sh. Soc.), p. 5.
5 Harman, *Caueat* (N. Sh. Soc.), p. 60.
6 Dekker, *O per se O*, 1612, sig. N. Concerning the authorship and trustworthiness of this pamphlet see Chapter VI.

or of the Generals of her Maiesties forces beyond the Seas, or of the Captaines of companies and other Officers, thereby to defraude her Maiesties subiects, and sometimes repaire to the Churches at the time of Diuine seruice, to make and gather collection by coulour of these counterfeit licences: of which sort, there are a great number dispersed in diuers Counties of the Realme, conspiring also, and combyning themselues together in very tumultuous sort to euill purposes: For the auoyding of which abuses, and iust punishment of such wicked and base people, her Maiesties pleasure is, that all Parsons or Vicars of Parishes, Churchwardens, or other her Maiesties Officers, and louing subiects, to whom these kinde of euill disposed persons may resort, shall consider well of the said licences, and finding cause to suspect the same, they shall bring them before the next Justice of the Peace to be strictly by them examined, and upon further cause of suspicion, he shall commit them to some Prison untill hee may be certainely informed from such, whose names are subscribed to the said Pasports or licences, whether the same bee true or counterfeite.' [1]

Pedlars and tinkers were so useful that, in spite of their thieving habits, they were always welcome to the country people, and these two trades became a common cloak for rogues, as did that of tinker in Scotland for gipsies.[2] If the tinkers of pamphlet literature represent the class, the members of that calling were merry rogues who did a great many things besides mend old pots and kettles. Greene, in a favourite and often copied story, describes one who added to his income by picking locks and stealing in every inn where he stopped. A Justice of the Peace who had proof of this entertained the tinker kindly, gave him some work, and sent him on an errand to the next jail carrying, instead of a letter, his own *mittimus*. Christopher Sly, in the *Taming of the Shrew*, is Harman's 'Dronken Tinckar' drawn to the life. He has the same fondness for 'bene bowse'. The hostess of the 'bowsing ken' knows him well enough for a rogue, and with the help of the third-borough would doubtless soon have put him in the stocks had the author not saved him for a merrier purpose.

[1] See Bodleian volume, *Proclamations by Elizabeth*, under date, May 3, 1596. Press-work, Arch. F. C. 11, fo. 355.

[2] Harman, *Caueat* (N. Sh. Soc.), pp. 59 and 60; Rid, *Art of Iugling* (1612), sig. B_2 verso.

So far has Harman led us into the mysteries of roguery. He understood them extremely well; but he was, after all, a rather stern, serious-minded Justice of the Peace, and one class of vagabonds probably visited him very little: these were the fellows whose business it was to give the villagers amusement: gamesters, fortune-tellers, bearwards, players, jugglers, and minstrels.

FIG. 5. A Pedlar.
(*From a ballad in the Pepysian Collection.*)

The Minstrels, roaming up and down the land singing bawdy ballads and furnishing music in taverns, at fairs, and at country wakes and feasts, were in very bad repute. But at the same time they were very popular. They commonly sold copies of the ballads which they sang, as Autolycus does, and like him they combined with their trade various kinds of roguery. Stubbes thought the honest ones too rare to count, and heartily condemned the whole tribe in a passage which contains a good picture of their life.

'I think that all good minstrelles, sober and chast musicions (speking of suche drunken sockets and bawdye parasits as range the Cuntreyes, ryming and singing of vncleane, corrupt, and filthie songs in Tauernes, Ale-houses, Innes, and other publique assemblies,) may daunce the wild Moris thorow a needles eye. For how should thei bere chaste minds, seeing that their exercyse is the pathway to all vncleanes. Their is no ship so balanced with massie matter, as their heads are fraught with all kind of bawdie songs, filthie ballads and scuruie rymes, seruing for euery purpose, and for euerie Cumpanie.'[1]

Even Sidney, who had no Puritan prejudices and was alive to poetry wherever he met it, speaking of the minstrels of his day, could only praise the song and not the singer.

FIG. 6. A Minstrel.
(*From one of the Roxburghe Ballads.*)

'Certainly I must confesse my own barbarousnes, I neuer heard the olde song of *Percy* and *Duglas*, that I found not my heart mooued more then with a Trumpet: and yet it is sung but by some blinde Crouder, with no rougher voyce, then rude stile.'[2]

The invention of printing had killed minstrelsy as it was known in the Middle Ages. The name survived for all those whose business it was to furnish popular musical entertainment: fiddlers, pipers, singers of songs and ballads. When these were attached to great households or licensed by other authorities they were considered respectable members of society; when not, they were defined by the law as vaga-

[1] *Anatomie of Abuses* (N. Sh. Soc.), p. 171.
[2] Sidney, *Apologie*, Arber's reprint, p. 46.

bonds and sturdy beggars.[1] Their character and habits were much the same in either case. Dependence upon a noble family evidently meant for a minstrel very little constant attendance, and the protected and unprotected wandered up and down the land entertaining the public, 'changing music for money' where they could. They played in the streets, visited great households on the occasion of a wedding or a feast, haunted taverns and more questionable resorts, either in bands (as Sneak's noise) or singly. They were merry fellows; some of them were decent and sang songs which rather tended to edification, others were the reverse. Curious vignettes of individual minstrels are preserved: of these Richard Sheale's account of himself and Deloney's of Anthony Now-now will serve as examples of the better sort, and Chettle's invective against the sons of old Barnes of 'Bishop's Stafford', put into the mouth of this same Anthony Now-now's ghost, of the lower.

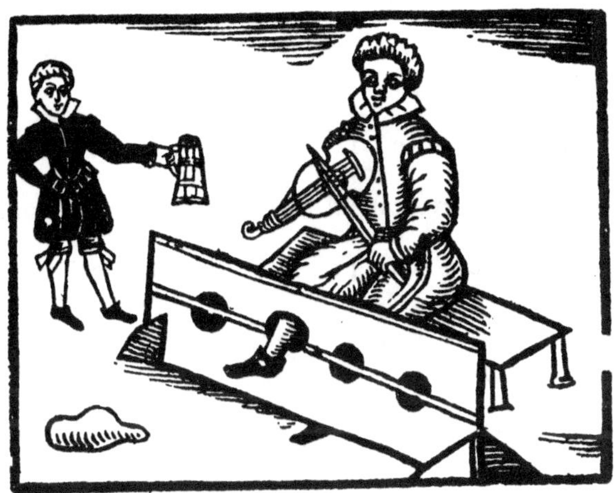

FIG. 7. A Minstrel in the Stocks.
(*From one of the Roxburghe Ballads.*)
BEGGARS they are with one consent,
And ROGUES by act of Parliament.

[1] Chambers, in his *Mediaeval Stage*, vol. ii, App. F, mentions several courts of minstrels and guilds which gave, or claimed to give, those licensed by them protection from the law against vagabonds. There was the Court of Minstrels held by the Duttons in Cheshire, that established by letters patent from John of Gaunt at Tutbury, and city guilds in London, Canterbury, and Beverley.

Sheale was a minstrel-retainer of the Earl of Derby about the middle of the century. He was not technically a vagabond, but he was evidently a skilful beggar and gained a large part of his living on the road. He was respectable enough to wish to pay his debts, and he was able, with the help of his wife, to amass sixty pounds with which to do it, but unfortunately he was waylaid by thieves on Dunsmore Heath and his money taken from him. A song which he made to recount this event and move good people to help make up his loss gives us a very good idea of him and of his class. He thought himself secure in carrying the money because of the reputation of his calling for poverty.

> And withowt company I ryde alone, thus was I folisshe bolde.
> I thought beth reason off my harpe no man wolde me susspecte ;
> For minstrels offt with mony the be not moche infecte.

But the thieves got wind of it and lay in wait for him on Dunsmore Heath,

> Wher many a man for las mony hathe ofte tymys cought his dethe.

He has grieved so much over it that he can hardly follow his calling ; he cannot play the merry knave for thinking of his loss :

> After my robbery my memory was so decayde,
> That I colde neathar syng nore talke, my wyttes wer so dismayde ;
> My awdacitie was gone, and all my myrry tawke.
> Ther ys sum hear have sene me as myrry as a hawke ;
> But nowe I am so trublyde with phansis in my mynde,
> That I cannote play the myrry knave accordynge to my kynde.

But after all he thanks God it was no worse ; his patron has given him letters, friends everywhere have contributed, and he hopes present company will do the same. So he ends,

Desyryng youe all to bear this tayle in mynde,
That I among your pursis nowe sum frendshipe may fynde.
Every man a lyttell wold satisfye my nede,
To helpe a poor man owt off dett, it ys a gracious dede.[1]

Sheale was characteristic of his trade in that his talents lay more in the direction of begging than of poetry. In the volume from which this poem is quoted is preserved the doggerel formula which he evidently used constantly to thank his host for hospitality and, at the same time, ask leave to come again.

Deloney's story of how Anthony Now-now got his name occurs in the tenth chapter of the second part of *The Gentle Craft*:

'The greene king (a shoemaker—the hero of this particular story. He is now on his way to Flanders) hauing thus taken his leaue, went toward *Billingsgate*, of purpose to take Barge: where by the way hee met with *Anthony* now now, the firkin Fidler of *Finchlane*:

What master (quoth he) well met, I pray whither are you walking? and how doe all our friends in saint *Martins*? Will you not haue a crash ere you goe?

Yfaith, *Anthony* (quoth he) thou knowest I am a good fellow, and one that hath not been a niggard to thee at any time, therefore if thou wilt bestow any musick on me, doe; and if it please God that I return safely from *Flanders* againe, I will pay thee well for thy paines; but now I haue no money for musick.

Gods-nigs (quoth *Anthony*) whether you haue money or no, you shall haue musick, I doe not allways request coyne of my friends for my cunning: what, you are not euery body, and seeing you are going beyond sea, I will bestow a pinte of wine on you at the Salutation:

Saist thou so *Anthony* (quoth he) in good sooth I will not refuse thy curtesie, and with that they stept into the Tauern, where *Anthony* cald for wine: and drawing forth his Fiddle began to play, and after he had scrapte halfe a score lessons he began to sing.

When should a man shew himselfe gentle and kinde,
When should a man comfort the sorrowful minde?

[1] Wright, *Songs and Ballads . . . chiefly of the reign of Philip and Mary*, 1860. The quotations are from No. xlvi, pp. 156–61.

O Anthony *now, now, now.*
O Anthony *now, now, now.*
When is the best time to drinke with a friend?
When is it meetest my money to spend?
O Anthony *now, now, now.*
O Anthony *now, now, now.*
When goes the King of good fellowes away?
That so much delighted in dauncing and play?
O Anthony *now, now, now.*
O Anthony *now, now, now.*
And when should I bid my Master farewell?
Whose bountie and curtesie so did excell?
O Anthony *now, now, now.*
O Anthony *now, now, now.*

Loe ye now Master (quoth he) this song haue I made for your sake, and, by the grace of God when you are gone I will sing it euery Sunday morning vnder your wiues window, that she may know we dranke together ere you parted:

I pray thee do so (said the Greene king) and do my commendations vnto her, and tell her at my returne I hope to make merry.

Thus after they had made an end of their wine, and paid for the shot, *Anthony* putting vp his Fiddle departed, seeking to change musicke for money: while the Greene king of Saint *Martins* sailed in *Grauesend* Barge. But *Anthony* in his absence sung this song so often in Saint *Martins*, that thereby he purchast a name which he neuer lost till his dying day, for euer after men called him nothing but *Anthony* now now.'[1]

In his tract called *Kind-Harts Dreame*, written at the end of 1592, three months after Greene's death, Chettle represents the ghosts of various people coming back to earth to bring denunciations of abuses in their professions. One of these is old Anthony Now-now, come back to protest against the abuses in ballad-singing which have sprung up since his day. Vile, indecent ballads are printed in large numbers; boys are taught to sing and sent out to sell them, escaping, because of their youth, the notice of the authorities:

'This error (ouer spreding the realme) hath in no small measure increased in Essex, and the shires thereto adioyning,

[1] *Deloney's Works*, ed. Mann, pp. 204–5.

by the blushlesse faces of certaine Babies, sonnes to one *Barnes*, most frequenting Bishops Stafford. The olde fellow their father, soothing his sonnes folly, resting his crabbed limes on a crab-tree staffe, was wont (and I thinke yet he vses) to seuer himselfe from the Booth, or rather Brothell of his two sons Ballad shambels: where, the one in a sweaking treble, the other in an ale-blowen base, carrowle out such adultrous ribaudry, as chast eares abhorre to heare, and modestie hath no tongue to vtter.

While they are in the ruffe of ribaudrie, (as I was about to say) the olde ale-knight, their dad, breakes out into admiration, and sends stragling customers to admire the roaring of his sonnes: where, that I may showe some abuses, and yet for shame let slip the most odious, they heare no better matter, but the lasciuious vnder songs of Watkins ale, the Carmans whistle, Chopingknives, and frier foxtaile, and that with such odious and detested boldnes, as if there be any one line in those lewd songs than other more abhominable, that with a double repetition is lowdly belowed. . . . The father leapes, the lubers roare, the people runne, the Diuell laughs, God lowers, and good men weepe.'[1]

These graceless imps of old Barnes, Anthony's ghost informs us, have before now been employed by cutpurses to gather a crowd and keep them amused while the thieves plied their trade.

'Where, yer [ere] a leaud songe was fully ended, some mist their kniues, some their purses, soome one thinge, soome another . . . how euer they sung, it is like they shared: for it hath beene saide, they themselues bragge, they gayned their twenty shillinges in a day.'[2]

Singing in public, Anthony proposes, should be allowed only to the aged and poor, who have this as a last resort before they come to beggary. These are the men—Richard Sheale, Anthony Now-now, the sons of Barnes, and their like—who in the sixteenth century inherited the name and, to some extent, filled the place of the courtly minstrel of the Middle Ages.

The tricks which wandering jugglers and conjurers performed

[1] Chettle, *Kind-Harts Dreame* (N. Sh. Soc.: *Shakspere Allusion Books*, i), pp. 48–9. The town is probably Bishop's Stortford.

[2] Ibid., p. 50. Cp. the section devoted to pickpockets in Chapter V below.

are described by Reginald Scot in his interesting *Discouerie of Witchcraft* published in 1584. Scot was moved to investigate the subject by his hatred of the horrible cruelties used against poor old women accused of being in league with the Devil, and he studied the art of juggling in order to expose the practisers of it, who often claimed supernatural power. He is loath, he says, to spoil the trade of poor men who practise juggling honestly for a living, but too many use it as a means of cozenage and to keep up the false belief in witchcraft. He gives careful directions for performing various amusing and wonderful feats of legerdemain—making balls multiply, dissolve, or combine into a large one; passing a coin through the table, or from one spectator's hand to another's; tricks with cards, tying the knot called 'fast and loose', which would resist the strongest pull, but loosen instantly when the conjurer blew on it; telling whether one cast 'crosse or pile' (i.e. heads or tails) by hearing the ring of the coin; altering grain in a box from one sort to another by magic words, burning a thread and making it whole again, making a book which would show the pages white, red, blue, green, or painted with pictures, at the owner's will. If you do not understand his description of this, 'you shall (if you be disposed) sée or buie for a small value the like booke, at the shop of *W. Brome* in Powles churchyard, for your further instruction'.[1]

In the section about 'desperate or dangerous iuggling knacks' he explains how to eat a knife and produce it again, to thrust a dagger into your hand or through your tongue without injury, to put a piece of lead into one eye, push it with a stick across the forehead under the skin and out of the other eye, to cut your nose half in two and heal it instantly, to cut off a man's head, lay it on a platter, and then restore it again, 'which the iugglers call the decollation of John Baptist'. There are pictures of the specially made daggers, tables, rings, &c. with which these tricks are performed. One of the best is 'To thrust a dagger or bodkin into your guts verie strangelie, and to recouer immediatlie'. The device is to construct a pasteboard breast and abdomen painted exactly to resemble the

[1] *Discouerie of Witchcraft*, book 13, chap. 33.

To cut off ones head, and to laie it in a platter,
which the iugglers call the decollation of Iohn Baptist.

The forme of ẏ planks, &c.

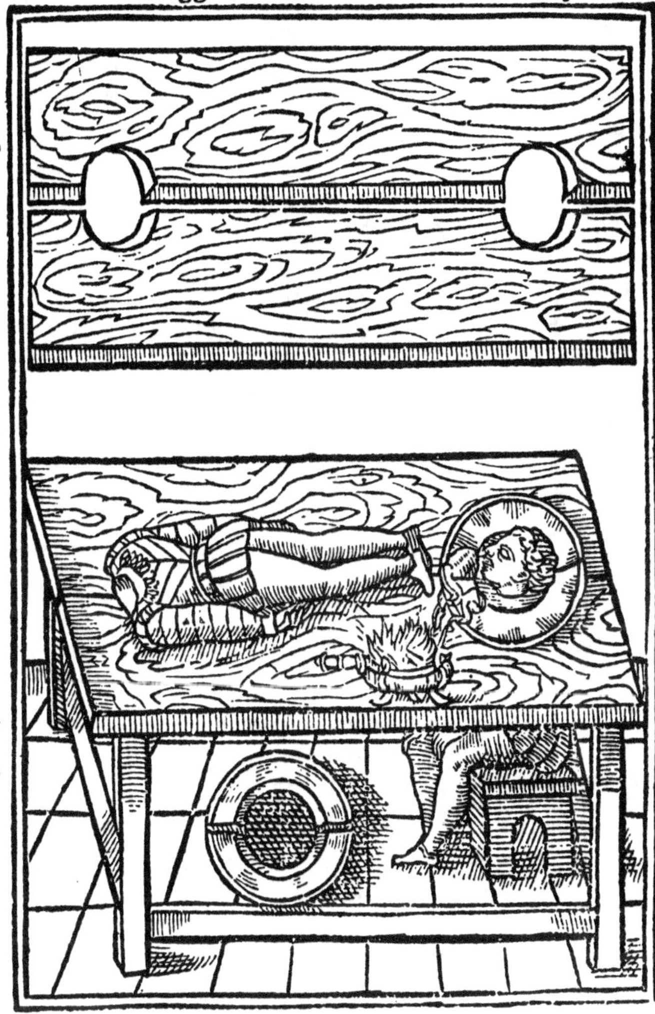

The order of the acti-on, as it is to be shew-ed.

FIG. 8. A Juggler's trick.
(*From Scot's Discouerie of Witchcraft.*)

skin and put on under the clothing; under this was worn a bladder full of blood, 'which bloud must be of a calfe or of a shéepe; but in no wise of an oxe or a cow, for that will be too thicke,' and under this bladder was a metal plate to protect the body. Thus equipped, the conjurer got himself stabbed and made the blood squirt from the wound by pressing against the plate with his body, at the same time acting the part of a dying man, so as to excite the wonder and horror of the beholders. At this trick, Scot tells us, 'not long since a iuggler caused himself to be killed at a tauerne in cheapside, from whence he presentlie went into Powles churchyard and died. Which misfortune fell vpon him through his owne follie, as being then drunken, and hauing forgotten his plate, which he should haue had for his defense.'[1] These were the tricks of the vagabond jugglers who wandered up and down the land, reaping a harvest in every market, fair, and tavern; they are mentioned in every statute against vagabonds, and doubtless had a prosperous life, in spite of the constables and judges.

During the period from 1547 to 1575—the palmiest days of vagabond life in England—we hear of some wanderers who did more than obtain a living by clever deception or thieving. These were the spreaders of discontent in regard to social and political conditions,

> moody beggars, starving for a time
> Of pell-mell havoc and confusion.

It has been shown how terribly hard conditions were for the poor about the middle of the century. One is not surprised to learn that some of the victims of enclosures, evictions and rent-raisings, driven out to wander as homeless vagabonds, were men of too fiery a substance to be able to set to work tamely to acquire the wretched vagabond arts of begging and stealing. Instead they went about spreading as best they might the discontent which was in the air and which is expressed forcibly in the various socialistic writings mentioned in the first chapter of this book. M. Jusserand conjectures that the sudden and mysterious presence of revolt on every hand in 1381 was due

[1] *Discouerie of Witchcraft*, book 13, chap. 34.

to the vagrants who swarmed on every highway and who spread the idea of discontent and rebellion from shire to shire.[1] It seems quite certain that this was true in 1549.

In this way the vagabonds became a serious menace to the peace of the realm. The worst days were perhaps in the time of Edward VI, but during the first twenty years of Elizabeth's reign this army of idle, discontented vagrants, ready to join in any rebellion, kept the government in constant danger. It was this danger which was responsible for the rapid development of the English poor law between 1530 and 1600: it was this danger which made the Privy Council devote so much personal attention to all sorts of petty details of its enforcement. The legal measures taken in response to this menace on the part of the vagabonds will be described in the next chapter; here we shall try only to throw what dim light is possible on their actions.

Several proclamations were issued in 1548 and 1549 against wandering Tale-tellers. One of these (issued July 8, 1549) calls them rogues, vagabonds, prison breakers and seditious run-a-gates.[2] Strype describes the conditions (largely in the words of this proclamation) as follows:

'There was now a sort of leud idle Fellows, the most part whereof had neither place to inhabit, nor sought any stay to live by, Persons many of them condemned of Felony, or Prison-breakers, run from the Wars, and Sea-rovers departed from the King's Garisons, and Loiterers; These Persons ran from Place to Place, from County to County, from Town to Town, to stir up Rumours, raise up Tales, imagin News, whereby to stir and gather together the Kings Subjects, of simplicity and ignorance deceived. And by that pretence such leud Ruffians and unruly Vagabonds became Ringleaders and Masters of the Kings people; seeking to spoil, rob and ravin where, or whom they listed, or might: And so lived, waxed rich, and fed on other Mens Labour, Mony and Food. And when the Poor of one part of the Country raised up by these Fellons, repented and saw their Folly, acknowledged their Faults, and returned themselves to their Duty, and

1 *English Wayfaring Life*, pp. 271–5.

2 In the library of the Society of Antiquaries in London. *Proclamations*, iii (39).

received the Kings Pardon; the said Runnagates escaped from the Places of their first Attempts, and daily resorted to new Places; and so from Place to Place, Shire to Shire, never quieting themselves, but devising slanderous Tales, and divulging to the People such kind of News as they thought might most readily move them to Uproars and Tumults; and pretending the same time they sought the redress of the *Commonwealth.* The King sent a Proclamation after these, dated *July* 8, Charging all Justices, Sheriffs, Bailiffs, and other his Officers, to be diligent to take some good special Order for the Apprehension and Attaching of such Persons, whether as Vagabonds, Wayfaring Men, Straglers or otherwise. And that whosoever should discover any of them should have the Kings hearty Thanks, and 20 Crowns for a Reward.'[1]

The Privy Council punished divers such persons by ordering them to be set on pillories, with the words 'Movers of Sedition and Spreaders of Falce Rumores' on their backs, and certain of the worst offenders had their ears cut off.[2] There are occasional notices of tale-tellers and movers of sedition later in Elizabeth's reign, but peace, prosperity, and workhouses together seem to have silenced most of them.

There was a similar state of affairs in regard to religion. The vagabond law of 1547 was especially severe against wandering monks and friars. Bishop Burnet (writing in 1681) says of Edward VI's time that 'these vagrants did every where alienate the people's minds from the government, and persuaded them that things would never be well settled till they were again restored to their houses. Some of these came often to London on pretence of suing for their pensions, but really to practise up and down through the country.'[3] Against no vagabonds were the efforts of the Privy Council more determined. The most extensive and thorough measures used against them during Elizabeth's reign—the whipping campaign of 1569–72—were caused by the rebellion of the Catholic nobles in the north in 1569.[4] Watches for vagrants were

[1] *Ecclesiastical Memorials* (1721), vol. ii, book i, chap. 21, p. 169.
[2] *Acts of Privy Council*, vol. for 1552–4, p. 168.
[3] *History of the Reformation*, 1865, ii. 100.
[4] See letter ordering these searches. (Transcribed in Appendix A, 6.)

PLATE IV

Two of Rembrandt's beggars.
(*From the British Museum collection.*)

ordered in every shire and the sheriffs and justices were instructed to send in the names of all vagabonds apprehended, probably in order that the Privy Council might trace Popish agitators and spies.

After the Armada there was continual fear lest Popish spies should slip into the country to prepare the way for a second invasion. A proclamation of October 18, 1591, against disguised Popish priests and agitators mentions among their various disguises: 'many of them in their behauiour as Ruffians, farre off to be thought, or suspected to be Friers, Priests, Jesuits, or Popish schollers.'[1] And Lodge, in 1596, gives a description of these seditious malcontents, which confirms what has just been said. According to him a young man of good wits who was tired of living so long in England, 'where men of good wits are most neglected,' would go abroad in search of better entertainment, or more freedom in religion, and return later 'with seditious bookes, false intelligences, and defamatorie Libels, to disgrace his Prince, detract her honourable counsell, and seduce the common sort'. In Paul's he told of the fortune awaiting shrewd fellows abroad; in the country he railed against enclosures and racked rents, calling for revolt, insurrection, and commotion.[2]

So much for the life of the wandering vagabonds. Enough has been said to give some idea of the variety of their devices for begging and stealing, to show how much they contributed to the amusement of the lower classes, and in what ways they were a serious danger to the peace of the realm. The vagrants included many kinds of harmful and harmless persons, but they were so hard to distinguish that they were all included in the one comprehensive term, Vagabond, and were legislated against in common.

[1] Bodleian volume, *Proclamations by Elizabeth*, fo. 316.

[2] Lodge, *Wits Miserie and the Worlds Madnesse*, 1596 (Hunterian Club), p. 67.

CHAPTER III

LAWS AGAINST VAGABONDS

THE object of this chapter is to outline the laws against rogues and vagabonds from 1530 to 1597 and to describe the methods used to execute them. This is worth doing for the sake of the information it gives about the vagabond class in its relation to society as a whole. Before 1530 there was almost no legislation on this subject, although a few towns and cities had already for half a century been wrestling with the problems presented by the increasing numbers of idlers and vagrants. From that year, however, until the end of the century the rogues and beggars received constant attention from Parliament. The legislation against vagabonds which is important for us falls into three periods, (1) from 1530 to 1547; (2) from 1547 to 1572; and (3) from 1572 to 1597. The discussion is divided according to this simple scheme and in connexion with each period is considered not only the laws enacted but also the measures taken to enforce them. However, before beginning the discussion outlined above, it may be worth while to sum up in one or two paragraphs the general tendencies in legislation and in execution of the laws against rogues and vagabonds during the entire period.

At the beginning of the sixteenth century the laws against vagrancy were of the simplest character; they directed that all suspicious vagrant persons should be punished by stocking and imprisonment until sureties could be found for their good behaviour. The next step was to divide these vagrant persons into two classes, sturdy and impotent. The first were forbidden to wander on pain of various punishments, stocking, whipping, loss of one or both ears, or even death. The second were given permits allowing them to beg for their relief. This plan of punishment and aid was modified at various times through the century, the changes tending always (except for one law which was in force only a few years) to make the punishments for vagabondage less severe, to make more and more ample provision for setting able-bodied vagrants to work, and to provide compulsory instead of voluntary payments for the aid of the impotent. Apparently the sixteenth-century law-makers drew three conclusions from their experiments in making laws against rogues and vagabonds: (1) that severe and cruel punishments did not suppress vagabondage but only made it more exciting; (2) that the one effective punishment for sturdy vagabonds and beggars was to set them to work; and (3) that for the relief of impotent poor it was far better to levy a regular tax than to depend on charity. These brief general statements sum up what was in reality a great legislative triumph. Goaded on by the discomfort and danger from the swarms of vagrants which infested the land, English law-makers, in a period of seventy years, developed from the rudest of beginnings a code of laws which were the foundation of English poor relief for the next two hundred years.

Great as was the contribution to legislation concerning the poor during this period, it was not more important than the progress in methods of enforcing the laws. The credit for this belongs to the Privy Council of Elizabeth. The old method of enforcing the poor laws had been to issue emphatic proclamations to Justices of the Peace, explaining their duties and directing that they should perform them as they wished to avoid their sovereign's displeasure. These proclamations are valuable to the historian for the way in which they describe conditions, but they seem to have had little effect. The same pressure which caused Parliament to seek constantly to improve the Poor Laws drove the Government to seek more effective ways of executing them. The members of Elizabeth's Privy Council directed the punishment of vagrants and the relief of the poor by means of personal letters to the sheriffs and justices of each shire. They ordered privy watches and searches for vagabonds and required certificates of the names of all who were punished. They personally examined vagabonds caught with false licences, investigated the complaints of persons who, for any extraordinary reason, demanded permits to beg, reproved the University of Cambridge for allowing wandering gamesters to settle near it, and altogether seem to have exercised a minute supervision over every detail. The machinery which Elizabeth's Council organized, improved by thirty years of use, enabled Charles I to enforce the poor law more thoroughly, it is said, than it has ever been executed since.[1] But in the reign of Elizabeth all this vigilance was barely sufficient to restrain the multitudes of rogues and vagabonds from grave disorder and rebellion: the evil would have been terrible without it.

1530–47. Legislation.

In order to understand the Elizabethan laws against vagabonds it is necessary to go back to the year 1530. The statute for the punishment of vagabonds in force at the beginning of Elizabeth's reign (22 Henry VIII, c. 12) had been made in 1530–1 and had continued in force since then except for three years of unsuccessful experimenting, 1547–9. This law provided that impotent beggars should have licences signed and sealed by the Justices of the Peace, allowing them to beg within certain limits. All vagabonds and beggars without such licences, and all persons able to labour, who were found begging, were to be stripped from the waist upward and whipped until bloody, or set in the stocks three days and three nights on bread and water; they were then to be sent to the place of their usual residence, to be relieved if impotent or set to work if able-bodied. Begging scholars, without licence from the Vice-Chancellor of their University, shipmen, proctors, pardoners, fortune-tellers, fencers, minstrels, players, and the like, without proper licence, were to be whipped two days in succession: for the second offence this punishment was to be repeated, and in addition they were to stand one day in the pillory and have an ear cut off; for the third offence they were to undergo like punishment and lose the other ear. The statute specified

[1] Leonard, *Early History of English Poor Relief*, p. 132.

one form of licence for deserving beggars and another for discharged prisoners begging for money to pay their jailer's fees; finally, it threatened any one harbouring a sturdy vagabond with a fine of 100*s.* and imprisonment at the King's will. This statute was slightly modified by another enacted in 1535–6 (27 Henry VIII, c. 25), which provided for regular collections

FIG. 9. Two pretended fortune-tellers in the pillory.
(*From The . . . Cousnages of Iohn West and Alice West, in the Bodleian.*)

of voluntary gifts to relieve the impotent poor and to set able-bodied vagrants to work, and made it a felony (punishable by death) to be guilty of vagrancy a third time. However, the 27 Henry VIII, c. 25, remained in force only until 1547, and was not renewed with the 22 Henry VIII, c. 12, in 1549.

1530–47. ENFORCEMENT OF THE LAWS.

A good many attempts were made to see that the law of 1530–1 was executed. In the year it was passed the King rebuked the Court of Aldermen of the City of London for allowing great multitudes of vagabonds to infest the streets.[1] A law was passed in 1541–2 (33 Henry VIII, c. 10) directing Justices of the Peace to proclaim and enforce the law of 1530–1 along with others against petty disorders; and there are in the Public Record Office papers referring to four or five letters from the Privy Council to Justices and other officers between 1537 and 1541, directing them to make special efforts to repress the multitude of idle vagabonds.[2]

In June 1530 a royal proclamation against vagabonds[3] recited that in spite of the efforts to restrain them, they were increased 'into great rowtes and companies', and ordered every vagrant to ask the nearest Justice of the Peace for a 'billet', i. e. passport, to his home. After two days every vagabond taken without such a billet was to be whipped and then given one (of a form specified in the proclamation), signed by the Justice, or, if he could not write, by some honest householder living near. On June 16, 1531, another proclamation was issued,[4] directing the due execution of the statute just enacted, and between this year and 1547, the date of the next law, half a dozen others—most of them against vagabonds in London and about the court. There is no trace, in such records of punishments as happen to be preserved, of any result from these proclamations, unless it be in the superior vigilance exercised against vagabonds in London.

Vagabonds were more strictly punished in the cities than anywhere else, as one would expect. Chester had a code of ordinances on this subject in 1540.[5] In the records of the Borough of Leicester is preserved an ordinance of Henry VII for the punishment of rogues and vagabonds, dated 1486, which compliments the rulers of the city for past diligence in

[1] *Repertory*, viii, fo. 218, March 5, 1530–1.

[2] *Calendar of Letters and Papers of Henry VIII*, vol. xii, pt. ii, No. 14 (to Justices of Peace and religious houses); vol. xii, pt. ii, No. 364 (to Duke of Suffolk); vol. xiii, pt. ii, app. 5 (to Justices of Peace); vol. xvi, No. 945 (to Justices of Peace).

[3] Bodleian volume, *Proclamations before Elizabeth*. Press-mark, Arch. F.C. 10 (2). Transcribed in Appendix A, 2.

[4] In library of Society of Antiquaries, London. *Proclamations*, i (58, 59).

[5] Referred to in *Calendar of State Papers*, Henry VIII, xv. 141.

this respect.[1] In 1520 there was another from Henry VIII ordering weekly watches and searches during the time of the king's invasion of France.[2] Interest in the subject was likely to be suddenly stimulated by the depredations of a troop of wandering rogues, as in Nottingham, where two or three Justices were presented in 1544 for not punishing a band of 'valliaunt beggers that hes newle and latle comyn in to ower towne'.[3]

In London a good deal had been done before 1530. The records of these proceedings are found in the *Repertories of the Court of Aldermen*, the *Journals of the London Common Council*, and other documents preserved in the Town Clerk's Office in the Guildhall. These records show that frequent searches had been made for vagabonds and for harbourers. The rogues caught were imprisoned in stocks and cages, had yellow V's stitched on their clothing, and were conducted out of the city with a basin ringing before them and a proclamation at the Standard in Cheapside. There is preserved in the Guildhall an extremely interesting set of orders devised by the mayor and aldermen in 1517, at the command of the Privy Council, for the repression of sturdy beggars and vagabonds. A list had been made for each ward of the beggars and poor who really belonged there and for whose support the city was responsible. The total number was over 1,000. Round tin badges with the arms of the city of London stamped on them were ordered, one was to be given to each beggar on the list, and no one else was to be allowed to beg. At the decease of each person having a token, his badge was to be returned to the alderman of the ward, to be kept until another impotent poor person was found in that ward. Any new vagabonds coming into the city were to be severely punished according to the statute of Henry VII. In order to carry this into effect Henry Barker, carpenter, and three persons with him were made surveyors of the beggars; they were to oversee the poor folk having tokens to beg, as well as to drive out

[1] *Records of Borough of Leicester*, vol. ii, pp. 308 ff.
[2] Ibid., vol. iii, p. 14.
[3] *Records of the Borough of Nottingham*, vol. iii, pp. 399–400.

vagabonds and mighty beggars repairing to the city. The surveyors of the beggars wore a livery; they were put in charge of a master of the beggars, about whom there are occasional entries in the records of the Court of Aldermen throughout the sixteenth century.[1]

The beggars who had tokens were expected to help to expel and keep out strange vagabonds, on pain of forfeiting their right to beg. The directions given to the licensed beggars for this police duty are amusing. Evidently it was desired that they should not break the peace, but, on the other hand, should not be so mild as to fail in their efforts. They were to 'do their laufull endeuour to expelle and kepe out the seyd vagabundes and myghty beggers out of the Citie by exclamacions, expulcions and puttyng out of thym' and, if that failed, to notify an officer. In asking alms of citizens, beggars were ordered to use good manners. If a person denied them by word, countenance, or gesture, they were not to trouble him further for that time—a provision which suggests that the ordinary beggar's behaviour was just the reverse. Beggars with horrible pocks or loathsome sores and diseases were forbidden to beg openly; instead, they were to be confined in hospitals and lazar houses and a proctor wearing the city token was allowed to beg for them.

These orders illustrate the early sixteenth-century ideas of the proper method of poor relief. They were far in advance of their time and differ very little in essence from the statutes in force until 1572. After the law of 1530–1 the vigilance in London was increased, judging from the number of punishments recorded, but the methods were not materially changed. Several vagabonds were commanded to leave the city on pain of losing both ears, according to the statute, and this punishment was no doubt resorted to occasionally, though no instances of it are recorded.

1547–72. Legislation.

Between 1547 and 1572 the vagabonds increased largely in numbers or, at any rate, the troubled times caused the bad

[1] These orders of 1517 are recorded in *Journal XI*, fo. 337 ff. They are transcribed in Appendix A, 1, below.

effects of their presence to be felt more keenly, and in consequence there was new (though not successful) legislation against them, and real improvement in methods of enforcing the laws. In 1547 the laws of 1530–1 and 1535–6 were repealed and a new and much severer statute (1 Edward VI, c. 3) was passed. This decreed that all able-bodied persons not working should be adjudged vagabonds; they might be seized by their former masters, branded with a V on the breast, and made slaves for two years. These slaves could legally be chained, given only the coarsest food, driven to work with whips or subjected to any other cruelty. Vagrants for whom no master could be found were to become slaves of the Borough or Hundred, which could employ them at road-making or any public work. If they ran away and were caught, they were to be branded S on the chest and made slaves for life. The punishment for a second running away was death as a felon. This statute was too severe to be enforced,[1] and for this reason was repealed after two years, and the 22 Henry VIII, c. 12, revived, which law continued in force until 1572.

1547–72. Execution of the Laws.

The twenty-five years from 1547 to 1572 mark a determined effort on the part of the Privy Council to see the laws regarding vagabonds enforced. The troubles of 1548 and 1549 brought forth ten public proclamations against tale-bearers and spreaders of seditious rumours, who were classed as rogues and vagabonds.[2] During the next decade there were proclamations commanding the vagabonds to leave London. At the same time began the series of letters to officers in different shires commanding them to do their part in suppressing the

[1] Cp. Preamble to the law repealing it—the 3 & 4 Edward VI, c. 16, 'thextremitie of some whereof have byn occation that they have not ben putt in ure.'

[2] For example see proclamation of July 8, 1549, in the library of the Society of Antiquaries, London. *Proclamations*, iii. 39. Other evidences of activity in London during this period are that the aldermen were provided with seals for passports, and that blank forms for these and for permits to beg were printed. *Repertory*, xii, Pt. 1, fos. 226, 230, and 233.

multitude of rogues. Part of the knowledge upon which these letters were based the Privy Council obtained by actually examining vagabonds caught in London.[1] On April 15, 1551, directions for watches and for the punishment of vagabonds were issued to the Justices of the Peace in all the shires:[1] letters were sent to Lord Russell and other gentlemen in Bucks. directing them to enforce the statute for relief of the poor Nov. 5, 1552,[1] to the Lord Mayor of London directing him to punish vagabonds September 16, 1554,[1] to the Justices of the Peace in Norfolk March 26, 1555,[2] to the Lord Lieutenant of Sussex and Surrey in 1559,[3] to the Archbishop of York in 1561,[4] to the sheriffs and justices of Southampton, Devon, Cornwall, Hereford, Stafford, Chester, Berks., Bucks., and Oxon., and to Lord Rutland, Lord President of the North, July 23, 1562.[1]

In 1569 began a still more thorough whipping campaign inspired mainly by the desire to restrain a class of idlers who were too easily enlisted by the leaders of the religious revolts which took place that year in many parts of the country, and especially in the North. In this year the Council issued a commission to Thos. Andrews, to inquire into and enforce the punishment of vagabonds,[5] and directed the Earl of Sussex (who was employed in putting down the rebellion in the North) to do the same.[6] A letter had been sent to the London Court of Aldermen in March 1569, and this being unnoticed another followed June 20,[7] rebuking them sharply for their negligence and commanding searches to be held at least monthly during the summer; all rogues punished were to be given passports directing them to their homes, or the place where they last resided for a space of three years; these passports to be discreetly written and sealed so as to be difficult to counterfeit ('as it ys reported

[1] Cp. *Acts of Privy Council*, October 16, 1551, and under dates mentioned in text. The date is the most convenient reference to any entry.

[2] Burnet, *History of the Reformation*, v. 427. (From Cotton MSS. Titus B. II, fo. 116.)

[3] *D. S. P. Eliz.*, xciii, No. 18, p. 52.

[4] *Cal. D. S. P. Eliz.*, add. 1547-65, p. 510.

[5] *D. S. P. Eliz.*, li. 11 (1 & 2).

[6] Ibid., Elizabeth, add. xiv. 67, 80.

[7] *Journal*, xix, fo. 171b. Quoted in Appendix A, 6.

some of theime can readely doo'), and to name in them the different towns by which the rogues should pass in their direct way home. Certificates of these searches and punishments were to be returned promptly to the Privy Council.

Copies of the same letter were sent to many shires, and it was intended that watches should be held throughout the country. It is very difficult to determine how extensively

FIG. 10. Whipping vagabonds at the cart's tail.
(*From the Bodleian copy of Harman's Caueat.*)

this was done.[1] A contemporary unsigned letter to Sir James Croft (concerning a small rebellion in Suffolk the same year) asserts that in the watches held all over the country 13,000 masterless men and vagabonds were apprehended, by means of which the rebellion in Suffolk was destroyed.[2] Strype accepts the statement,[3] and it has been

[1] At least three copies of these letters ordering watches and searches during the whipping campaign of 1569–72 are readily accessible. They may be found in the following places:

Strype, *Annals*, vol. i, pt. ii, Appendix, No. 43 (Clarendon Press ed., p. 554). The original is in Cotton MS. Titus B II, fos. 278–9.

Journals of the London Common Council, xix, fo. 171 b (this and the one above dated June 20, 1569).

Shrewsbury Muniments, No. 2,621, Pet. to Bail., &c. (July 30, 1571).

The second and third, which differ in one or two interesting particulars, are transcribed in full in Appendix, Nos. 6 and 8.

[2] Quoted in Strype, *Annals*, vol. i, pt. ii, chap. lv (Clarendon Press ed., p. 346). The original statement is in Cotton MS. Titus B II, fo. (ink) 471.

[3] *Annals*, vol. i, pt. ii, chap. liii (Clarendon Press ed., pp. 295–6).

often copied since, but not the least reliance can be placed on it. It is impossible to know whether the writer made it from an inspection of the certificates returned to the Privy Council or simply by guess. Some idea of the lack of means for making exact statistics may be obtained from the fact that the Privy Council had no accurate list of the names of the smaller towns in each shire. The letter ordering watches and searches to be held was sent only to the chief officers in the northern counties on account of uncertainty as to the names of the smaller towns.[1] It is very difficult to check the contemporary estimates by any evidence now obtainable. Only a few of the certificates required by the Council are preserved, but these are from districts as far apart as Devon, Cornwall, Norfolk, and York. In all there are certificates from only one-half of the counties of England, and usually from only a few hundreds in each county, so that they furnish very little basis for statistics, although they show very well the methods employed.[2] It is probable that a large number of vagabonds were apprehended, and that their apprehension did something to defeat the rebellions breaking out everywhere in this year.

Watches and searches of a similar kind were held in 1570,[3] 1571, and in the spring of 1572. The fullest official returns preserved are those concerning watches held in August, September, and October 1571, in response to a general letter from the Privy Council dated July 30.[4] Watches were held usually from nine o'clock at night until three or four o'clock the next afternoon. The vagabonds were examined by the Justices of the Peace, stocked or whipped at a cart's tail—sometimes both—and given the usual passports. Had these measures been efficiently carried out vagabondage in England would have received a severe check. But plenty of evidence

[1] See the letter quoted by Strype, *Annals*, vol. i, pt. ii, Appendix, No. 43 (Clarendon Press ed., p. 556).

[2] A table of the returns for 1571 and 1572 will be found in Appendix A, 10. Characteristic certificates of the punishment of vagabonds are printed in Appendix A, 9. In Appendix A, 7, will be found the articles agreed upon by Justices in Devon, which give a good account of their procedure.

[3] *Domestic State Papers, Elizabeth*, lxvii. 45 (April 7, 1570).

[4] The letter to Shrewsbury is quoted in Appendix A, 8.

exists to prove that Dogberry and Justice Shallow are not uncharacteristic pictures of Elizabethan officers of the law. Even the London Court of Aldermen had been fooled by a counterfeit crank, and in the country the rogues probably fared much better. A letter from Burghley to Walsingham, describing the watches set to apprehend three members of Babington's conspiracy in 1586, points its own moral. Burghley saw watchmen standing in groups near each village, by the roadside or under a shed; he stopped near one group and asked why they were watching. They said, 'To take three young men.' Asked further how they were to know them, they replied, 'One of the parties hath a hook'd nose.' When Burghley demanded whether they had any more information about him, they said, 'No.'[1] This watch was set for a conspirator against the life of the Queen. How much less vigilance may we imagine in the watches for common vagabonds, with whom half the countrymen sympathized. A certificate from Gloucestershire sends no names, but only alludes to 'such poore beggerlye persons as we think vnmette to troble your Honnors withall, whoo haue receyued condigne punyshement according to the lawes in suche case provyded'.[2] One may be sure that only a small proportion of the rogues were caught, and that for the most part their counterfeit diseases and counterfeit licences got them a fairly untroubled passage up and down the land. As long as they were not set to work, 'of which punishment', says Harrison, 'they stand in greatest feare,'[3] occasional watchings and whippings furnished them only with an element of adventure and a means of exciting compassion.

In London the period from 1550 to 1570 was one of great activity in whipping vagabonds. There was more effort than formerly to make each alderman find out the harbouring places and restrain the vagabonds in his ward: the alderman or his deputy committed the rogues to Bridewell on their own authority, and towards the close of the period less is

[1] *Domestic State Papers, Elizabeth*, cxcii. 22 (August 10, 1586).
[2] *Domestic State Papers, Elizabeth*, lxxx. 52 (August 27, 1571).
[3] *Description of England* (N. Sh. Soc.), Book ii, p. 103.

heard of ordinary cases in the city courts. Means were sought to put the vagabonds imprisoned in Bridewell to some useful labour. In the summer of 1564 they were employed in cleaning the pond in Smithfield,[1] and frequently during the decade following, committees were appointed to find out other work for them.

The letters of the Privy Council in 1569–72 increased the activity of the city officials still more, with the result that there were many watches and searches; finally, the Lord Mayor and Bishop of London presented a memorandum of orders for dealing with vagrants to the Council, March 9, 1571–2, and the Lords promised to appoint a commission to execute them.[2]

1572–97. LEGISLATION.

At the same time that the Privy Council had been so active in its efforts to repress vagabondage and disorder by enforcing the existing laws, there had been a great deal of discussion in Parliament about a new and better law on the subject. The result of six years' thought and debate was the statute of 1572 (14 Eliz. c. 5), which provided a stricter punishment for sturdy beggars and inaugurated a compulsory poor rate to aid the deserving poor. This measure contains the well-known definition, which reflects vividly the varied character of the Elizabethan wayfarers. It places in the ranks of rogues and vagabonds all proctors without sufficient authority, idle persons using subtle, crafty, and unlawful games, and all able-bodied persons who are not working and have no good excuse for being idle. To these are added all fencers, bearwards, players, and minstrels not belonging to any baron or honourable personage of greater degree, all jugglers, pedlars, tinkers, and petty chapmen, unless such fencers, bearwards, &c., have licences from two Justices of the Peace, one of whom is of the quorum in the shire where they are wandering. Finally, the law enumerates, in addition to

[1] *Repertory*, xv, fo. 367.

[2] *Acts of Privy Council.* The entry on the subject is exceptionally full.

the above, common labourers refusing to work, counterfeiters of passports and licences and users of the same knowing them to be counterfeit, scholars of the universities wandering and begging without licence from their Vice-Chancellor, shipmen pretending losses at sea, discharged prisoners begging for money to pay their jailers' fees or for support on their way home to their friends, unless they have a licence from a Justice of the Peace in the shire where they were imprisoned. A proviso is made for soldiers and sailors on their way home after they have been discharged from Her Majesty's service, for harvest workers, for persons who have been robbed on the highway, and for servants who have been turned away or whose masters have died. All the rest, being over fourteen years of age, the law declared were to be whipped and burned through the gristle of the right ear with a hot iron one inch in circumference, unless some master could be found to take them to service for a year. For wandering, loitering, idling, or begging a second time, the penalty was death as a felon, unless some one could be found to take the culprit to service for two years. For running away from this service, or for a third offence the penalty was death without benefit of clergy. The principal defect in the law was that it provided no effective means for setting sturdy rogues to work. An attempt was made to remedy this three years later by an act (18 Eliz. c. 3) ordering stocks of wool, hemp, iron, &c., to be provided in each parish for the poor to work on, and also directing that one or more houses of correction should be established in each county. The famous poor law of 1597 was nothing but a modification of these two statutes, moderating the punishments while it made more explicit and practicable the directions for collecting and distributing the poor rate, and for setting the able-bodied to work.

1572–97. Execution of the Laws.

The statutes of 1572 and 1575 mark the beginning of the end of the old free, merry, vagabond life. The houses of correction and the provision of wool and hemp did what the whips and stocks, and even the gallows, could not do. The Mayor of London himself went to Southwark on the day the 14 Eliz. c. 5 was proclaimed to oversee its execution, and the Court of Aldermen prepared a book of orders to enforce the 18 Eliz. c. 3, which were printed in 1579 or 1580 and again in 1587.[1] Committees were continually appointed to devise new means for setting idlers to work; some rogues were taken from Bridewell to be impressed as soldiers; and in 1591 when the ditches about the city were badly in need of cleaning, a search was made for vagabonds, they were set to work, and actually paid 4*d.* each a day for their labour.[2] London and the large cities were of course far ahead of the rest of the country, and their practice no doubt fell behind their 'orders', but the resolutions show the trend of the efforts for reform.

The whipping and branding punishments of the 14 Eliz. were promptly administered in some places at least. In the accounts of the Chamberlain of the city of Leicester, between 1570 and 1575, there are several records of payments to 'Richardson the burneman' for his cart about town to whip vagabonds.[3] In the Middlesex sessions, between 1572 and 1575, forty-four vagabonds were sentenced to be branded, five to be hanged, and eight set to service;[4] several of those hanged had been set to service previously and had run away. One remarkable case is that of Joan Wynstone, who was whipped and branded as a vagabond February 6, 1576. The 26 July following she was caught wandering again and only saved from hanging by being taken to service for two years by Thos. Wynstone her husband. On October 3 she was caught wandering again, having run away from her husband, and was sentenced to be hanged.[5]

[1] *Journal*, xx, pt. ii, fo. 325. The pamphlet was called 'Orders appointed to be executed in the cittie of London for setting roges and idle persons to worke and for releefe of the poore.' A copy is to be found in the Guildhall Library.

[2] *Repertory*, xxii, fo. 268 verso—269.

[3] *Records of the Borough of Leicester*, vol. iii, pp. 133, 137, 160, and 161.

[4] See entries in printed volume between these dates.

[5] *Middlesex Sessions' Rolls* (*Middlesex County Records*, I). The exact date is the most convenient reference to any entry.

Immediately after the defeat of the Armada the number of vagabonds in England was greatly increased by poor soldiers and sailors on their way home from the wars. Continual proclamations testify to the multitudes of these thronging the streets of London. The Records of the Middlesex Sessions furnish grim confirmation of their numbers. In 1589, between October 6 and December 14, seventy-one rogues were sentenced in this court to be whipped and burned

FIG. 11. A Hanging.
(*From a ballad in the Pepysian Collection.*)

through the ear. Much is heard of vagrant soldiers, real and pretended, throughout the remainder of Elizabeth's reign. Provost-marshals were appointed with the special duty of apprehending and punishing them, and occasionally special tribunals were held to inquire into their complaints. The council finally ordered that they should be given, along with their discharge at the port towns, an allowance of money for their expenses homewards and a licence permitting them to travel unmolested so long as they followed a specified route and arrived within a definite limited time.[1]

[1] A statute (35 Eliz. cc. 3, 4) made a general provision for pensions, aid to soldiers on the way home, &c., and ordered that any soldier found begging should forfeit his pension. During the ten years after the Armada

THE POOR LAWS OF 1597 AND 1601.

The poor laws of 1597 and 1601 had little influence on conditions during Elizabeth's reign, and hence need no detailed notice here. They only carried out the principles of the statutes of 1572 and 1575; the greatest advance was made in methods of enforcing them. The task of instructing the Justices of the Peace and Overseers of the Poor in their duties and of making them feel a responsibility to the Privy Council for performing them was not adequately performed until 1630–1. But this task the Privy Council of Elizabeth had begun with the order for searches and certificates in 1569–72. Searches were held and certificates returned occasionally through Elizabeth's reign.

the following proclamations were directed against vagrant soldiers. They show, in the most graphic way, the disorder which followed the war with Spain. Hundreds of rogues, assuming the rôle of discharged soldiers, took advantage of the gratitude and patriotism of the people to commit all manner of depredations.

November 13, 1589 (found in Bodleian volume, *Proclamations by Elizabeth*). Recites depredations of vagrant soldiers and commands them and all vagabonds to apply to a Justice of the Peace within two days for a passport to their homes.

November 5, 1591. (Ibid.) Many vagabonds pretend to be soldiers who are not; all are to be examined, undeserving ones punished, and others given help to go home. After this all discharged soldiers will be given money at the port where they are dismissed, to pay their expenses home. The Lieutenants of the different counties are to appoint Provost-marshals to help in apprehending vagrants.

February 28, 159½. (Ibid.) The streets of London are infested with idle soldiers. The Justices of the Peace, Treasurers of War, and other discreet persons are to be formed into a special court to try them at the Sessions Hall, Old Bailey. All idle soldiers commanded to appear there Saturday next at 1 p.m. and such as cannot prove themselves genuine will be committed and punished.

No. 349 in the same volume is a set of orders for the behaviour of soldiers, for provisions for their relief, for fortnightly searches for rogues, and for two special courts—one to examine pretended soldiers, the other to try rogues—to sit twice a month in the Sessions Hall near Newgate. It is dated July 4, 1595.

1596 (?) (*Domestic State Papers*, *Eliz.* cclxi. 70.) The court and city still crowded with vagabonds and pretended soldiers. Certain days in each month will be set aside to search for and imprison them. Some soldiers being armed have committed robberies and murders; the Queen will appoint Provost-marshals to apprehend and execute them without delay.

September 9, 1598 (Bodleian volume, *Proclamations by Elizabeth*). Vagabonds who pretend to be soldiers still disturb the peace of London and surrounding country. A Provost-marshal is to be appointed to assist in catching them, and those apprehended are to be executed by Martial Law.

Justices met in various shires and devised Books of Orders for dealing with vagabonds and beggars. Workhouses were established here and there, and gradually the new ideas of poor relief took hold.

Meanwhile conditions remained in many places very bad. It seemed as if all the laws and all the trouble taken to have them enforced had been in vain. In 1596 Edward Hext, a Somersetshire Justice, wrote a letter to one of the members of the Privy Council giving a very discouraged account of the vagabonds and disorder in his shire. He encloses in it the calendar of the Somerset assizes for that year, showing that forty felons had been executed, and one hundred and eighty persons, committed or bound over for felony, were turned loose to live by spoil. Furthermore, Hext says that as a rule only one-fifth of the persons who committed felony were apprehended, and many that were taken escaped before their trial. Thieves when detected often obtained freedom by restoring the stolen goods, and many simple people would refuse to swear a thief to death for any goods whatsoever, even though their own had been stolen. The escaped thieves infected the rest until the whole country was pestered with them. Many of the vagabonds were not suffering from poverty. Hext encloses a forged passport used, he says, by a young man who was heir to land worth 40 pounds. The blame for all this disorder Hext places on the inferior ministers and justices, who were careless, selfish, and corrupt in the discharge of their duties. The letter suggests a terrible picture of the state of England socially at the time when Elizabethan literature was at the height of its greatness.[1]

Conditions in London were no better than those in the country. In 1594 the Lord Mayor, Sir John Spencer, in a letter to the Council, asserted that Kentish Street, Newington, and other places on the south side of the river were very nurseries and breeding-places of the begging poor who swarmed the streets of the city. For this he blamed covetous landlords who rented their houses to several families, tenement fashion,

[1] The letter is found in the British Museum, MS. Lans. 81 (62). It is printed as Appendix A, 14, below.

for so-called 'penny-rents', which were paid weekly and usually got by begging. The Mayor estimated the number of these beggars at 12,000, and he asked for a meeting of the justices of Sussex and Surrey to take measures to banish them from the city or prevent them from crossing the bridge.[1] One of the last proclamations of Elizabeth's reign is directed against rogues and vagabonds, and contains practical directions to the justices for enforcing the laws.[2] In 1613 Sir Thomas Middleton, when he became Lord Mayor, set to work to rid the streets of the beggars. There is in the City Records in the Guildhall a copy of an interesting letter from him to the Lord Chamberlain describing his methods and reflecting the conditions as he found them. He punished no one for begging, but set them to work, which, he says, was worse than death to them. He sent spies to find out lewd houses, and even visited some of them himself in disguise. Bawds, as many as he could catch, he carted, whipped, and banished. He made a list of all the ale-houses and victualling-houses in the city, of which there were more than 1,000. In some of these he found more than 300 barrels of strong beer and about 40,000 barrels in them all. These ale-houses he regulated by making strict rules as to the amount of beer each house could use, with the result that the prices of corn and malt fell. He made some other reforms, and intended, he said, to go on to restrain the thieving brokers or broggers who encouraged theft by receiving stolen goods.[3]

All this proves that neither the laws of 1572 and 1575 nor those of 1597 and 1601 worked immediate reform. But many things show that conditions gradually improved in the latter part of Elizabeth's reign. There are fewer orders from the Privy Council to justices concerning vagabonds, fewer precepts about them in London. The measures of restraint became regular instead of being violent and spasmodic as they had been. Particularly striking is the fact that although rogues

[1] *Remembrancia*. ii. 74.

[2] January 14, 1599/1600. Bodl. Arch. F.C. 11 (391). See also one dated February 15, 1600/01, B.M. Press mark G. 6463 (383).

[3] *Remembrancia*, iii. 159. The letter is dated July 8, 1614.

and vagabonds were much more popular in pamphlet literature after 1590 than before, the descriptions of their life are mainly copied from the old books—especially from Harman. The merry, wicked, resourceful vagabonds of the middle of the century had become merely tame beggars. The interesting and dangerous element in the early part of Elizabeth's reign had been not the impotent poor, but the sturdy beggars. These were the fellows who had been strong and keen-witted enough to make vagabond life exciting and pleasant. Whippings and even worse punishments they had been able to evade or endure, but work was another matter: with the advent of this punishment in 1575 the poetry of their life began to decline, and the literature of rogues and vagabonds to fall back upon tradition.

CHAPTER IV

THE ART OF CONNY-CATCHING

> *Falstaff.* Well, sirs, I am almost out at heels, . . .
> There is no remedy ; I must conny-catch ; I must shift. . . .
> *Pistol.* Let vultures gripe thy guts ! for gourd and fullam holds,
> And high and low beguiles the rich and poor.
>
> *Merry Wives of Windsor*, Act III, sc. i.

IN Elizabethan London there was a band of rogues and sharpers very different from the race of vagabonds we have just been describing, although they were all united in the common bond of roguery and freely borrowed each other's tricks. The city rogue lived as a gallant, haunted taverns, ordinaries, and theatres, beat the watch, took purses, and outwitted gulls. When he had sunk a stage lower he played the roystering boy and bullied the punk he lived on, or, if he was a fellow of more courage or desperation, he became a professional ruffian and murderer, of the type depicted in *Macbeth* and *Arden of Feversham.*

These rogues had more brains and more daring than the ordinary vagabonds, and they played for bigger stakes. They formed the gallant company of shifters who lived by their wits ; their business was not begging, but cozening. Elizabethan literature is full of them : Jack Wilton, Falstaff and his conny-catching companions, Subtle, Edgeworth, Knockem. Cutting, and so on ; in Middleton's plays we find them on every page, and the list might be extended indefinitely.

The accounts of the city rogues and sharpers were written not by honest, substantial gentlemen like Harman, Harrison, and Scot, but by Bohemian pamphleteers with more cleverness than honesty, many of whom lived the same life as the rogues they were describing. The purpose of the writers of conny-catching books was not the reformation of the commonwealth, their pretences notwithstanding, but rather the selling of pamphlets. Like all popular literature these pamphlets followed the prevailing fashions, and this fact must be allowed for in estimating what the rogue life which lay behind their descriptions really was. They worked quite as often from earlier accounts of rogue tricks as they did from the life around them. Some of the rogue pamphlets of Thomas Dekker and Samuel Rowlands, for example, resemble the Latin verses made from old vulgus-books in *Tom Brown's School Days*. Even Greene, the realest Bohemian of them all, is guilty of some plagiarisms.[1] These facts must make the reader wary. Are the pamphleteers to be believed at all? Is not the whole conny-catching world with its manners and customs a literary fiction? Or is it not, at any rate, an inextricable tangle of fiction and fact?

Let us consider these questions separately. In the first place, to reject the whole of conny-catching lore as fiction is to go, I believe, quite contrary to the evidence which we find outside the pamphlets themselves. From many sources in Elizabethan history and literature, the statements of Greene and his fellows are confirmed. We find on the statute books a law directed against the combination of pickpockets which Greene describes. All the satirists of the day inveigh against the cheating tricks which Greene explains. In the plays dealing with contemporary life are hundreds of conny-catchers, pickpockets, cheaters, and lifters, who practise exactly the tricks which the pamphleteers attribute to them. Foreigners travelling in England corroborate the pamphlet descriptions of the methods of English horse thieves. The cheating tricks are still practised in our city streets and dives, and many words of the sixteenth-century rogue cant are still used by thieves and sharpers. Nowhere is there a contemporary statement that these rogue customs are a literary fiction. Nevertheless the pamphleteers, as we shall see later, are not slow to criticize each other for inaccuracies, and to point out the widespread plagiarism which certainly existed in this kind of literature. Had the whole thing been a myth some pamphleteer or many would have hastened to say so.

[1] For details see Chapter VI below.

On the other hand, it is clear that some of the tricks recounted by the pamphleteers are impossible, obviously made to sell and not to practise. Greene admits as much (see Chapter VI below), but one need not stretch this admission too far. The main outlines of the life which he and his fellows describe are clear and authentic enough. With these we can rest satisfied and reconcile ourselves to some uncertainty in regard to details. One statement must be added to the foregoing. It seems pretty clear that many of the rogue pamphlets are somewhat behind the times. The greatest vogue for these exposures followed the conny-catching series of Robert Greene published in 1591 and 1592, and continued for about twenty-five years. Most of these later works are made up of borrowings; they describe conditions more as they were in the middle of the reign of Elizabeth than as they were in the time of James I.

The prey of the cozeners was the tribe of gulls, of whom Dekker has given, in the *Guls Horne-booke*, the most vivid and convincing picture to be found in Elizabethan literature. Jonson painted his idea of the type in the play of *Bartholomew Fair*, but Cokes is too much of a caricature, too much of a fool, too helpless, and too easily gulled. Dekker's account is full of humour and even sympathy. He shows us the Elizabethan fop walking in St. Paul's, sitting on the stage of the theatre to display his clothes, and dawdling, pipe in hand, among the booksellers' shops, 'where, if you cannot reade, exercise your smoake, and inquire who has writ against this diuine wéede'.[1] The Gull pretends to wit, fashion, or wealth in the ordinary, lets a sonnet drop from his glove, or inquires who has need of help to obtain a suit at court; he feasts in a tavern on a tapster's credit, and directs his link boy, hired for one night, to call him 'Sir' as they pass the watch going home. The cozeners, who pretended to be men of fashion themselves, found these gulls easy prey. When a young heir came to the city, after the 'worme-eaten Farmer, his father,' had died and left him 'five hundred a yeare, onely to keepe

[1] *Guls Horne-booke*, 1609, p. 19 (Temple edition, p. 33).

PLATE V

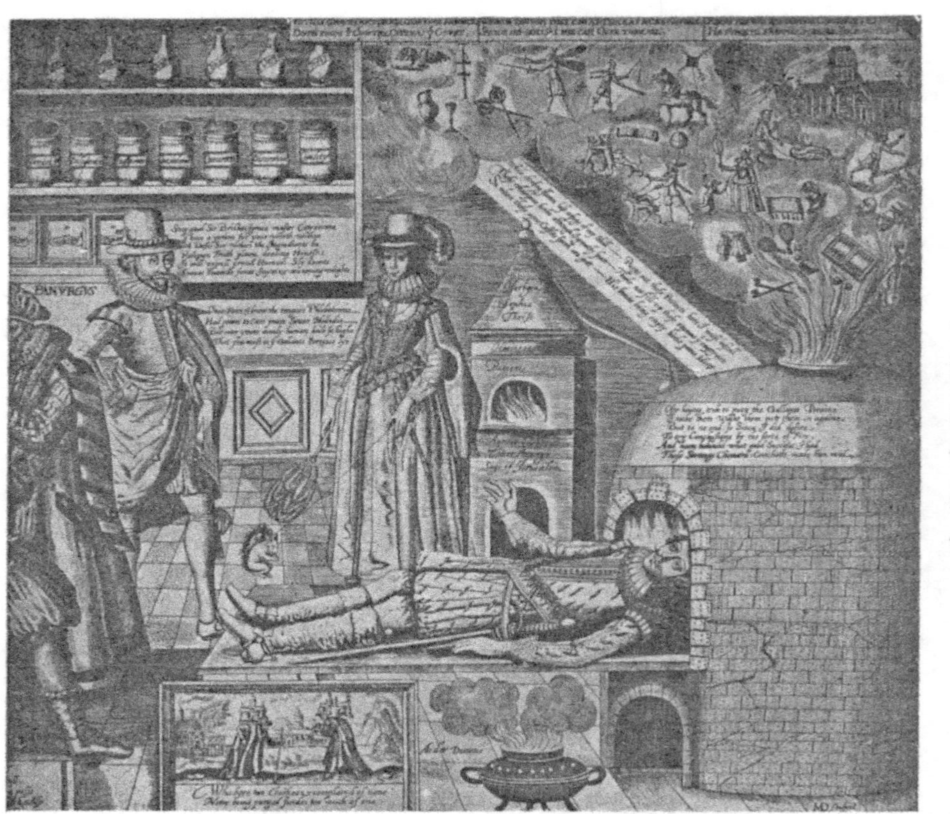

'Ofte having tride to purg the
  Gallants Braine
I tooke them, washt them: putt
  them in againe,
But to no end: so since I did
  desire
To try Conclusions by the force
  of Fire,
And heere behould what good
  successe I had
These strange Chimaera-crot-
  chetts made him mad.'

an Irish hobby, an Irish horse-boy and himself like a gentleman', they showed him the haunts of fashion, taught him to be a gallant and a gamester, and eventually absorbed a good part of his money. If at any time he found his purse bare before his rents were due, he could easily get as much as he needed from a money-lender 'without usury', which was illegal above 10 per cent., by taking one-half or three-fourths of his loan in commodities,[1] and putting a piece of land to forfeit if he did not pay by a certain time. Woe unto him if he failed to keep his day! The usurer could seize not merely enough of the land to satisfy his debt, but the whole.[2] It would not take many transactions of this kind to leave the young heir penniless. After he was ruined, if he was dishonest enough, he was ready to make a capital conny-catcher's assistant, to hunt for gulls among his own friends from the country, and thus eke out a living helping to cozen others as he had been cozened himself. This was the typical 'rake's progress' from the state of gallant, gaily feathered gull to that of poor and needy cozener, who lived from hand to mouth by the practice of the various cheating 'laws'.

The places in which this fleecing process was carried on were, as has been indicated, the fashionable resorts of London. There were first of all regularly licensed gaming-houses, for a description of which the reader is referred to the next chapter. In addition, gambling was carried on in every ordinary, bowling alley, inn, or tavern. George Whetstone's *Touchstone for the Time* (1584) describes the different kinds of ordinaries. The most expensive ones were the resorts of the gentleman cheater. Here he posed as a man of wealth and fashion, or a soldier, or a wit, and impressed the gull with his conversation before dice were mentioned. When the dishes were cleared away play began, and sooner or later the

[1] See the 37 Henry VIII, c. 9, which was in force from 1545 to 1551–2, and again from 1571 to 1623–4. The custom of making part of a loan in commodities was common because of the lack of ready money. It was not necessarily dishonest, but it multiplied the opportunities for sharp dealing. Lutestring (luster, a kind of silk) and paper, which were often used, were valuable and readily saleable articles.

[2] Cp. *Defence of Conny-catching*, Grosart's edition of Greene, vol. xi, pp. 52 ff.

new-comer's money was lost. However, fleecing a gull was a business not of one afternoon, but of many, during which time his new friends went with him to the theatre, to the Bear Garden, or to walk in Paul's; and in their gaming, in order to give more appearance of honesty, they freely lost large sums to each other, but not to the gull. The Pander and Usurer haunted the best ordinaries no less constantly than the Cheater, ready to complete the young Prodigal's ruin.

There were cheaper ordinaries, dicing houses, and bowling alleys where dice and cards were kept for the citizens, who

FIG. 12. A Tavern Scene.
(*From a ballad in the Pepysian Collection.*)

were addicted to gaming no less than gallants. Dekker describes the citizens' ordinary very well:

'There is another Ordinary to which your London Usurer, your stale Batchilor, and your thrifty Atturney do resort: the price three-pence: the roomes as full of company as a Iaile, and indéede diuided into seuerall wards, like the beds of an Hospital. The complement betwéene these is not much, their words few: for the belly hath no eares, euery mans eie héere is vpon the other mans trencher, to note whether his fellow lurch him or no: if they chaunce to discourse, it is of nothing but of *Statutes*, *Bonds*, *Recognizances*, *Fines*, *Recoueries*, *Audits*, *Rents*, *Subsidies*, *Suerties*, *Inclosures*, *Liueries*, *Inditements*, *Outlaries*, *Feoffments*, *Iudg-*

ments, *Commissions*, *Bankerouts*, *Amercements*, and of such horrible matter, that when a Lifetenant dines with his punck in the nexte roome, hee thinkes verily the men are coniuring.'[1]

These places were patronized so extensively that Whetstone advocated a law prohibiting any citizen from taking a meal outside his own house except when he visited a friend.

A third great class, composed of rogues, thieves, and ruffians, was addicted to gaming, and had still cheaper and more secret eating and gaming houses—ruffians' ordinaries.

'Nowe remayneth the discouerie of the thirde sort of these hauntes, which are placed in Allies, gardens, and other obscure corners out of the common walks of the Magistrate. The dayly guests of these priuie houses, are maisterles men, needy shifters, theeues, cutpurses, unthriftie seruants, both seruing men, and prentises. Heere a man may pick out mates for all purposes, saue such as are good. Heere a man may finde out *Brauoes* of *Rome* and *Naples*, who for a pottle of wine, will make no more conscience to kill a man, than a Butcher a beast, heare closely lie good fellowes, that with a good Northren Gelding, will gaine more by a halter, than an honest yeoman will with a teame of good horses . . . the most of these idle persons haue neither landes nor credite, nor will liue by an honest occupation: forsooth they haue yet handes to filch, heades to deceive, and friendes to receive: and by these helpes, shift meetely badly well.'[2]

In Middleton's *Black Book* we have an account of the company at Master Bezle's, which was just such a rogues' ordinary.

'There was your gallant extraordinary thief that keeps his college of good fellows, and will not fear to rob a lord in his coach for all his ten trencher-bearers on horseback; your deep-conceited cutpurse, who by the dexterity of his knife will draw out the money, and make a flame-coloured purse show like the bottomless pit, but with never a soul in't; your cheating bowler, that will bank false of purpose, and lose a game of twelvepence to purchase his partner twelve shillings in bets, and so share it after the play; your cheveril-gutted catchpoll, who like a horse-leech sucks gentlemen; and, in all, your twelve tribes of villany.'[3]

[1] Dekker, *Guls Horne-booke*, 1609, pp. 26–7 (Temple edition, pp. 45–6).
[2] Whetstone, *Touchstone for the Time* (an addition to *A Mirour for Magestrates of Cyties*, 1584), leaf 33 and verso.
[3] Middleton, *Black Book* (Bullen's edition), vol. viii, pp. 30–1.

It is difficult to find out exactly the conditions in the sanctuaries of Elizabethan London, but they do not seem to have been especially the haunts of rogues and conny-catchers. One finds some mention of them but no evidence indicating that they were the scenes, more than other places, of such life as that which Shadwell describes in Alsatia (the cant name for Whitefriars) during the Restoration, and which Scott has transferred to the reign of James I.[1] Shadwell and Scott's Alsatia is not a real sanctuary as that term was understood before the Reformation and, to some extent, throughout the sixteenth century, but only a criminal quarter such as one finds in modern cities, where the immunity from arrest was based partly on custom but mostly on the strength of the criminals and the weakness or indifference of the officers of the law. Alsatia was not the only such refuge in the city. The law of 1696–7 mentions as well the Savoy, Salisbury Court, Ram Alley, Mitre Court, Fuller's Rents, Baldwin's Gardens, Montague Close, the Minories, the Mint, the Clink, and Deadman's Place.[2] Several of these and other places like them, some sanctuaries, others not, are mentioned as haunts of rogues in the reign of Elizabeth. William Fletewood, Recorder of the city of London from 1571 to 1591, writes to Lord Burghley August 8, 1575, reporting the progress he has made in the suppression of rogues: 'As for Westminster, the Duchie (the district about the Savoy), St. Giles, Highe Holborn, St. Johne's streate, and Islington, were never so well and quiet, for neither roge nor masterles man dare once to looke into those parts.' In January 1581 he writes, 'The chiefe nurserie of all these evell people is the Savoye and the brick-kilnes nere Islington.' In July 1585 he sends a list of eighteen 'Harboring-howses for maisterles-men, and for such as lyve by thefte and other such like shifts'. Two of these are in the sanctuary of Westminster, one in Southwark, one at Newington Butts; the others are scattered all about the city and

[1] See Shadwell, *Squire of Alsatia*; and Scott, *Fortunes of Nigel*.

[2] 8–9 William III, c. 27, s. 15. Against those who resisted arrest for debt in these pretended liberties.

suburbs.[1] The 'manor of Pickthatch' he does not mention, but it was doubtless another of the same sort. My point is that there was no necessary connexion between the conny-catchers and the sanctuaries. In the early part of the sixteenth century, before the privilege of sanctuary was seriously curtailed, the men who sought refuge there were likely to be more important criminals in danger of their lives for murder or felony. Machyn gives us a glimpse of this old sanctuary life which was even then (1552) passing away.[2] Elizabethan rogues and sharpers herded together anywhere, in the old sanctuary precincts, on the Bankside, or in any tenements or stews, sallying forth to pursue their calling among the haunts of better men.

It is a curious fact that even the jails served now and then as a refuge for Elizabethan rogues and as a basis for their operations. We hear of fellows who lived in jail and would not be persuaded to leave, who kept themselves loaded with suits for debt to cover their other knaveries. In the King's Bench and the Marshalsea, as we shall see later in this chapter, they had their workshops for the manufacture of false dice; to the Counters they returned for safety after committing highway robberies. A prison is a place to learn more villany, Mynshul tells us, than twenty dicing houses, bowling allies, brothels or ordinaries.[3] The knowing prisoner did not suffer too much restraint. He could go abroad at any time with a keeper (who doubtless was not above winking at a trick now and then, of which he would receive part of the proceeds) on

[1] These three quotations are from Fletewood's letters, printed by T. Wright in his *Queen Elizabeth and her Times*, vol. ii, p. 18 (from MS. Lans. 20, 8); p. 166 (from MS. Lans. 34, 3); p. 249 (from MS. Lans. 44, 38).

[2] *Diary*, Camden Soc., p. 121. A reference to the sanctuary men in Westminster.

[3] On the points mentioned see the following pamphlets, at the pages given and *passim*: *Oeconomy of the Fleet*, Camden Soc., p. 9; William Fennor, *Compters Commonwealth*, 1617, pp. 56–7, 73, and 83–4 (the meeting of the governing council in the 'Hole' sounds very much like the deliberations of Duke Hildebrod and his advisers in *The Fortunes of Nigel*); Geffray Mynshul, *Essayes and Characters of a Prison and Prisoners*, 1618, pp. 3, 7, 19, 27–9; *Manifest Detection*, Percy Soc., p. 27.

the payment of a stated price per day or half-day.[1] In jail he could receive freely the visits of friends, confederates, and mistresses, he could have readily any luxury he could pay for, and he could live on charity or on the donations of friends when his money was gone. Even here there were gulls to be fleeced, and gaming went on from morning till night. One reads a great deal about the miseries of Elizabethan jails, and conditions in them were certainly from our point of view terrible, but not all the prisoners were innocent debtors or recusants exposed to the cruelty of merciless keepers. There were not wanting conny-catchers who could make life in a debtor's prison tolerable, and who, if they were not regular jail-birds, were yet glad now and then, when the Aldermen were active, to pay something for a night's lodging in one of the Counters to escape 'privy watches and searches' without.[2]

Conny-catching went on all the year round, but it had its busy and its dull seasons. The best time was during the terms of court, when hundreds of countrymen came to London on business or pleasure, with purses well stocked with money. Then Paul's walk swarmed with crowds of honest men and knaves, and all kinds of business, honest and dishonest, went on merrily. Dekker has a description of London in term time, done in his best style. The pamphlet in which it occurs, *The Dead Tearme*, is in form of a dialogue between St. Paul's and Westminster. Paul's church is speaking:

'What whispering is there in *Terme* times, how by some slight to cheat the poore country Clients of his full purse that is stucke vnder his girdle? What plots are layde to furnish young gallants with readie money (which is shared afterwards at a Tauern) therby to disfurnish him of his patrimony? what buying vp of oaths, out of the hands of knightes of the Post, who for a few shillings doe daily sell their soules? What layinge of heads is there together and sifting of the brains,

[1] This was in the Fleet, in the time of James I, 20*d.* per day, 10*d.* for the half-day. See *Oeconomy of the Fleet*, quoted above, pp. 76 ff.

[2] See Stow's *Survey*, ed. Kingsford, i. 350–1: 'Being of a Iury to enquire against a Sessions of Gaile deliuery in the yeare 1552 we found the prisoners hardly dealt withall, for their achates and otherwise, as also that theeues and strumpets were there lodged for foure pence the night, whereby they might be safe from searches that were made abroad.'

still and anon, as it growes towardes eleuen of the clocke, (euen amongst those that wear guilt Rapiers by their sides) where for that noone they may shift from Duke *Humfrey*, and bee furnished with a Dinner at some meaner mans Table? What damnable bargaines of vnmercifull Brokery, and of vnmeasure-able Vsury are there clapt vp? What swearing is there: yea, what swaggering, what facing and out-facing? What shuffling, what shouldering, what Iustling, what Ieering, what byting of Thumbs to beget quarrels, what holding vppe of fingers to remember drunken méetings, what brauing with Feathers, what bearding with Mustachoes, what casting open of cloakes to publish new clothes, what muffling in cloaks to hyde broken Elbows, so that when I heare such trampling vp and downe, such spetting, such halking, and such humming (euery mans lippes making a noise, yet not a word to be vnderstoode,) I verily beléeue that I am the Tower of *Babell* newly to be builded vp, but presentlie despaire of euer béeing finished, because there is in me such a confusion of languages.

For at one time, in one and the same ranke, yea, foote by foote, and elbow by elbow, shall you sée walking, the Knight, the Gull, the Gallant, the vpstart, the Gentleman, the Clowne, the Captaine, the Appel-squire, the Lawyer, the Vsurer, the Cittizen, the Bankerout, the Scholler, the Begger, the Doctor, the Ideot, the Ruffian, the Cheater, the Puritan, the Cut-throat, the Hye-men, the Low-men, the True-man, and the Thiefe: of all trades and professions some, of all Countryes some; And thus dooth my middle *Isle* shew like the *Mediterranean Sea*, in which as well the Merchant hoysts vp sayles to purchace wealth honestly, as the *Rouer* to light vpon prize vniustly. Thus am I like a common Mart where all Commodities (both the good and the bad) are to be bought and solde. Thus whilest deuotion kneeles at her prayers, doth prophanation walke vnder her nose in contempt of *Religion*. But my lamentations are scattered with the winds, my sighes are lost in the Ayre, and I my selfe not thought worthy to stand high in the loue of those that are borne and nourished by mee. An end therefore doe I make heare of this my mourning.'[1]

So much for the Gull to be fleeced and the time and place of his fleecing. Now for the methods. These were the so-called conny-catching 'laws'. The word 'law' was the cant term for any cheating trick; it had been used in this sense at least

[1] Dekker, *The Dead Tearme*, 1608, sig. D_4 verso—E (ed. Grosart, vol. iv, pp. 50–2).

as early as the middle of the sixteenth century. Greene describes, in his first and most reliable pamphlet, eight 'laws', and in his second one adds five more [1]; they are:

High Law.	Barnard's Law.
Sacking Law.	Black Art.
Cheating Law.	Courbing Law.
Crossbiting Law.	Vincent's Law.
Conny-catching Law.	Prigging Law.
Versing Law.	Lifting Law.
Figging Law.	

Two of these are methods of cozenage with cards, one is cheating with dice, two more are methods of blackmailing with the help of whores, one a cozenage at bowls, and the others different kinds of theft: horse-stealing, pocket-picking, shop-lifting, and so on. In nearly every case the methods and tricks are full of ingenuity, and worthy of detailed description, especially since various legal records, reports of trials, &c., are full enough to prove that the tricks which the pamphleteers describe were actually practised.

The method of cozenage with cards Greene called Conny-catching Law.[2] It was so common that the word 'conny-catching' became the name for the whole varied art of cozening. Conny-catching proper was played by four persons: the first of these was a Setter, whose duty was to entice into a tavern the destined Conny, some countryman visiting the city, or a farmer up for the term of court. He had many ways of doing it, which he adapted to his prey. He began perhaps by greeting him warmly in the street, and upon the farmer declaring that he did not know him, the Setter—guessing what part of the country he was from by his accent—would say, 'You come from such and such a shire, do you not?' If he missed he would ask the farmer's name, and when he had heard it and perhaps those of one or two other gentlemen living near him, would beg his pardon and leave, to impart the information to the Verser—the fellow

[1] *A Notable Discouery of Coosnage*, 1591; *The Second Part of Conny-catching*, 1591.
[2] Greene, *Notable Discouery of Coosnage* (Grosart, x. 15–29).

whose duty it was to play the game in any case—who, thus equipped, would probably be more successful. Perhaps the Verser would claim kinship with some gentleman in the farmer's neighbourhood and say he had often called at the good man's house. If all failed, there were other tricks to get the Conny into a tavern. One was to drop a shilling in

FIG. 13. Conny-catching law.
(*From Greene's Notable Discouery of Coosnage.*)

front of him and, when he picked it up, to cry 'half part', and then, quoting the proverb, ''Tis ill luck to keep found money,' induce him to go into a public-house to spend it. Another was to pretend to want him to carry a letter to some one in his neighbourhood, and to ask him to step in while the letter was written. Once inside, a game was started, perhaps the Setter and the Verser playing for the wine, the Conny looking on or helping one to cozen the other at some apparently sure trick. Then the Barnacle blundered in, pretending to be drunk, and the Conny helped one of his companions to strip the new-comer of some trifling amount. They won a few times perhaps, but the Barnacle doubled the stakes each time he lost, and finally, when the amount was high enough, the luck turned and the poor Conny was caught.

According to Greene the game most commonly used for this villany was called Decoy, or Mumchance-at-cards.[1] It was very simple: the pack was shuffled and cut, each player called a card, and the man whose card came first won. The trick was in cutting to bring a card which you had seen yourself or shown to a confederate near the top of the pack. Every card-player understands such tricks, and doubtless did in Greene's time. Reginald Scot explains how to shuffle and manipulate the cards for tricks of this kind, and describes a number of similar sleights: 'How to deliuer out foure aces, and to conuert them into foure knaues;—how to tell what card anie man thinketh;—how to make one drawe the same or anie card you list, etc.' The success of the game depended upon the skill with which the trick was performed and upon the eagerness of the Conny to fleece the drunken Barnacle. Scot evidently understood this part of the conny-catching game also, for he warns his readers against it.

'If you plaie among strangers,' he writes, 'beware of him that séemes simple or drunken; for vnder their habit the most speciall couseners are presented, and while you thinke by their simplicitie and imperfections to beguile them (and therof perchance are persuaded by their confederats, your verie freends as you thinke) you your selfe will be most of all ouertaken. Beware also of bettors by, and lookers on, and namelie of them that bet on your side: for whilest they looke in your game

[1] Greene, *Notable Discouery of Coosnage* (Grosart, x. 21 and 25). 'Mumchance' is much commoner as the name of a game with dice, as the following quotations show: 'Ye must also be furnished with high men, and low men for a mumchance and for passage.'—*A manifest detection of the moste vyle and detestable vse of Diceplay*, 1552, sig. C_4 (Percy Soc., vol. xxix, p. 27).

> But leauing Cardes, lett's goe to dice awhile,
> To Passage, Treitrippe, Hazarde, or Mumchaunce.

—*Machiuells Dogge*, sig. B verso. Greene's name 'Mumchance-at-cardes' may indicate this. I have not seen the game mentioned explicitly as a game of cards elsewhere except in Dekker's *Belman of London*, which is copied from Greene.

PLATE VI

Conny-catching at cards by the use of a mirror, as pictured by Callot.

(*From the British Museum collection.*)

without suspicion, they discouer it by signes to your aduersaries, with whome they bet, and yet are their confederates.'[1]

Conny-catching was simply a new name for an old trick which was practised half a century or more before Greene wrote. It is described in the pamphlet called *A manifest detection of the moste vyle and detestable vse of Diceplay* (1552) under the name of Barnard's Law.[2] Greene says that conny-catching is a much more detestable villany than Barnard's Law, but there is really little difference—the most surprising thing about the history of cozening tricks is that they change so little. In Barnard's Law there is the Taker-up—an affable fellow, able to converse engagingly on any subject, and to get the 'Cousin' (the ancestor of Greene's Conny) into a tavern and into a game, no matter how determined he is against it. The other confederates—the Setter, the Verser, the Barnard (whom Greene calls the Barnacle), and the Rutter, agree exactly in the parts they perform. The change in name is only a common alteration of rogue's cant. Pamphleteers following Greene ten years later describe the same trick under the name of Batfowling with suitable changes in the names of the characters.[3] In a similar way Figging Law became the art of Fool-taking,[4] and the seventeenth-century pamphlets on villany have an almost endless variety of cant terms for the same old tricks.

The art of using false dice, called Cheating Law, was no less popular and no less well supplied with its own proper vocabulary. Greene refused to describe the dicing tricks, for what reason I do not know. 'Pardon me Gentlemen,' he says, 'for although no man could better then my selfe discouer this lawe and his tearmes, and the name of their Cheats, Barddice, Flats, Forgers, Langrets, Gourds, Demies, and many other, with

[1] *Discouerie of Witchcraft*, Book xiii, chaps. 27 and 28.

[2] Percy Society edition (vol. xxix), p. 37—copied by Greene in the *Introduction to a Notable Discouery of Coosnage*. See Chapter VI for discussion of Greene's debt to this pamphlet.

[3] *Greenes Ghost Haunting Conie-catchers* (1602), by S. R. Also *Belman of London*, sig. F_3.

[4] Greene, *Thirde and Last Part of Conny-catching*, 1592 (Grosart x. 156).

their nature, and the crosses and contraries to them vpon aduantage, yet for some speciall reasons, herein I will be silent.'[1] Reginald Scot avoids it also; he speaks of dice play as a means 'whereby a man maie be inevitablie cousened', and dismisses it with this declaration: 'I dare not (as I could) shew the lewd iuggling that chetors practise, least it minister some offense to the well disposed, to the simple hurt and losses, and to the wicked occasion of euill dooing.'[2]

The principal authority on cheating law is the *Manifest Detection* mentioned above. At least three later descriptions of this art are, as we shall see, copied verbatim from it. This pamphlet informs us that dicing has grown from a game to a profession with a whole army of followers. Any one of these is able to make a fool of any dice-player of the generation gone by. Hodge Setter, who forty years ago was thought 'pereles in crafty playe', would be nothing in a modern game:

> 'Lyke as all good and lyberall scyences had a rude beginninge, and by the industrye of good men, beeinge augmented by lytell and by litell at laste grewe to a iuste perfection: so this detestable priuy robery from a few and deceytful rules is in few yeres grown to the body of an arte, and hath his perculiar termes, and therof as great a multitude applied to it, as hathe Gramer or Lodgicke, or any other of the approued sciensis.'[3]

This improvement in the art of dicing has come about from the many new and ingenious varieties of false dice which have been invented, and from the skill with which the gamesters substitute one kind for another, juggler fashion. False dice of a good quality were made, the author informs us, in the two jails, the King's Bench and the Marshalsea: 'yet Bird in Holburn is the finest workman, acquaint your self with him, and let him make you a bale or ii. of squariers of sundry sisis, some lesse, some more, to throw into the first play, til ye perceiue what your company is. Then haue in a redines to

[1] *Notable Discouery of Coosnage*, 1591, sig. C_4 verso (Grosart, x. 37).

[2] *Discouerie of Witchcraft*, Book xiii, chap. 27.

[3] *Manifest Detection*, sig. B_3 and verso. (Percy Society reprint, vol. xxix, p. 16. In this reprint the spelling is modernized and there are many mistakes.)

be foisted in when time shalbe, your fine chetes of all sorts.'[1] There were fourteen varieties of 'fine chetes', i.e. false dice, necessary for the cheater's outfit:

A bale of barde sinke deuxis.
A bale of flatte synke deuxis.
A bale of flatte sixe eacis.
A bale of barde syxe eacis.
A bale of barde cater trees.
A bale of flat cater trees.
A bale of fullans of the best making.
A bale of light grauiers.
A bale of Langretes contrary to the vantage.
A bale of Gordes with as many hyghe men as lowe men for passage.
A bale of demies.
A bale of long dyce for euen and odde.
A bale of brystelles.
A bale of direct contraries.[2]

It is rather difficult to tell just what all these terms mean. Barred and flat cinq-deuces, six-aces, and quater-treas seem to be dice forged slightly longer one way or the other so as to make it easier or more difficult for certain numbers to turn up, barred cinq-deuces, six-aces, and quater-treas tending to prevent the numbers in question, while flats turned them upward. That this is the correct explanation is proved by a passage in this pamphlet:

'Lo here saith the chetor to this yong Nouisse, a well fauored die that semeth good and square: yet is the forhed longer on the cater and tray, then any other way, and therefore holdeth the name of a langret, such be also called bard cater tres, bicause commonly the longer end will of his owne sway draw downwards, and turne vp to the eye sice sinke, deuis or ace, the principal vse of them is at Nouem quinque. So long as a paier of bard quater tres be walking on the bord

[1] *Manifest Detection*, sig. C_3 verso. (Percy Society, vol. xxix, p. 27.) I have changed the reading 'roysted' of the copy printed by Abraham Veale to 'foysted', for which it was evidently intended. The mis-reading of 'quartiers' for 'squariers' in the Percy Society reprint spoils the meaning of the passage.

[2] Ibid., on reverse of title-page. I have changed the reading 'contrarnes' to 'contraries', for which it was evidently meant. This list is copied in *Mihil Mumchance* and the *Belman of London.*

so long can ye cast neither .v. nor .ix. onles it be by a great mischance that the roughnes of the bord, or some other stay, force them to stay and run against their kind. For without quater trey, ye wot that, v. nor .ix. [the pamphlet has x, an obvious mistake] can neuer fall.' [1]

A langret, according to the above, was the same as a barred quater-trea. A langret cut contrary to the vantage was evidently the opposite, and most readily showed three or four: 'when the Chetor with a langret, cut contrarie to the vantage, will cros-bite a bard cater tray.' [2]

Fullams were dice loaded with quicksilver or lead: bristles were those with a short hair set in one side to prevent that face lying on the table. Capell conjectures that gourds were dice hollowed out on one side to accomplish the same result as loading. 'As for Gords and bristle dice, [they] be now to grose a practise to be put in vse,' says the *Manifest Detection.*[3] However, the worthy Pistol still reposed confidence in gourds at any rate. High men and low men were names used for various dice according to the numbers they turned up; high fullams and low fullams are common terms. Sometimes the dice were wrongly numbered, high or low as the case might be. A story quoted by Strutt from the Harleian MSS. will illustrate this:

'Sir William Herbert playing at Dice with an other gentleman, there arose some question about a cast: The other swore it was a 5 and 4: and he swore it could not be so, for it was 6:5: the other swore againe, and curst himselfe to the pitt of Hell, if it were not 5 and 4: Well sayes Sir Will: now I see plainly th'art a damn'd periurd Rogue; for giue me but *6d*, and if there be e're a 4 in the Dice, i'le giue the 1000 l.: at which the other was presently blanch't; for indeed the Dice were false, and of an high cutt, without a 4.' [4]

Concerning demies, light graviers, direct contraries, and long dice for even and odd, I have no information to offer, and shall

[1] *Manifest Detection*, sig. C_1 (Percy Society reprint, vol. xxix, p. 24).

[2] Greene, *A Notable Discouerie of Coosnage*, 1591, sig. A_4 verso (Grosart, x. 12).

[3] Sig. C_4 (Percy Society, vol. xxix, p. 28), where fullams are also explained.

[4] Strutt, *Sports and Pastimes*, ed. Cox, p. 247 (from Harl. MS. 6395, Art. 69). The story as given here is from the MS.

venture no conjecture further than that they also doubtless 'beguiled the rich and poor'.

The accomplished cheater did not make the advantage in his dice too great, but was content to win slowly. Perhaps he would use 'squares' to begin with, in order to give his intended victim a chance. It was a proverb that the cheater always lost to the gull if the dice were fair. But gradually the langrets, gourds, and fullams came walking on the board, one kind in the box when the cheater was casting, and another when the turn came for his opponent. The dice were changed by a sleight of hand which took long practice to learn. Indeed, *ars longa* could be applied to the whole art of conny-catching.

> 'Is it a small tyme, thinke yow,' asks Harington, 'that one of these cunninge gamesters spendes in practysinge to slurre a dye sewerly, to stop a card cleanly, to laye a pack cunningly? I have herd some (and those no novyses in these misteryes) affyrme, that the devyser of the sett at the new cutt, (that did cut so many ere the edge was fully discovered,) coulde not spend so little as a moneths earnest study, beatinge his brayns ere hee could contryve it,—if it colde be donne withowt the help of the devell, for, indeed, whom the devill should the devill assyst, but soch as labor and study night and day in his service?'[1]

It was no small task merely to recognize the different forms of false dice by their looks and to know immediately what numbers they would turn up in combination. But when all this was mastered, the sharper had his opponent at his mercy; his difficulty then was to avoid the unsavoury reputation of always winning. The best way to manage this was to play into the hands of a confederate, for which office no one was better than a ruined gull. The gull might have a good acquaintance in the country, and could bring in his friends to be fleeced. The old gamester in the *Manifest Detection*, who is coaching a ruined young heir in the mysteries of the art by which his inheritance had been rattled away, instructs him especially to avoid swearing in his play, rather giving up a point than making a quarrel.

[1] Sir John Harington, *Nugae Antiquae*, 'A Treatise on Playe' (*c.* 1597), i. 214 (ed. Park, 1804).

Bowling was almost as common in Elizabethan London as cards and dice. It was very popular among the citizens, and the alleys were thronged with them, even the poorer men who could ill afford the money they spent in play and lost in betting. Sir Nicholas Woodrofe, Lord Mayor in 1580, in a letter to the Privy Council described alleys as places of the most vicious and disorderly character. There are far too many of them in the city, he says, both open ones for summer and closed ones for winter; all kinds of people resort to them, and such is the fascination of the sport that the poor labourers neglect their work, and play away their money and even their household goods, while their wives and children are in want at home. Drink is commonly sold, and dice, cards, and table play kept in addition to bowling; the alleys are dangerous in time of plague owing to the great crowds in them, and they are the scene of daily drunkenness, blaspheming, picking, cozening, and all kinds of disorder.[1]

One cozening trick used in bowling alleys, Greene describes. It was called Vincent's Law. Certain sharpers, apparelled like honest substantial citizens, would begin a game, apparently for the sake of a little honest recreation, while their confederates stood among the spectators, waiting for an opportunity to bet. If any man offered a wager, these fellows took it, no matter how small the chance of their winning. Perhaps the play would go still further against them, and the gull—here called the Vincent—would lay bets more freely and at greater odds, but in the end the game swung round, the sharpers won their bets, and, at the close of the day, shared the spoils with the players.[2]

Picking pockets was an art or mystery. Every writer about it speaks of the fraternity of cut-purses, to which they paid dues for insurance when they were caught, and through which they apportioned their territories and privileges. A statute of 1564 (the 8 Eliz. c. 4) mentions this reputed association of pickpockets and prescribes severe punishments for any

[1] See Chapter V below. His letter is recorded in *Remembrancia*, i. 133.
[2] *Second Part of Conny-catching* (Grosart, x. 82).

members of it who shall be caught, these to be administered without benefit of clergy.[1] 'I remember their hall', says Greene, 'was once about *Bushops gate*, neere unto fishers follie, but because it was a noted place, they have remooued it to *Kent-street*, and as far as I can learne, it is kept at one *Laurence Pickerings* house, one that hath bene if he be not still, a notable Foist.'[2] Recorder Fletewood was very likely the man who 'noted' it; he was always in hot pursuit of pickpockets and conny-catchers of all kinds. Among the jolly letters from him to Lord Burghley printed by Wright in his *Elizabeth and her Times* is one dated July 7, 1585, which gives us a picture of a cut-purse hall and training school much better than Greene's. Fletewood shall speak for himself:

'The same daie my Lord Maior being absente abowte the goods of the Spanyards, and also all my Lords the justices of the benches being also awaye, we fewe that were there did spend the same daie abowte the searching owt of sundry that were receptors of felons, where we found a greate many as well in London, Westminster, Sowthwarke, as in all other places abowte the same. Amongst our travells this one matter tumbled owt by the way, that one Wotton, a gentilman borne, and sometyme a marchaunt man of good credyt, who falling by tyme into decay, kepte an alehowse at Smart's Key, neere Byllingsgate, and after for some mysdemeanor being put downe, he reared up a new trade of lyfe, and in the same howse he procured all the cuttpurses abowte this cittie to repaire to his same howse. There was a schole-howse sett up to learne young boyes to cutt purses. There were hung up two devyses, the one was a pocket, the other was a purse. The pocket had in it certain cownters, and was hung abowt with hawkes' bells, and over the top did hang a little sacring bell; and he that could take out a cownter without any noyse was allowed to be a publique foyster, and he that could take a piece of sylver out of the purse, without the noyse of any of the bells, he was adjudged a judiciall nypper. Nota, that a foyster is a pick-pokett, and a nypper is termed a pickpurse, or a cutpurse.'[3]

[1] Cp. Chapter V below.

[2] *Second Part of Conny-catching* (Grosart, x. 109).

[3] Wright, *Elizabeth and her Times*, ii. 245–51 (from Lansdowne MS. 44, 38). Fletewood appends a list of the names of forty-five masterless men and cut-purses, and mentions the eighteen harbouring houses for them in London and the suburbs referred to above. Maitland, in his *History of London*, 1756, vol. i, p. 269, prints this extract.

It was the long schooling and apprenticeship required to become an expert in this profession, we are told, that kept it so well organized:

'Their craft of all others requireth most slyght, and hath a meruelus plenty of terms and strange language, and therfore no man can attayne to bee a workman therat, till he haue had a good time of scoling, and by that meanes they do not only know eache other well, but they be subiecte to an order, suche as the elders shal prescribe. No man so sturdy to practise his feate but in the place apoynted, nor for any cause once to put his fote in an others walke.'[1]

The pickpockets are the heroes of the best stories of the pamphleteers, and their manners are described at length. There were two classes, each of which disdained the other: the Nip who cut purses with a knife and a horn thumb, and the Foist who drew them with his fingers, scorning to carry a knife even to cut his meat, lest he should be suspected of using it in the profession. Further, there were city foists and country foists, who were very jealous of any infringement of territory. A pickpocket was often followed by a 'cloyer' who claimed a part of each haul as 'snappage' on pain of exposing the theft if he was denied.[2] Their best fields of operation were St. Paul's at the crowded hours, Westminster during term, the theatres, the Bear Garden, Fleet Street, the Strand, Tyburn on the day of an execution, and all fairs and celebrations. Sometimes, in order to draw a crowd, they would hire a fellow to sing ballads and sell them (as in the case of the sons of old Barnes of 'Bishop's Stafford'), the Foists in the crowd watching where each buyer put his purse in order to filch it before he left,[3] or they hired a nimble fellow to climb a steeple, and, while the crowd watched him with heads in the air, they nipped a fine lot of purses[4]; or they exhibited some freak or curiosity at a fair. There were not lacking bold spirits who

[1] *Manifest Detection*, sig. D_6 (Percy Society, vol. xxix, pp. 40-1). The whole account of the pickpockets' corporation here and their ways of helping each other is most interesting.

[2] *Greenes Ghost Haunting Conie-catchers*, 1602, Hunterian Club edition of Rowlands, i. 16–17.

[3] Greene, *Thirde and Last Part of Conny-catching* (Grosart, x. 161). Cp. also p. 49, above.

[4] *Mihil Mumchance*, sig. D_2.

could take a purse under the most difficult circumstances. One fellow, meeting a gentlewoman who had a purse hanging from her girdle, pretended to mistake her for a relative, greeted her warmly, kissed her, drew her purse, apologized for his mistake, and retired before she perceived her loss. Another coming up to a lawyer from behind, clapped his hands over his eyes, and cried, 'Who am I?' while a confederate who had pretended to retain the lawyer for a case and had paid the fee in advance, secured the purse with the fee and all. The first rogue then made an apology, pretending to have mistaken the lawyer for a friend, and departed, followed soon after by the second to share the booty.[1]

Greene's Crossbiting Law[2]—cozenage with whores—was only a new name for the Sacking Law mentioned in the *Manifest Detection*. A common woman enticed a young gull into a room with her, then a Roystering Boy who pretended to be her husband or brother swaggered in, sword in hand, threatening murder in revenge for the wrong done to his honour, which wrong the trembling culprit appeased with all the money in his purse in order to save his life or his reputation. The Crossbiter was considered the lowest possible type of rogue; he was more contemptible than the professional murderer, and fit only to swagger in the stews, hold the door for the customers he procured, and live on mouldy stewed prunes.

Prigging Law and Courbing Law have been described in another chapter. Lifting Law (that is, shop-lifting) and the Black Art (picking locks) need no detailed account.[3] Theft of all kinds was encouraged by the large number of brokers, or broggers, who flourished in every part of the city, and who were ready to buy any kind of booty without asking questions. Many of them were no better than thieves themselves. They kept their houses open all night, aided the thieves in every way they could, and disposed of articles which it was

1 Greene, *Thirde and Last Part of Conny-catching* (Grosart, x. 156–60).
2 *Notable Discouery of Coosnage* (Grosart, x. 39).
3 *Second Part of Conny-catching* (Grosart, x. 118 and 128).

unsafe to sell in England, to Dutch and French brokers who conveyed them secretly out of the country.[1] The trade of brokage flourished in spite of a storm of protest and in the face of the strictest prohibitive legislation.

There remains one kind of villany which could be used against persons who would not be caught by any bait set for

FIG. 14. The Black Art—picking locks.
(*From Greene's Second and Last Part of Conny-catching.*)

gulls. This was High Law, or highway robbery. It was a kind of thieving which seems to have been considered fit for a gentleman. It was one way for the ruined heir to work poetic justice on the wealthy merchant who had his land.

Whetstone says that many a fellow who played the gallant at the fashionable ordinaries, waited behind a hedge on the high-

[1] See Greene, *Thirde and Last Part of Conny-catching* (Grosart, x. 155); and compare with it the letter from the Lord Mayor of London to the Attorney-General on this subject, which is transcribed in Appendix A, 12.

way in a green mask to get his living.[1] A large proportion of the men convicted of highway robbery in the Middlesex Sessions during the sixteenth century called themselves gentlemen. It is reasonable to suppose that they were superior to the conny-catchers and cozeners heretofore described. It required more courage to rob a man on the highway than to cheat him at cards or pick his pocket. 'All the former Lawes are attained by wit,' says Dekker, 'but the *High Law* stands both vpon *Wit* and *Manhood*.'[2] The stories told of the sixteenth-century highwaymen have a little of the same code of ethics, so delightful to the popular mind, as the tales of Robin Hood. Gamaliell Ratsey is a good example. A little pamphlet about his life and death, published in 1605, narrates divers of his adventures, showing his wit and daring: how he robbed nine men alone in Northamptonshire; how he robbed a Cambridge scholar and made him afterwards deliver an oration on the sinfulness of theft; how he robbed two men and knighted them.[3] But some of the stories also illustrate his kindness of heart. On one occasion Ratsey robbed a poor man of five nobles, his entire fortune, which he had saved for several years to buy a cow. But when the poor old man told him this, the gallant highwayman returned the money, gave him forty shillings in addition, and sent him joyfully on to the fair to buy two cows instead of one.[4] Another time he held up a poor farmer who was carrying 150 pounds to pay on a bond for which all his land and goods were pledged as forfeit. The whole sum due was 200 pounds, but the poor man was able to pay only 150, and with that he intended to try to save his farm, although he had great fear of losing it, because he could not make up the full sum. When Ratsey understood the poor fellow's situation (and could find no convenient place for the robbery), he lent him fifty pounds in addition to pay the bond. The next day when the landlord

[1] *Touchstone for the Time* (an addition to *A Mirour for Magestrates of Cyties*, 1584), leaf 28. (The numbering is mixed; it runs 25, 28, 27, 26, 29, &c.)

[2] *Belman of London*, 1608, sig. G_4 verso (Temple edition, p. 142).

[3] *The Life and Death of Gamaliell Ratsey* (1605).

[4] Ibid., sig. C_3.

was carrying this, along with some additional money, to make a purchase at the next town, Ratsey robbed him, getting back his own fifty pounds, the poor man's 150, and 100 besides.[1] These stories are manifestly fiction—borrowings from Robin Hood ballads and traditional highwaymen stories. The trade had perhaps lost some of its poetry by the sixteenth century, but it was still flourishing nevertheless.

Harrison says that few highway robberies were committed without the help of the inn-keepers and chamberlains, who found out which men were worth robbing, what direction they were going, and perhaps even sent a confederate along with the intended victim. This confederate would guide the rest of the party into the highwayman's hands, and would for appearance' sake be robbed along with them.[2] The robbery on Gad's Hill in *Henry IV* follows the traditional method exactly.

Richard Sheale, the minstrel (see Chapter II), thinks that something of the same kind happened to him.

> And sum hath bene robde in ther yns, as I have hard men tell:
> The chamberlayne or ostelare, when the have a bowgyt spyede,
> May gyve knowlege to fals knavis whiche way ther gest wyll ryde;
> And he him selffe wyll byd at hom, and his office styll aplye.
> Many a man thus hathe be robde, and so I think was I.[3]

Highway robberies were not so common in the sixteenth century as they had been in the fourteenth and fifteenth, and they were not so often accompanied by murder as they had been in earlier times. But they were still very frequent. The little hundred of Benhurst on the road from London to Reading, paid £255 in one year in damages for robberies committed within the hundred when the hue and cry failed to catch the malefactors.[4] The Privy Council was frequently occupied in investigating important robberies committed in

[1] *The Life and Death of Gamaliell Ratsey* (1605), sig. C_4 verso.
[2] *Description of England*, Book iii, chap. xvi (N. Sh. Soc., pp. 108–9).
[3] Wright, *Songs and Ballads, &c.*, 1860, p. 159.
[4] Cp. 39 Eliz. c. 25 (1597–8).

different parts of the country. During the reign of Elizabeth there are frequent convictions for highway robbery recorded in the Middlesex Sessions' Rolls.

This completes the list of cozening 'Laws' reported by Greene. There are hundreds of variations and illustrations of them in the pamphlets which follow him, but all of these add very little to his account, whilst his writing has a certain convincing ring usually wanting in his imitators. As was said earlier in this chapter, the main outlines of this vagabond life are clear and convincing. Of course, one would not care to vouch for the authenticity of every trick nor of every story, but this credit must be given to the pamphleteers, that their account has a certain reality not to be found always in mere facts. They reproduce the spirit of conny-catching life. This mad merry rogue spirit is illustrated nowhere better than in a short, dateless, nameless sermon reprinted by Viles and Furnivall from a Cotton MS. in the British Museum—a sermon in praise of thieves and thieving. A certain Parson Hyberdyne, so the document states, was robbed by a band of thieves at Hartley Row in Hampshire. After the robbery the thieves compelled their victim to preach them a sermon in praise of thieves and thieving. This the merry parson did so well that they restored his money again and in addition gave him two shillings to reward his eloquence. The sermon recites the manly qualities demanded for the trade of thieving—especially for highway robbery; it encourages boldness, fortitude, and courage. Thieving is practised by all men, and has precedent in Scripture. Jacob stole his Uncle Laban's kids and his father's blessing; David stole the hallowed bread from the temple, and even Christ took an ass and a colt that were none of his. With a burst of eloquence the preacher concludes:

'But moste of all I marvell that men can dispyse yow theves, where as in all poyntes almoste yow be lyke vnto christe hym selfe: for chryste had noo dwellynge place; noo more haue yow. christe wente frome towne to towne; and soo doo yow. christe was hated of all men, sauynge of his freendes; and soo are yow. christe was laid waite vpon in many places; and soo are you. chryste at the lengthe was cawght; and soo shall yow bee. he was browght before the iudges; and soo shall yow bee. he was accused; and soo shall you bee. he was condempned; and soo shall yow bee. he was hanged; and so shall yow bee. he wente downe into hell; and soo shall yow dooe. mary! in this one thynge yow dyffer frome hym, for he rose agayne and assendid into heauen; and soo shall yow neuer dooe, withowte godes greate mercy, which gode grawnte yow! to whome with the father, and the soone, and hooly ghoste, bee all honore and glorye, for euer and euer. Amen!'[1]

[1] *The Rogues and Vagabonds of Shakespere's Youth* (N. Sh. Soc.), p. 95. (From MS. Cott. Vesp. A. xxv, leaf 53.) The sermon is also reprinted in Wright and Halliwell's *Reliquiae Antiquae*, 1841–3, ii. 111. They assign to it the date *c.* 1573. Ribton Turner, *History of Vagrants and Vagrancy*, p. 40, tells a story (without giving the reference) which looks as if it might be a fourteenth-century form of this one.

CHAPTER V

LAWS AGAINST CONNY-CATCHING

Slender. Marry, sir, I have matter in my head against you, and against your conny-catching rascals, Bardolph, Nym, and Pistol.

Merry Wives of Windsor, Act I, sc. 1.

THE history of the sixteenth-century legislation against vagabondage and begging is the story of a great legislative triumph. In a space of seventy years the Parliament and Privy Council of England devised a set of laws and a system for putting them in force which harassed the poor vagrants on every side and visited thousands of them with that most effective of all punishments—work. The history of the legislation against conny-catchers, on the other hand, is the story of an absolute failure. Slender's remark quoted above represents the attitude of the laws, but, despite many clumsy attempts, the matter went very little further. The problem was more complicated, of course; the conny-catchers were far more clever than the wandering beggars; it was obviously difficult to legislate against a tribe whose pride it was to have a new trick for every occasion. It was also true that the conny-catchers were far less numerous than the vagabonds, and their doings were more carefully hidden from the public: without a detective force and a rogues' gallery it was hard to catch them.

But the most important reason for the conny-catchers' immunity from legal interference was what we should call in modern American parlance 'graft'. They had influence in high places. Gaming-houses and bowling-alleys were licensed, bales of dice were approved and sealed, and playing-cards were sold—all under monopolies granted by royal patents, so that the protection of gaming yielded a good revenue to favourites of the Queen. Hence it is that our study of the relation in which this kind of roguery stood to society in the reign of Elizabeth leads us not as in the case of vagrants and beggars to a study of laws and reports of trials, but instead to a study of the legal machinery by which this gaming was licensed and protected.

The laws against gaming were strict enough. At the beginning of Elizabeth's reign bowling, quoits, closh, kayles, half-bowl, tennis, dice, tables, and cards were forbidden by numerous statutes and proclamations; the people were commanded to practise, instead, archery and such other exercises as were calculated to preserve the ancient strength of English soldiery. These statutes went into such detail as to prescribe that bowmakers (whose high prices had been alleged in divers petitions as the chief reason for the decline of this manly sport in favour of the more decadent cards, dice, and bowling) should not demand more than six shillings and eight pence for a longbow of the best quality.[1]

However, the royal patents permitted what the laws forbade. It was an age which loved gaming; in spite of the laws and proclamations and the seduction of six shilling and eight-penny bows, all manner of games of chance were increasing. Hence the government saw fit to license what it could not restrain. The official excuse is expressed very well in Elizabeth's patent of 1576 allowing Thomas Cornwallis, her Groom-porter, to license gaming-houses in London: 'seyng the inclination of menne to be geven and bent to the aforesayd pastymes and playe, and that secretlye or openlye they do commonly playe, and that no penaltye of the lawes or statutes aforesayd hath heretofore restrayned them.'[2] The laws against all manner of games remained on the statute books, but their only effect was to benefit the owners of the patents.

There was continual opposition by the city government to this royal protection of gaming, just as there was to the royal protection of the theatres. The profits all went to the favourites of the Crown while the trouble and disgrace fell on the city, in consequence of which there was more than one sharp dispute between the Aldermen and the Privy Council.

[1] 8 Eliz., c. 10 (continued ten times during the next sixty years). The prices, as fixed by this law, ranged from 6*s*. 8*d*. down to 2*s*.

[2] P.R.O. Patent Roll, 18 Eliz., pt. 1, m. 31.

Gaming-houses, so licensed, were the principal field of operation of the sharpers and cozeners with whom this chapter and the preceding are concerned. We shall begin our explanation of the system by looking for a moment at the history of these permits granted in direct opposition to the statutes and proclamations forbidding 'unlawfull games'.

Licensed gaming-houses had existed at least since the reign of Henry VIII. In 1540 the king made Gilbert Clerc and Nicholas Damporte 'Keepers of the Plays' in Calais, which plays were, as specified in the patent, 'Hande oute and Keiles without the Lantern Gate,' and dice, cards, and tables in the market-place.[1] This office Robert Donyngton had occupied before them. In 1545 John Swynerton, *alias* Vennet, had a licence to keep gambling-houses in London.[2] Groom-porter Lewknor, under Philip and Mary, held public gaming at his house at Christmas time, under the protection of the sovereigns. All such licences were revoked by the 2 and 3 Philip and Mary, cap. 9, in 1555, on account of the great disorders arising from gaming-houses, only to be reissued early in the reign of Elizabeth.

It was one of the perquisites of the Groom-porter of the Household to arrange cards, dice, and other games for the royal family and courtiers to play at Christmas time, and to make what profits he could from them. The play at the Groom-porter's at Christmas is alluded to frequently, and is well described by Pepys in the entry in his *Diary* for January 1, 1667–8.[3]

It was by a natural extension of this privilege that Elizabeth granted, by a patent dated July 9, 1576, to her Groom-porter, Thomas Cornwallis, the right to issue licences to gaming-houses in London.[4] He was to require persons whom he licensed not to suffer any frauds or cozenage in their gaming-

[1] Rymer, *Foedera*, vol. xiv, p. 707.

[2] Patent Roll, 36 Henry VIII, pt. 17, m. 16 (Dec. 21).

[3] For other allusions see Evelyn's *Diary*, January 6, 1661–2; Jonson, *Alchemist*, Act III, sc. 2; *Ordinary*, Act II, sc. 3 (Hazlitt's *Dodsley*, xii, p. 247); Harington, *Nugae Antiquae*, ed. Park, i. 187; Lilly, *A Collection of Seventy-nine Black Letter Ballads*, &c., 1867, pp. 123 ff. 'The Groome-porters lawes at Mawe.'

[4] Patent Roll, 18 Eliz., pt. 1, m. 31.

places, nor to allow any apprentices or suspected persons to frequent them. Cornwallis was also empowered to moderate or compound such fines and penalties as should be levied on any person under the laws in respect to unlawful games, or under this patent, and he could sue out process compulsatory on any offenders who refused to compound. All licences granted by him were to be in tripartite indenture, one copy for each party concerned, and one to be deposited in the records of the High Court of Chancery. In the Public Record Office three of these licences are preserved, very much defaced, from which the form quoted in Appendix A, 13 has been reconstructed.

This protection of gambling brought profit to the favourites of the Crown, but it made the city harder to govern and was resented by the city authorities. The Lord Mayor in 1580, Sir Nicholas Woodrofe, stopped the building of a licensed bowling alley, because there were two more very disorderly ones adjoining it on the same half-acre of ground. The keeper appealed to Sir James Croft, Comptroller of the Royal Household (to whom he stood in some relation denoted by the vague word, servant), and the outcome of the correspondence was that the Mayor wrote to the Privy Council the letter mentioned in Chapter IV above, complaining indignantly that licensed gaming-places violated habitually all the provisions of the Queen's patents, and asking the Council to give him power to restrain them, or else to do it themselves, 'for if such alleys are allowed to continue, the work of dayly looking to them will be infinite.' [1]

Cornwallis's patent of 1576 was revoked in 1596, and a new one granted to him designed to give him more power to prevent the wholesale deceit and cozenage, which had been found to accompany the gaming.[2] This new patent gave Cornwallis practically the same privileges as the first one, for thirteen years following, and, in addition, enabled him or his deputies to search gaming-houses, in order to discover violations either of the law or of this patent, and directed that no dice-makers

[1] For three of the letters see *Remembrancia*, i. 131, 132, 133.
[2] Patent Rolls, 38 Eliz., pt. 6, m. 35.

(who, says the patent, are responsible for most of the cozenage) should make or sell any dice not examined and sealed by the said Thomas Cornwallis. It fixed the penalty for making or selling false dice at 3*s*. 4*d*. for each one. This patent confirms strikingly the stories of the pamphleteers about dice play, and indicates that the use of unfair dice was extremely common.

The new power of surveillance given to the Groom-porter was one step in a strenuous effort made in 1596 by the Privy Council and the London Court of Aldermen, to restrain the use of false dice. In the proceedings of the Court of Aldermen for April 20, there is an allusion to letters from the Council, calling the Aldermen's attention to the manufacture of such dice in the city.[1] A committee was appointed to investigate. On July 22 Cornwallis's new patent was granted, and another committee appointed by the Aldermen to consider it.[2] On August 27 several haberdashers were added to this committee to devise means for searching for false dice in the haberdashery shops.[3] The means devised seem to have been inadequate, for two years later (December 30, 1598) the court drew up new and elaborate orders for search for false dice.[4] Perhaps Cornwallis's deputies had at first charged an extravagant fee for sealing bales of good dice, for this order provides that searchers, agreed upon by Cornwallis and the Board of Aldermen, shall seal dice found to be correctly made for a charge not exceeding one halfpenny per bale of nine pairs. After March 1 following no unsealed dice were to be offered for sale, on pain of forfeiting them. All this supervision may have checked the open sale of unfair dice; less is heard in the later pamphleteers of such fine workmen in that trade as Bird, of Holborn, who flourished in the middle of the century;[5] but, whether the vending of them was secret or open, false dice were still made and used on every hand.

Playing-cards were supplied by a monopoly granted under a patent. The monopoly of importing them was first granted

[1] *Repertory*, xxiii, fo. 523.
[2] *Repertory*, xxiii, fo. 560 b.
[3] Ibid., fo. 570 b.
[4] See Appendix A, 11 for transcription.
[5] Cp. Chapter IV, above.

to Raphe Bowes and Thos. Bedingfield, July 28, 1576, in consideration of 100 marks a year.[1] Their patent prohibited the manufacture of playing-cards in England. The privilege was regranted June 4, 1578, given up June 13, 1588, and the monopoly vested in Raphe Bowes alone for twelve years, he to pay 100 marks a year and one-half the fines collected for violations.[2] The records of the Borough of Leicester contain a notice of a visit of two deputies of Bowes, September 18, 1593, with licence to search everywhere touching playing-cards.[3] It seems that these searches were common enough to make a good opportunity for fakers, since we are told on the same page that some pretended deputies had visited the town a short time before. It is easy to see what an excellent chance for booty such rogues would have; blackmailing other rogues in the card business, and compounding for fines and penalties as Bowes was allowed to do under the patent.

Bowes's patent expired in 1600. Two years before the Queen granted to Edward Darcy, Groom of the Privy Chamber, a similar patent to extend for twenty-one years from the expiration of that of Bowes, out of which grant arose the famous 'Case of Monopolies' (Darcy *v.* Allen) which is still cited in English courts. Darcy brought suit in 1602 against T. Allen, a haberdasher, for making and selling playing-cards contrary to the patent. The decision handed down by Chief Justice Popham in the Easter term, 1603, declared the patent null and void as creating a monopoly contrary to common law and as being against divers Acts of Parliament.[4]

Another patent for playing-cards, granted to Sir Richard Coningsby June 24, 1615, was the occasion of one of the many conflicts with James I over the right of the King to grant monopolies. Coningsby was empowered to search and seal all cards sold in the realm, for which he exacted a fee of five shillings a gross. This, in addition to the customs and

[1] Patent Rolls, 18 Eliz., pt. 1, m. 32.

[2] See *Proclamations*, vol. iv, No. 12, in library of Society of Antiquaries, London. (The date at the end of the proclamation 'the thirtenth yeare' is an evident mistake for 'thirtieth yeare'.)

[3] *Records of the Borough of Leicester*, iii. 291.

[4] J. W. Gordon, *Monopolies by Patents*, 1897, pp. 193–232.

imposts, destroyed all profit in importing cards, with the result that the haberdashers and merchants trading into France objected. The Privy Council temporarily suspended the patent June 30, 1616, whereupon both Coningsby and the King asked for a rehearing, but I have found no record of the end of the dispute.[1]

In connexion with these patents one request for a still more valuable grant has some interest. In 1592 Thomas Bedingfield asked the Queen to give him a monopoly of all the gaming-houses in London, Westminster, and the suburbs, arguing that this would offer a means of controlling the number of houses, now grown very great, and of ensuring that none but fitting persons—'noblemen, gentilemen, marchants, and such others as shalbe ceased in the books of subsedye at x^{l} in land or goods'—should have access to them, and 'guylaful and deceightfull playe' suppressed.[2] Such a monopoly would have been a mine of wealth, but the Queen did not see fit to grant it. She could not have done so without rendering void the patent held by Thomas Cornwallis, if for no other reason.[3]

Next to the users of unlawful games, the members of the conny-catchers' tribe to receive most attention from the law-makers, were the cutpurses and pickpockets. The most singular and interesting of all the laws against conny-catchers of any sort is the 8 Elizabeth, c. 4 (1566), directed against these thieves. As was pointed out in Chapter IV, the act recognizes that picking pockets has become a trade or craft, the practisers of which are bound together for mutual support, and it goes on to give an interesting description of their fields of operation. In church during the time of divine service (one thinks immediately of the stories about Paul's), at court, at fairs and markets, at executions 'ordeined chieflye for Terrour and Example of evill doers', and in all sorts of

[1] The papers from which this account is made are preserved in the British Museum, Lansdowne MSS. clx. fos. 291–301.

[2] *Domestic State Papers, Elizabeth*, vol. 243, No. 58.

[3] One of Cox's additions to Strutt's *Sports and Pastimes*, 1903 (p. 86), says that this monopoly 'was apparently granted'. I have been able to find no trace of it in Patent Rolls or elsewhere. Cox puts the date 1597; there is no date in the document but it is assigned in the Calendar to October 1592.

public assemblies these light-fingered gentry, the law asserts, are busy reaping a harvest of purses from the pockets of honest men. The passage is so interesting that it is worth quoting in full.

'Where a certayne kynde of evill disposed persons commonly called Cutpurses or Pyckpurses, but in deede by the Lawes of this Lande very Fellons and Theeves, doo confeder togethers making among themselves as it were a Brotherhed or Fraternitie of an Arte or Mysterie, to lyve idellye by the secrete Spoyle of the good and true Subjectes of this Realme, and aswell at Sermons and Prechings of the Woorde of God, and in places and tyme of doing service and common Prayer in Churches Chappelles Closettes and Oratories, and not only there but also in the Princes Palace House, yea and presence, and at the Places and Courtes of Justice, and at the tymes of Mynystracion of the Lawes in the same, and in Fayres Markettes and other Assemblies of People, yea and at the tyme of doing of Execucion of suche as ben attaynted of anye Murder Felonye or other crimynall Cause ordeined chieflye for Terrour and Example of evill doers, do without respect or regarde of anye tyme place or person, or anye feare or dreade of God, or any Lawe or Punyshment, under the cloke of Honestie, by their owtwarde Apparell Countenance and Behaviour subtiltie privilye craftelye and felonyously take the Goodes of dyvers good and honest Subjectes from their persons by cutting and pycking their Purses and other felonious Slaightes and Devices, to the utter undoing and impoverishment of many: BEE it therefore enacted by the aucthorite of this present Parliament,' &c., &c., to the effect that persons convicted of this crime shall be executed as felons without benefit of clergy.

The sixteenth-century court records indicate that no part of the country was free from pickpockets,[1] but London was their best field, and there are frequent entries on the Middlesex Sessions' Rolls of male and female pickpockets sentenced to be hanged. Sometimes such fellows were not left for the tender punishments of Constable Dogberry and Justice Shallow. If one was caught in a theatre the custom was to tie him to

[1] For example, in 1598 three pickpockets were hanged at the midsummer sessions at Exeter Castle (Hamilton, *Quarter Sessions*, p. 33); and in 1606 some suspected cutpurses and rogues were whipped at Malton in the North Riding of Yorkshire (*North Riding Records*, vol. i, p. 52).

a post on the stage to let the people jeer at him through the rest of the play. 'I remembred one of them to be a noted Cut-purse,' says Will Kemp in his account of his Morris dance from London to Norwich, 'such a one as we tye to a poast on our stage, for all people to wonder at, when at a play they are taken pilfring.'[1] Another allusion to the same custom occurs in the old play *Nobody and Somebody*.

> *Somebody*
> Once pickt a pocket in this Play-house yard,
> Was hoysted on the stage, and shamd about it.[2]

The authorities sought in other more or less clumsy ways to restrain the shifty tribe of conny-catchers and cozeners. There were numerous attempts to restrain the number of taverns and ale-houses. Lists of tavern-keepers were made, and reported to the sessions in different shires, and to the Board of Aldermen of London in the Wardmote presentments, and these persons were repeatedly sworn not to keep their houses open during hours of church service, to allow no unlawful games, and to serve no meat on fish days.[3] There were proclamations against the stews and against the crowds and traffic in Paul's Walk—all of which seem to have been very little enforced.[4]

A few stray records of punishment will show what was considered adequate penalty for a cozener when caught. The law was not definite, and the penalties, compared with those covered explicitly by statute, seem very light. In 1537 a man who had obtained a horse 'per fraudem deceptionem et astutiam vocat' Cosenyage' was fined 40*s*. and put in Cheapside pillory.[5] Had he stolen it directly, he would of course have been hanged. At Leicester in the year 1575-6 two 'cosoners' were set on the pillory with printed papers

[1] *Kemps Nine Daies Wonder*, 1600 (Camden Soc. edition, p. 6).
[2] Simpson, *School of Shakespeare*, i. 352.
[3] See *Middlesex Sessions' Rolls*, pp. 10-11 (June 20 to September 5, 6 Edward VI), and MS. Wardmote presentments in Guildhall Record Office.
[4] *Proclamations*, ii. 164, April 13, 1546, in library of the London Society of Antiquaries; also Proclamation of October 30, 1561, in Bodleian volume, *Proclamations by Elizabeth*.
[5] *Middlesex Sessions' Rolls*, June 9, 19 Eliz.

(evidently describing their offences) above their heads.[1] The same thing was done in London in 1571, and a proclamation by the mayor was posted on the pillory reciting how,

FIG. 15. A man in the pillory with a paper over his head describing his offence.

(*From a ballad in the Pepysian Collection.*)

'theis towe personnes here present with diuerse other there Complices and confederates yet not apprehended, have bynne Cointis (?)[2] Cosiners and Deceyvers of the Quenes Maiesties

[1] *Records of the Borough of Leicester*, vol. iii, p. 166 'for pentinge 2 papers for the cosoners that were sett on the pillorye 8*d*.'

[2] Word not legible: it may be some spelling of quaint, i.e. cunning, in a bad sense.

liege people, beinge symple, with false cardes and false play at the same. Whereby they haue spoiled diverse personnes of their monies, as they themselues have confessed. And therefore it hath bynne thought good by my Lord Maior and his brethren, thaldermen of this Cytie, that for their punishment in that behalf, they shuld stand here apon the pillory, for an example to all such like malefactors, Cosyners and Deceyvers. If they be not vtterly destitute and void of grace; to desist and from hensforth leave of the like false vnlaufull and develish exercise. And also for that all suche personnes as shuld behold and loke vpon them shuld beware of them and such like at all tymes hereafter, and gyve warning to all their Friends and neighbors to beware of the like deceat.

God save the Queene.'[1]

These might well have been members of a band of conny-catchers, and it is doubtful whether the punishment used would have any effect either in reforming the two caught or in frightening their fellows 'still at large'. It may have helped a little to teach the public to be wary of their tricks. It is interesting to note that the authorities, in punishing offences such as these, were usually most concerned to give the people warning to escape such fellows in the future, by exhibiting their persons and describing their methods. The actual punishment for getting a man's money by some cozening trick seems very light compared with the legal penalties for stupidly stealing the same amount.

Hence it was that conny-catching, shielded by royal protection on the one hand, and by the vagueness of the laws and stupidity of the officers on the other, went on practically unchecked. The Elizabethans loved gambling. No men ever cherished a stronger belief in the possibility and advisability of getting something for nothing: this idea was a natural result of the age of expansion in which they lived, and on this task their greatest minds were bent. It is not surprising, then, that the tribe of conny-catchers, who were only trying the same thing in their own way, flourished and prospered among them.

[1] *Journal*, 19, fo. 353 verso.

CHAPTER VI

THE ROGUE PAMPHLETS

IN this chapter it is my purpose to give some account of the Elizabethan pamphlets in which the lives of rogues and vagabonds are treated. That does not mean that I shall attempt to criticize all the works which have been drawn upon for material for the preceding parts of this essay. I shall limit my discussion to books belonging to two classes: (1) those early pamphlets (down to 1592) upon which this study is primarily based—the *Manifest Detection* and the works of Awdeley, Harman, and Greene; and (2) the late pamphlets (from 1592 to 1616) which followed the fashion of exposing rogue life. These make twenty or twenty-five pamphlets in all; other books of which I have made use (and some, like Scot's *Discouerie of Witchcraft*, although not rogue pamphlets, have furnished important material) are mentioned in foot-notes or in the text. The earlier pamphlets have the interest that belongs to honest and real descriptions of a little-known phase of sixteenth-century life. The later ones are mostly borrowed from the earlier, and the interest and value which they have for us is in the light they shed upon the unscrupulous methods of Elizabethan hack-writers. Before beginning the discussion it is necessary to make a short digression in order to consider the influence of foreign rogue literature of the period on the English.

During the sixteenth century rogue literature became popular in Spain, France, and Germany. In Spain early and in France late in the century the prevailing type was the picaresque novel; in Germany late in the fifteenth century and early in the sixteenth arose the type represented by the English jest-book. This foreign literature had its effect upon English humour and satire; the curious reader will find the lines of influence admirably traced in Chandler's *Literature of Roguery* and in Herford's *Literary Relations of England and Germany in the Sixteenth Century*. A very brief summary will be enough to indicate its relations to the pamphlets with which we are dealing.

The two Spanish rogue books which mainly influenced English literature of this kind in the sixteenth century, the *Celestina* and *Lazarillo de Tormes*, are quite different in nature from the books we are studying, much better as works of art and much less prosaically realistic. Their influence tended more in the direction of such work as Nash's *Vnfortunate Traueller*, though the opinions of those entitled to speak differ as to how much that novel owes to Spanish sources. So far as one can judge from translations and from the accounts of the history of the picaresque novel there is nothing in this quarter to take away the credit of originality from the most important sixteenth-century English exposures of rogue life.[1] The Spanish influences upon seventeenth-century English works do not concern us here.

The German influence on English jest-books concerns us almost as little. Professor Herford points out the debt of such compilations as the *C. Mery Talys*, *Tales and Quicke Answeres*, *Scogin's Jests*, and *Skelton's Jests*, to the Eulenspiegel cycle of jest-books in Germany. But while these contain many anecdotes of clever knavery, there is in them practically nothing illustrating the peculiar life and manners of English rogues and vagabonds. When one comes to the later *Peeles Jests* and Dekker's *Iests to make you Merie*, which do contain native vagabond lore, the authors have done what Dekker truthfully says he did in the *Guls Horne-booke*—'of a Dutchman fashioned a meere Englishman'.

It is the *Narrenschiff* of Sebastian Brandt, published in 1494 and translated into English by Alexander Barclay as the *Shyp of Folys* in 1508, which comes nearest to the literature with which we are dealing. It contains a great deal about rogues, beggars, gamesters, and other knaves, but its

[1] The best treatment of this subject is to be found in Chandler's *Romances of Roguery*, and in his *Literature of Roguery*, vol. i.

statements are so general that they are as true of the rogues of one country as of another. It had a great vogue in England as in the rest of Europe. One finds in *Cocke Lorelles Bote,* in Copland's *Hye Way to the Spyttel Hous,* and in one part of Awdeley's *Fraternitye of Vacabondes,* an unmistakable debt to the general and artificial satire of the *Shyp of Folys,* and sometimes, mixed with this, definite references to English rogue life. The two elements are quite distinct; as the second increases the first declines. A brief examination of the three works mentioned will make the point clear.

Cocke Lorelles Bote (n.d., printed by Wynkyn de Worde) represents a ship of fools and knaves under the command of Cock Lorell setting out on its voyage. The crew contains members of every trade, from goldsmith to rat-catcher, all of whom are rascals. In one place we are told that

> They sayled fro garlyke hede to knaves in,

and in another

> They sayled England thorowe and thorowe,
> Vyllage, towne, cyte, and borowe.

The poem is rudely interesting, but throws no light on contemporary rogue manners. Cock Lorell, the hero, has been regarded by many early and modern writers as a real person—a famous leader of rogues and vagabonds. But there is no convincing evidence in support of this. E. F. Rimbault, the editor of *Cocke Lorelles Bote* for the Percy Society, quotes from *Martin Mark-all,* where, however, the name of Cock Lorell occurs in the midst of a jumble of evident myth and hopelessly inaccurate history, which makes most untrustworthy evidence. The five or six other contemporary references to Cock Lorell that I have seen are of the same character. The word 'lorel', meaning rogue or rascal (a variant of 'losel'), was in common use after the fourteenth century, and Cock Lorell as a chief or leader of rogues is apparently the invention of the author of this poem.

Copland's *Hye Way to the Spyttel Hous* (which is usually dated about the middle of the reign of Henry VIII) represents an interview between the author and the porter of an almshouse. The porter describes the various kinds of fools whose deeds put them on the high road to dependence on public charity. The poem contains interesting bits of description of contemporary life and some rogue tricks and beggars' cant. It is mainly, however, a warning against various kinds of foolishness which will lead one to beggary, evidently based on the *Shyp of Folys,* not primarily an exposure of rogue life. There is a mention of the apparently traditional 'ordres VIII tyme thre of knaves only', a description of which forms one portion of Awdeley's tract, his 'Quartern of Knaues confirmed for euer by Cocke Lorell'.

Awdeley's *Fraternitye of Vacabondes* (1561) is a compound of this foreign satire, of the type inspired by the *Shyp of Folys,* with native English vagabond lore, the result of observation of contemporary manners and customs. It illustrates strikingly the difference between the two. The pamphlet divides clearly into two parts: the first is 'The Fraternitye of Vacabondes, as wel of ruflying Vacabondes as of beggerly, of women as of men, of Gyrles as of Boyes, with their proper names and qualities, with a description of the crafty company of Cousoners and Shifters'. This is a description of real vagabonds and conny-catchers—drawn apparently from life. The second part is 'literary' rogue satire, drawn not from life, but, as Herford points out, from Barclay's *Shyp of Folys* via *Cocke Lorelles Bote.* The rest of the title-page reads: 'Whereunto also is adioyned the .XXV. Orders of Knaues otherwyse called a Quartern of Knaues. Confirmed for euer by Cocke Lorell.' The connexion between the two Awdeley attempts to establish in poetical fashion by the following stanzas underneath the title.

The Vprightman speaketh.
Our Brotherhood of Vacabondes,
If you would know where dwell:
In graues end Barge which syldome standes,
The talke wyll shew ryght well.

Cocke Lorell aunswereth.
Some orders of my Knaues also
In that Barge shall ye fynde:
For no where shall ye walke I trow,
But ye shall see their kynde.

In the first part the pamphlet gives brief descriptions of nineteen orders of beggars comprised in the Brotherhood of Vagabonds, explaining the cant names for them—Upright Man, Rogue, Palliard, Counterfeit Crank, &c.—for the first time. It then describes at some length the tricks of three of the company of cozeners and shifters (thus making a distinction between wandering rogues and London sharpers). Awdeley says that the information in his pamphlet came from a vagabond who had confessed before some justices.

> Which at the request of a worshipful man,
> I haue set it forth as well as I can.

There is no reason to doubt the truth of this assertion: his classes of knaves, their methods of begging, and the tricks of the 'Cousoners and Shifters' are confirmed in almost every detail by Harman and Greene.

In the second part the 'XXV Orders of Knaves' are so many different kinds of unruly, idle, gluttonous, thieving serving men—knaves but not necessarily vagabonds—described under such titles as 'Obloquium', 'Nichol Hartles', 'Simon soone agon', 'Mounch present', 'Choplogyke', 'Esen Droppers', 'Unthrift', 'Nunquam', &c. The artificial satire of the 'Quartern of Knaves', the vagueness of the statements, the straining for a moral, all contrast sharply with the plain realistic tone of his description of the 'Fraternitye of Vacabondes'. The one is the manner of the foreign works we have just been considering, the other the manner of Harman and Greene.

The contrast just pointed out brings me to my thesis concerning the rogue literature upon which the foregoing essay is based. This literature is not founded upon Spanish or German accounts of rogue tricks, but is instead a trustworthy picture of the terrible social conditions of the early part of Elizabeth's reign. In the seventeenth century, when these conditions had been somewhat improved by legal administration, and still more by economic adjustment, rogue literature fell back upon tradition and imitation, sometimes of earlier English works, sometimes of foreign. These later borrowings are explained in detail in Professor Chandler's book, which follows the history of rogue literature from the sixteenth century down to the present time. We are here concerned only with those sixteenth-century studies which were founded upon actual life.

One other work demands mention here, the *Liber Vagatorum*, first published about 1512 and edited by Martin Luther in 1528. This book describes various orders of beggars and illustrates their tricks. Its plan is something like that of Awdeley and Harman, but its material is as distinctly German as Harman's is distinctly English. In the preface to his translation of the *Liber Vagatorum*, J. C. Hotten maintains that Awdeley and Harman show influences of the German work, and Chandler takes the same view.[1] However, I find it very difficult to believe this; there are only such vague resemblances in material as would exist in the art of begging in all countries, and while it is of course impossible to prove that the English books do not owe their existence to the suggestion of the German one, there is nothing except the subject and the common use of a very natural and simple form to indicate that either Harman or Awdeley ever saw or heard of the *Liber Vagatorum*.

The most important and trustworthy English rogue pamphlets, those upon which this study is principally based, and of which it is now time to give a more detailed account, are the following:

1. *A manifest detection of the moste vyle and detestable vse of Diceplay*, 1552, attributed to Gilbert Walker.
2. *The Fraternitye of Vacabondes*, 1561, by John Awdeley.
3. *A Caueat or Warening for Commen Cursetors Vulgarely Called Vagabones*, 1566, by Thomas Harman.
4. *A Notable Discouery of Coosnage*, 1591.
5. *The Second Part of Conny-catching*, 1591 (reprinted in 1592 as *The Second and Last Part of Conny-catching*).
6. *The Thirde and Last Part of Conny-catching*, 1592.
7. *A Disputation Betweene a Hee Conny-catcher and a Shee Conny-catcher*, 1592.

[1] Hotten, *The Book of Vagabonds and Beggars*, 1860, preface; Chandler, *Literature of Roguery*, vol. i, pp. 27–8. Hotten's preface is full of mistakes in regard to the English rogue books which he mentions.

8. *The Blacke Bookes Messenger*, 1592, all five by Robert Greene.

The *Manifest Detection* was printed by Richard Tottyl, 1552, and by Abraham Veale without date. It is clear from internal evidence that it was written about the year 1552.[1] It was reprinted by Halliwell in 1850 for the Percy Society from a copy of the Veale edition. In this reprint the spelling is modernized and there are misreadings which in many places spoil the sense, mistakes which are due to the fact that Halliwell was unable to collate his proofs with the original. The Veale edition itself is very carelessly printed. My quotations follow the copies of it in the Bodleian and the library of the University of Cambridge, but because of the importance and rarity of the tract I have given references in the notes to the Percy Society reprint as well. Both the Tottyl and Veale copies were anonymous, but a manuscript note (said to be in an ancient, perhaps contemporary, hand) in a volume of tracts formerly belonging to Topham Beauclerc attributes the *Manifest Detection* to Gilbert Walker, about whom nothing is known.

The pamphlet is important as being the first exposition of the art of conny-catching as it was practised in the second half of the sixteenth century. It explains cheating with dice and cards, picking pockets, and cozenage with whores substantially as they are described by Greene and his fellow pamphleteers forty years later, using many of the same cant words and recounting many of the same tricks. The later pamphleteers owe a great deal to it. In so far as Greene has a literary original for his conny-catching books, it is this pamphlet. He cribs from it now and then, and does, much better, it is true, the same thing which this pamphlet attempted. Other writers, as we shall see, use page after page of it verbatim.

[1] A reference to the battle of Boulogne (which occurred September 8, 1544) as a matter of recent news, and an allusion to the King's laws, prove that it was written between 1544 and 1553. Then the pamphlet refers to a pickpocket as a disciple of James Ellis. Ellis was tried and hanged for this crime in 1552 (Machyn's *Diary*, Camden Society, pp. 18 and 21–2), and the reference is probably an echo of this event. The 1834 Lowndes dates the Tottyl copy 1532, which mistake Halliwell copies in his introduction to the Percy Society reprint. Tottyl began business in 1552.

The *Manifest Detection* is a dialogue between two friends, M and R. R has been cozened by a band of cheaters, and M is revealing to him the tricks by which he has been deceived. The dialogue begins by R's account of the way he was cozened. A well-dressed gentleman accosted him in Paul's, and when they had conversed awhile invited him to dinner, where after the meal the company indulged in play for a little sport. R won at first, and became so enamoured of the engaging manners of his host that, at the latter's solicitation, he took up his quarters there. Each day he and other friends of the cheater played cards or dice after meals, paying a small fraction of each stake to the house for current expenses. R speedily began to lose, but played on hopefully, waiting for his luck to turn, as his new friends assured him it would sooner or later. M shows R that this was only a wicked cozening plot, and tells him how common cheating at dice has become in the last twenty years. The art was invented by Hodge Setter, but whereas his followers a score of years before had been few and poor, they were now many and rich. M explains the names of the false dice, where the best ones are made (as we have seen, in the King's Bench, the Marshalsea, and by the most excellent workman of all, Bird of Holborn), and tells something about their use. He then goes on to explain the various devices employed to attract the gull and hold him until he is entirely stripped. There were the bawds with whom all cheaters had a close alliance; and there were various means of getting his money besides dice play—by cheating at cards, by taking him to Paris Garden or an interlude to get his pocket picked; or, if all failed, by robbing him on a highway as he returned to his home. M describes the cut-purses' corporation and their craft, and ends with a warning against all these detestable villanies. The pamphlet is rather crudely written, and is very plain matter of fact in tone. It lacks the snap and spirit of Greene's conny-catching books and the homely, personal sincerity of Harman's *Caueat*, but it ranks with them as one of the best first-hand authorities on rogue life. It is the beginning of the Elizabethan literature of conny-catching.

We have already spoken of Awdeley's *Fraternitye of Vacabondes*, which chronologically follows the *Manifest Detection* and precedes Harman's *Caueat for Commen Cursetors*. Harman was a country gentleman of Kent who, as he tells us, was kept much at home by poor health, and who amused himself by questioning the beggars and vagrants who came to his door, and by preparing his exposure of their knaveries. He tells many amusing anecdotes about his own experiences with vagabonds and the devices he employed to outwit them. He was keen enough to extract from them a surprising amount of information about their lives; indeed, the rogues confided all sorts of delicate matters to him, confidences which the good man, in his zeal to protect the public, did not hesitate to betray. Everything points to the accuracy of his account. Many bits of evidence supporting his descriptions of begging tricks have been given already. His list of cant words is confirmed by the rogue dialect found in many Elizabethan plays and pamphlets, and even by the Thieves' Latin of the present day. One piece of evidence remains, more curious and striking, perhaps, than any. The worthy justice gives at the end of his book a list of the names of three hundred of the most notorious rogues who habitually passed his house in Kent at the time he wrote, in the year 1566. Among the certificates still preserved of rogues punished during the 'watches and searches' of 1571–2, in Southern and Midland counties, occur the names of fourteen of Harman's rogues, and five or six others of them are mentioned in the Middlesex Sessions' Rolls down to 1590.[1] A few correspondences could be attributed to coincidence, but so large a percentage in such fragmentary records makes it practically certain that Harman's list was a genuine one.

The *Caueat* was so popular that it went through three editions 1566–8, and another in 1573.[2] Viles and Furnivall were inclined to assign the first edition to 1567. But it is

[1] See Appendix A, 5 for a list of these, with references.

[2] The first has disappeared. There are two different issues, each calling itself the second edition, and both dated 1567, but, from internal evidence, both must have appeared early in 1568, new style.—See introduction to the edition of Viles and Furnivall, N. Sh. Soc., pp. iv–vii.

dated November 11, 1566, by Robert Burton (who evidently knew it well) in a manuscript note in his copy of the *Belman of London*, now in the Bodleian (Art. 4°, G. 8. BS), which date seems to fit every indication in the *Caueat.* The privilege of printing it seems to have been eagerly sought. One printer, Henry Bynnyman, was fined by the Stationers' Company for trying to obtain it by unfair means from William Griffith, to whom it was licensed. According to another entry in the *Stationers' Register* Gerard Dewes paid £2 6*s.* 4*d.* fine for printing it; this was evidently a penalty for having used it without licence.[1] It was copied freely by later Elizabethan writers, who added little to it except from their imaginations. The book is a plain, homely piece of work which inspires respect for its unpretending writer. It was useful then and it is interesting now as an honest picture of Elizabethan life near at hand.

Robert Greene was as good an authority on London sharpers and conny-catchers as was Thomas Harman on wandering beggars. He wrote five pamphlets describing their tricks, the titles of which are given in the list above. He had lived among the conny-catchers and perhaps practised their tricks himself in his wild days following his travels in France and Italy. The pamphlets exposing them he wrote during the violently repentant years (1591–1592) just before his death. They show evidence of great haste in composition, and are somewhat haphazard in their arrangement; one of them, *The Second Part of Conny-catching*, seems to have been garbled in the printing, since the paragraphs apparently intended to begin the pamphlet occur somewhere in the middle.[2]

The *Notable Discouery of Coosnage* is evidently an experiment undertaken with the double intention of satisfying his conscience and attracting the public. It contains a table giving the principal methods of cheating, a few of which Greene describes in detail, and a long discourse at the end on

[1] Arber's Transcript of the *Stationers' Register*, i. 345 and 369 (on 369 is a repetition of the entry crossed out p. 348).
[2] At p. 88 of vol. x of Grosart's edition.

the 'Coosenage of Colliars'. *The Second Part of Conny-catching* is manifestly the result of the success of the *Notable Discouery of Coosnage*, and the best part of it is an enlargement on matters merely outlined in the first pamphlet. *The Thirde and Last Part of Conny-catching* is a continuation of the series as a result of the great success of the first two parts. It is composed entirely of stories illustrating the methods which Greene has just been describing. One is tempted to say that here Greene leaves fact and begins with fiction, according to the words of his confession quoted below.

The same criticism applies to the *Disputation Betweene a Hee Conny-catcher and a Shee Conny-catcher* and the *Blacke Bookes Messenger*. The first is a discussion between a thief and a whore as to which can do the most harm. They maintain their arguments by describing their various tricks, telling many stories in illustration, till the woman finally wins the day. The *Blacke Bookes Messenger* was intended by Greene to herald the publication of a *Black Book* containing the names of all the conny-catchers and cozeners which were then operating in London. The *Messenger* is a pamphlet narrating the wicked life and shameful death of Ned Brown, a cut-purse, whom Greene represents as practising all kinds of conny-catching tricks. It shows carelessness in composition: on the title-page we are told that Brown died unrepentant, but the event is different, for he ends piously enough with a long exhortation to those disposed to follow in his footsteps.

It is evident that Greene, finding that conny-catching pamphlets paid well, worked them during that wretched last year of his life for all they were worth. In the address to 'The Gentlemen Readers' prefixed to his *Vision* (the address was probably written in 1592, though it is clear, as Churton Collins points out, that the *Vision* itself was written in 1590) Greene says, 'I haue shotte at many abuses, ouer shotte my selfe in describing of some; where truth failed, my inuention hath stood my friend.'[1] I believe that this statement was meant by him to apply especially to the fantastic stories and 'laws' of the *Thirde and Last Part of Conny-catching, Disputation*

[1] *Greene's Vision*, 'To the Gentlemen Readers' (Grosart, xii. 195–6).

Betweene a Hec Conny-catcher and a Shee Conny-catcher, and *Blacke Bookes Messenger*; but there is no reason for making from Greene's morbid confession too sweeping a condemnation of the three pamphlets. Their atmosphere is that of the earlier exposures which he gives himself so much credit for making, and a hundred details in them help to fill out the picture of rogue life. One can only guess which stories were true and which imaginative; this conjecture is hardly worth the trouble, since no importance attaches to the decision. One of them, the story of the 'Cutler and the Nip', was apparently told about the town for true, since Greene tells it a second time in the *Thirde Part of Conny-catching*, because he had made a mistake in his version of it in the *Second Part.* Although his pamphlets are not to be taken in the same literal way as Harman's *Caueat*, they are far more valuable than Harman's in suggesting the atmosphere of rogue life. Harman's book is plain, honest matter of fact: Greene's pamphlets are a part of the literature of roguery.

Greene's exposures seem to be made from the life, but in two or three places, as we have noted, he copies from an earlier work. The description of 'Barnard's Law', in the introduction to the *Notable Discouerie of Coosnage*, follows practically word for word the account in the *Manifest Detection.*[1] But Greene introduces this passage as a quotation (or at least as history), prefacing it with the words: 'There was before this many yeeres agoe a practise put in vse by such shifting companions, which was called the Barnards Law,' &c., and he quotes it only to show how much worse is the modern practice of conny-catching.

Later in the same pamphlet his explanation of the word 'law' as used for a method of cheating, and his conny-catcher's speech in self-justification, on the ground that there is deceit in all professions, are likewise borrowed word for word from the *Manifest Detection.*[2] These plagiarisms are all in comparatively unimportant passages, and, considering the

[1] Compare *Manifest Detection*, sig. D_3 verso f. (Percy Society, vol. xxix, p. 37 ff.), with Greene, *Notable Discouerie of Coosnage* (Grosart, x. 9 ff.).

[2] *Manifest Detection*, sig. B_4, f., and B_7 verso (Percy Society, xxix, pp. 17 f. and 22 f.); Greene, *Notable Discouerie of Coosnage* (Grosart, x. 33–5).

standards of the time, it would be a mistake, it seems to me, to argue from them any general impeachment of the truth of Greene's exposures.

Greene was a queer compound of idealist and rogue. He began, evidently, with aristocratic notions of literature, writing his early love pamphlets in elegant euphuistic language. For the Elizabethan popular drama he had a contempt for which we should have much more sympathy if we knew that stage only as it was in the early '80's. In a general way Greene's position at the beginning of his literary career was that of the classicists of his day, Webbe, Puttenham, and Sidney. But a reckless and dissipated life soon brought him to terms with the stage, and he became a fairly popular dramatist. His plays brought in money, but money only increased his dissipation, and he sank a step lower, from writing plays to roguery, or at least to association with rogues. From Euphuist to playwright, from playwright to conny-catcher: the second descent seemed no greater to him than the first. Dissipation soon played havoc with his bodily health, and at length, two years before his death, out of money, estranged from his wife and from whatever of good reputation he may have had, he began to write his confessions and his exposures of low life. He was prompted, perhaps, by a real, although sentimental repentance, perhaps by want of money, perhaps by love of notoriety—who shall untangle his motives? In any event the result was the conny-catching pamphlets, which, in spite of their carelessness and occasionally improbable stories, bear on their face the stamp of truth and are the most vivid and brilliant works of the kind which the age produced. So much for his work. Regarding the man himself—too brilliantly talented to be called unfortunate, and too weak to be called tragic—no sentence fits so well as Stevenson's comment on Villon: 'the sorriest figure on the rolls of fame.'

The unique interest and the popularity of the works described above, especially of Greene's conny-catching pamphlets, started a craze for rogue pamphlets the effect of which was to call forth a large number of imitations of Harman and

Greene. The most important of the works which followed this fashion and the ones I have selected for discussion are as follows:

1. *The Groundworke of Conny-catching*, 1592.
2. *The Defence of Conny catching*, 1592.
3. *Mihil Mumchance, His Discouerie of the Art of Cheating in false Dyceplay, &c.*, 1597.
4. *The Life and Death of Gamaliell Ratsey*, 1605.
5. *Greenes Ghost Haunting Conie-catchers*, by S. R., 1602.
6. *Martin Mark-all, Beadle of Bridewell*, by S. R., ? 1608 (both attributed to Samuel Rowlands, but the latter probably by Samuel Rid).
7. *The Belman of London*, by Thomas Dekker, 1608.
8. *Lanthorne and Candle-light*, by Thomas Dekker, 1608 (with the continuations of 1612 and 1616).
9. *The Art of Iugling or Legerdemaine*, by Samuel Rid, 1612.

A few sentences will give an idea of the wholesale cribbing in these late works. The first is almost entirely stolen, word for word, from Harman. The second is a satire on other trades and professions trying to ride on the wave of conny-catching popularity. The third is stolen verbatim from the *Manifest Detection*, the fourth is largely a rehash of the stories of the Robin Hood ballads, the fifth is made up of bits from Harman, Greene, and various other sources. For the most part the sixth is original. The seventh and eighth are cribbed from Harman, Greene, and such other sources as Dekker could find. The ninth is reprinted with only a change here and there from Reginald Scot. Conny-catching books would sell, and such were the methods by which hack-writers supplied the demand. As one goes on into the seventeenth century the situation remains the same, except that the borrowings cross and recross with increasing complexity. The four volumes of the *English Rogue* are one long tangled mass of pilferings from every possible source, English and foreign.

A prompt tribute to the popularity of Greene's work was a book called *The Groundworke of Conny-catching*, anonymous, which was printed in 1592, by John Danter for William Barley, with a woodcut on the title-page made by combining seven illustrations which had formerly been used for the conny-catching pamphlets. The title is almost the only part of the work which has anything to do with conny-catching. The main part of it is about beggars and vagabonds, reprinted word for word from Harman's *Caueat.* The opening sentence shows that it follows Greene's exposures and is issued as a continuation of that popular series, in order to describe abuses not noticed by Greene.

'Whereas of late diuers coossening deuises and deuilish deceites haue beene discouered, whereby great inconueniences haue beene eschewed, which otherwise might haue been the vtter ouerthrowe of diuers honest men of all degrees, I thought this, amongst the rest, not the least worthie of noting, especially of those that trade to Faires and Markets, that thereby being warned, they may likewise be armed, both to see the deceit, and shun the daunger.' [1]

The *Defence of Conny catching*, 1592, is another tribute to the selling power which Greene's works had given the title. The author of it calls himself Cuthbert Cunny-catcher, and he sets out to show that the members of his tribe are not the only thieves in the realm. There is conny-catching in all professions, as he proves by many examples, and even Mr. R. G. himself is accused of selling the same play twice, to two different dramatic companies. What is that but conny-catching? The pamphlet is often credited to Greene, but it is evidently not by him. Grosart saw this, although he reprinted it in his edition of Greene's works. In the *Second Part of Conny-catching* Greene asserts that the rogues, in revenge for his exposures, have hired a scholar to make an invective against him. 'Marry the good men Conny-catchers, those base excrements of dishonesty, they in their huffes report they haue got one (   ) I wil not bewray his name, but a scholler they say he is, to make an inuectiue against me, in that he is a fauourer of those base reprobates,' &c.[2] It is a tempting hypothesis that the *Defence* is this invective.

[1] N. Sh. Soc. edition, p. 100.
[2] Grosart's *Greene*, x. 101.

Another pamphlet which quickly followed the conny-catching fashion was *Mihil Mumchance his Discouerie of the Art of Cheating in false Dyce play* (licensed 1597). This is only a copy of the *Manifest Detection* discussed above. *Mihil Mumchance* was a bookseller's venture, like the *Groundworke of Conny-catching*, apparently intended to fill another gap left in Greene's exposures. It reprints its original almost word for word: one sentence in the *Detection* which mentions places where false dice are made is altered so as to leave out the names; references to the King's Court are changed to the Queen's; directions for making Ione Silverpin as good a maid as she was before she ever came to the stews are omitted in the later work for fear of offending chaste ears; one or two other cozening shifts are inserted; and the dialogue form of the *Manifest Detection* is changed into ordinary discourse. Except for these changes the two pamphlets run on page after page exactly alike, and they end together.

In order to discuss all the works of each man together, I shall depart a little from the chronological order here, leaving the pamphlet *Greenes Ghost Haunting Conie-catchers* (1602), by Samuel Rowlands, until I come to him, and begin with the works of 'honest' Dekker.

The Belman of London (1608), by Thomas Dekker, was one of the most popular of all the conny-catching books. It went through four editions the first year.[1] Its popularity is attested by a sentence in the *Compters Common-wealth* (1617), by William Fennor. 'Why sir,' says the author, when an old jail-bird from the Hole offers to expose some of the villanies of the time, 'there is a booke called *Greenes Ghost Haunts Cony-catchers*; another called *Legerdemaine*, and *The Blacke Dog of Newgate*, but the most wittiest, elegantest and eloquentest *Peece* (Master *Dekkers*, the true heire of *Apollo* composed) called *The Bellman of London*, haue already set foorth the vices of the time so viuely, that it is vnpossible the

[1] Hazlitt's *Handbook*, and Miss M. L. Hunt's *Thomas Dekker* (Col. Univ. Press, 1911) mention only three, but Mr. F. P. Wilson, who is making a Dekker bibliography, tells me that it is quite certain there were four. It was anonymous in all its editions.

Anchor of any other mans braine can sound the sea of a more deepe and dreadful mischeefe.' However, Dekker's book is a tissue of borrowings from earlier pamphlets—not even clothed in new language, but copied word for word—woven together and ornamented with liberal additions of his own swashing rhetoric and extravagant humour. There is no more entertaining pamphlet to be found, for Dekker had a wonderful knack, acquired by long practice in hack-work, of weaving small parings of other men's wit into an effective whole. But it lacks the air of reality.

The Belman of London opens with a surprising eulogy of country life, and a description of a wonderful grove in which the trees overarch so as to make a thick ceiling, while the ground to our surprise is covered with long grass thickly studded with yellow field-flowers and with 'white and red daizies', looking in the sunlight, which was apparently strong enough to pierce this leafy ceiling, like gold and silver nails. In the grove Dekker comes upon an inn where is to be held the quarterly feast of vagabonds, which he is allowed to watch and which he describes very well. So far, the pamphlet is entirely original. After the feast, the old wrinkled beldam hostess explains to him the orders of beggars and their various tricks and sleights, which explanation is taken direct from Harman. Returning to London, Dekker meets the Bellman on his rounds, who straightway discloses to him various villanies practised in the city—the tricks of conny-catchers—all of which is also borrowed, sometimes word for word, sometimes paraphrased. The art of cheating with false dice he copies from *Mihil Mumchance* (the author of which pamphlet had copied it from the *Manifest Detection*). The account of Sacking Law, and Barnard's Law, he copies and paraphrases from Greene's *Notable Discouery of Coosnage*; Figging Law, Courbing Law, Vincent's Law, Prigging Law, and the Black Art from the *Second Part of Conny-catching*. He borrows three stories from the *Thirde and Last Part of Conny-catching*, and the five tricks which he calls 'Five Jumps at Leap-Frog', from the pamphlet called *Greenes Ghost Haunting Coniecatchers* (1602) by Samuel Rowlands.

It is interesting to find that the MS. notes in Robert Burton's copy of the *Belman of London* in the Bodleian point out many of Dekker's thefts from Harman. Burton was as much interested in vagabond lore as in other curious knowledge; the *Anatomy of Melancholy* contains several references to the cant terms and begging tricks with which we have been occupied in former chapters.[1]

Lanthorne and Candle-light or the Bell-mans second Nights walke (1608) begins with a canting dictionary copied from Harman, and a canting song from Copland's *Hye Way to the Spyttel Hous.*[2] Dekker then goes on to describe things which he knows more about: Gul-groping in ordinaries, how gentlemen are undone by taking up commodities, the cozenages of literary men, the villanies of horse-traders, the infection of the suburbs, &c. The life in it is not such as it would require an extraordinary Bohemian experience to observe; and although Dekker probably did not know much about rogues and vagabonds, he understood very well cozening tricks practised by citizens, brokers, horse traders, needy poets, and hack-writers.

This pamphlet has special interest for the student of minor Elizabethan literature, because in it are described the various forms of literary cozenage—the hack-writer's methods of 'yarking' up a pamphlet, and of getting money by means of false dedications. A rogue who practises the latter deceit Dekker calls a Falconer. The ordinary way of working it was to buy up a whole edition of some old sermon, or other unsaleable work, print for it new dedications, every copy to a different man, and present each patron with the book containing his name in the hope of receiving a handsome fee from each. Sometimes the Falconer would patch up a whole book in praise of a wealthy gentleman, copy it out neatly, and present it to him, in return for such labour he might receive, if he were lucky, a gift large enough to keep him in gaming-money for a month. The pamphlet gives an interesting

[1] For Counterfeit Cranks, Dommerers, and Abraham Men see the *Anatomy*, Part I, Sect. II, Mem. IV, Subs. VI (York Library edition, vol. i, p. 409).

[2] Grosart, iii. 197; Copland, *Hye Way*, l. 1046 ff. (Hazlitt, *Remains of the Early Popular Poetry of England*, iv. 69).

but very unattractive idea of the position and character of an Elizabethan hack-writer.

Lanthorne and Candle-light was reissued frequently in revised and enlarged editions during the first half of the seventeenth century. The first of these is *O per se O*, 1612. This pamphlet follows the 1608 edition to the end and then begins the section called 'O per se O', from which this reprint takes its name. The style and tone of the addition are so different that one cannot avoid the suggestion that it is a continuation by a different author. That we may know that his material is genuine, this writer carefully tells us that when he was High Constable in the late Queen's time he examined many rogues and took one to service, a Clapperdudgeon whom he calls by the name of O per se O (this is the refrain of a beggar song which he gives). He then goes on to tell us what this rogue revealed to him about vagabond life. The most curious of these additions are perhaps those concerning artificial sores and counterfeit licences, which have been already noted in Chapter II. But all of the material is interesting, and, while it follows the main lines laid down by Harman, many details are new. In several places the writer hints that the Bellman was not entirely master of his subject, and that now we are to hear some revelations never made before.[1] This may be only Dekker playing with us, but the authorship seems to me at least open to question.

The next revision of *Lanthorne and Candle-light* was *Villanies Discouered*, &c., 1616. This contains all the material of the 1608 and 1612 forms, somewhat differently and rather confusedly arranged: the first chapter, 'On Canting,' now appears as chapter xvii, prefaced by one new sentence. The new part begins with chapter xi, 'Of a Prison' (the numbering in the table of contents is confused here). The description of prison life is very good, and sounds more like Dekker than do the additions which appeared first in *O per se O*.[2] Geffray Mynshul, in his *Essayes and Characters of a Prison and*

[1] Cp. sig. L_3, M and verso, N, and O.

[2] Compare for instance the references to prison life in *Iests to make you Merie*, and *Newes from Hell*, neither of which, however, is exactly followed in *Villanies Discouered*.

Prisoners, 1618, cribs largely from these chapters.[1] After the prison section the pamphlet follows *O per se O* to the end.

Grosart includes neither the additions of *O per se O* nor of *Villanies Discouered* in his reprint of Dekker's prose works, nor does he (in spite of promises in several notes) examine into the question of their authorship.

Not much is known about Dekker's life and character, but from these rogue pamphlets one or two things are clear. He was a typical hack-writer, following the fashion, writing what would sell, unscrupulous in borrowing other men's work, but brilliant in patching it together and dressing it out in the showy rhetoric which Elizabethans loved. Evidently he was more bourgeois than Bohemian, if one may judge from the fact that the *Guls Horne-booke* and *Shoemaker's Holiday*, both excellent pictures of city life, are his own work, while his rogue pamphlets are mainly borrowed.

Samuel Rowlands was also a hack-writer, with much less ability than Dekker and no perceptible honesty. The greater part of his work is a series of verse pamphlets which are a storehouse of material gleaned from jest-books and rogue pamphlets worked over into doggerel verse. They may deserve more consideration than I have given them, but because the stories are all old, nearly all borrowed, with no marks of original observation, and always badly told, I have chosen to leave them out of account and confine myself here to two prose pamphlets, one of which is interesting for its pilferings and the other for its original material. The first is *Greenes Ghost Haunting Conie-catchers* (1602) and the second *Martin Mark-all, Beadle of Bridewell* (? 1608). The works are both signed S. R. and are both included in the only reprint of Rowlands' works. However, as will be seen below, they cannot both belong to Rowlands, and it is the second and more original pamphlet which must be denied him, though the man to whom it must be ascribed is, in his only other known work, a more shameless plagiarist than Rowlands.

[1] Compare Mynshul's tract, pp. 7, 6, 9–14, 16–19, and 20–2, with *Villanies Discouered*, chapters xi, xii, xiii, xiv, and xv.

Greenes Ghost Haunting Conie-catchers is an excellent illustration of the kind of book-making practised by Dekker's Falconer, who 'scraped together certaine small paringes of witte', cut them into pretty pieces, and of these patched up a book.[1] Its title is an attempt to conjure up buyers with the magic name of Greene. The pamphlet itself is a *mélange* of stories borrowed from recent popular tracts on roguery. It copies some cut-purse material from the *Second Part of Conny-catching*; the 'who am I' story, and the trick of inviting a man to drink and departing with a silver cup, leaving him to pay the loss, from the *Thirde and Last Part of Conny-catching*; and an excellent courbing story from the *Blacke Bookes Messenger*. It uses two-thirds of what little material there was in the *Groundworke of Conny-catching* not borrowed from Harman, and has one trick which may possibly be worked over from *Mihil Mumchance*.[2]

On the other hand, *Martin Mark-all, Beadle of Bridewell* is an extremely interesting and remarkable work. It opens with a capital arraignment of Dekker for his pilferings from Harman in the *Belman of London* and in *Lanthorne and Candle-light*. The substance of this has been explained in the paragraphs on Dekker's works. It has also been pointed out that Dekker's *Belman of London* copies some passages verbatim from the pamphlet called *Greenes Ghost Haunting Conie-catchers*. The partial exposure of Dekker in the *Beadle of Bridewell* proves that Samuel Rowlands is not the author both of it and of *Greenes Ghost Haunting Conie-catchers*, although they are both attributed to him in the Hunterian Club edition of his works. If he had been, he certainly would have noticed Dekker's cribbing from *Greenes Ghost*, and have accused him of it as well as of the pilferings from Harman.

After soundly trouncing Dekker, *Martin Mark-all* goes on

[1] *Lanthorne and Candle-light* (Temple edition), p. 223.

[2] The trick of substituting a copper chain for a gold one is nearly the same as that described in *M.M.* (sig. E). The most complete list of the borrowings in *Greenes Ghost* is that in Mr. Edward D. McDonald's essay, 'An Example of Plagiarism among Elizabethan Pamphleteers', in Indiana University Studies, 1911. He finds in it cribbings from no less than ten different sources.

to give an account of the original of the Regiment of Rogues, narrating what seems to have been the traditional belief about their origin, giving a list of their leaders, and ends with a promise to complete the list down to the author's time: 'so that what betwéene them both (i.e. common rogues and gipsies), they were two pestiferous members in a Commonwealth: but I will leaue them both, and pray for a prosperous winde to bring my Barke to the wished port of her desire . . . which if good fortune fauour me so much, I shall be bouldened once more to play the Merchant venturer . . . wherein . . . I will procéed and set downe the successours from *Cocke Lorrell* vntill this present day.'

Another writer with the initials S. R. (Samuel Rid) published a vagabond book called the *Art of Iugling*, in 1612. From the opening of this pamphlet it is evident that the author had published one before on canting rogues and gipsies (which are treated in the *Beadle of Bridewell*) and had promised another pamphlet. 'Here to fore we have run over the two pestiferous carbuncles in the commonwealth, the Egyptians and the common canters: the poor canters we have canvassed meetely well, it now remaines to proceede where I left, and to goe forward with that before I promised.' For several reasons it seems clear that the author of *Martin Mark-all* was Rid. The ending of the earlier pamphlet fits neatly with the beginning of the later. The whole discussion of the gipsies and their captain, Giles Hather, in the last page or two of *Martin Mark-all* resembles closely that which begins the *Art of Iugling*: both are largely founded on Harman's dedicatory epistle and preserve the same bits of Harman's wording. The prefaces to the two pamphlets are addressed alike and signed with the same formula. In that to the *Art of Iugling* there are scornful allusions to 'caprichious coxecombes, with their desperate wits' which may be a survival of Martin Mark-all's quarrel with Dekker, since they close with what looks like a reference to *Lanthorne and Candle-light*: 'But I cannot stand all day nosing of Candle-sticks.' And at the end of the *Art of Iugling* the author refers to himself as the Beadle, an obvious reference to the sub-title of

Martin Mark-all: 'thou séest simplicity can not doubte, nor plaine dealing cannot dissemble, I could wish thée to amend thy life, and take heede of the Beadle.'

No edition of *Martin Mark-all* earlier than 1610 is known, but an earlier form of the pamphlet must have been published in 1608 since in *Lanthorne and Candle-light*, which appeared during the latter part of that year, Dekker replies to the Beadle of Bridewell's attack upon his *Belman of London*. Probably the lost 1608 edition of *Martin Mark-all* differed in many respects from that of 1610, since the pamphlet was newly licensed in that year (Arber, iii. 430) as '*Martyn Marke all his defence' beinge an answere to* '*the bellman of London*.'

The *Art of Iugling* is a treatise on Legerdemain copied verbatim from Reginald Scot's *Discouerie of Witchcraft* (1584) with a little discussion of cheating with cards and dice coming via *Mihil Mumchance* from the *Manifest Detection*. In order to illustrate more vividly the way in which not only ideas but the words of former writers were borrowed by Elizabethan pamphleteers I have quoted, in Appendix B, four versions of a passage from the *Manifest Detection*, which appears almost word for word in *Mihil Mumchance* and later in Dekker's *Belman of London* and in Rid's *Art of Iugling*.

It has seemed worth while to comment in detail in this chapter only on the most important pamphlets which were written directly about rogue life. But those selected are not sufficient to show the use made of this material by pamphleteers. The rogue stories were utilized freely in such books as *Tarltons Iests*, *Peele's Jests*, Dekker's *Iests to make you Merie*, Chettle's *Kind-Harts Dreame*, and later very largely by the writers of seventeenth century jest-books and chap-books.

There are a good many pamphlets following Greene's death which, like *Greenes Ghost Haunting Conie-catchers*, made use of his name in their title-pages with the hope of thus attracting purchasers, as *Greenes Newes both from Heauen and Hell*, and *Greene in Conceipt New raised from his graue to write the Tragique History of fair Valeria of London*. There were satirical works describing life in London, like Stubbes's *Anatomie of Abuses*, Whetstone's *Touchstone for the Time*,[1] Dekker's *Guls Horne-booke*, Lodge's *Wits Miserie and the Worlds Madnesse*, Nash's *Pierce Penilesse* and *Vnfortunate Traueller*, Gosson's *Schoole of Abuse*, &c. These, while they have been used freely in the account of rogue life, have not been thought to call for criticism as rogue pamphlets. Whetstone, one imagines, might have contributed a great deal more to our knowledge of low life in London had he wished. One of the magistrates of London to whom he dedicates his *Mirour for Magestrates of Cyties* is 'Mr. Seriant Fleetwood, Recorder of the same citie, his approued good Frende and Kinsman'; from Fleetwood Whetstone might have learned whatever his own experiences with cozeners (at the end of the *Touchstone* he says that the adventures of P. Plasmos in the *Rocke of Regard* were his own) had not taught him. But he evidently hated these caterpillars of the commonwealth too much to give us the detailed account of their ways that he could have otherwise. As it is, his works abound in allusions to cozeners and in invective against them, especially against dicers, brokers, and dishonest lawyers.

The chief merit of the works upon which this study is based is that they pulsate with the life of the time. From no other source could one get so true a picture of the lives of the men of town and country as from the prose pamphlets. They yield neither to the drama nor the poetry of the age. Most of the works I have been considering are, of course, satires, but in many of them the satire is so tinged with sympathy that it is almost disguised. There is in them more of the spirit with which Shakespeare drew Falstaff and his conny-catching companions than of the attitude of Ben Jonson in his comedies, or that of the later satirists. Greene tells stories of the wit and cleverness of his rogues with a gusto and sympathy not the less apparent for the moralizing and invective with which he conceives it his duty to end each pamphlet. Dekker enjoys

[1] This is copied almost entire in a tract called *Look on Me, London*, published in 1613.

his Gull too much not to like him a little. Nash reforms Jack Wilton at the end and tries to believe, and to convince us, that he made a good citizen after he married his courtezan and settled down. There are a few exceptions. To Stubbes the vices of his age are horror unrelieved. The merry books are only things which 'infect the soule, and corrupt the minde, hailing it to distruction, if the great mercy of God be not present'.[1] In him and in his fellows the Puritan age had already begun, and for them Bohemianism had no charms.

As to the form of these pamphlets the task of the critic is harder. It is easy to point out many ways in which the prose of earlier and of later periods is better. Elizabeth's reign was a time of experiment and transition in prose style. The chief factor in the change was Euphuism, a style in which the newly awakened feeling for order and form in prose ran to the greatest extremes. The immediate results of Euphuism were bad. No one, perhaps, enjoys the tortured antitheses and far-fetched comparisons which this style produced unless he has cultivated the taste. But when the follower of Lyly forgot his pseudo-science and his moral saws, his pyrite stones which when they looked coldest were most hot, his salamanders, and all the rest of this wonderful zoology and mineralogy, the effect of Euphuism on his style was good. At their best Dekker and Greene write with ease and clearness, and they put on their works the stamp of their own characters, full of the excess and confusion of their age, yet touched with its magic charm.

The style of the pamphleteers is as good as their thought; neither has any elements of greatness. Historical criticism usually tends to overrate these minor Elizabethans. As a matter of fact, most of them were lost in the intellectual confusion of the age, no less than in the social. They admired the literature of the Italian renaissance without perceiving its weakness. The mediaeval standards of art and of life they rejected; the classic they misunderstood; and the result was that, in the case of these men who had not the extraordinary power of intellect needed to map out right paths for themselves, their most careful art was grotesque, their views of life

[1] *Anatomie of Abuses*, N. Sh. Soc., p. 185.

superficial and false. They are interesting to us for what the times made them; we receive instruction from their failures rather than from their thought.

It is no wonder that they failed to 'see life steadily and see it whole.' No age in the history of England has offered to its thinkers such difficult problems with such scant help toward their solution. The greatest of them in his greatest work has done little more than put the question: 'What a piece of work is a man! How noble in reason! How infinite in faculty! In form and moving how express and admirable! In action how like an angel! In apprehension how like a god! . . . And yet, to me, what is this quintessence of dust?'

It is man the quintessence of dust that we find in these pamphleteers. Gay and attractive or sordid and mean, in either case it is only the outside that they show us, only their realism that is convincing. They loved life and could paint its externals: they did not trouble about its meaning. They had lost the old faith, but they could not formulate a new. They expressed the unrest of their time: they could not direct its aspiration.

APPENDIX

[In the documents which follow, ordinary abbreviations and contractions have been expanded, and in two or three instances accidental repetitions of a word have been silently corrected. The punctuation and capitalization of the manuscripts is followed except in a few places where it is so bad as to make the meaning difficult. *ff* is transcribed *F* or *f* as occasion demands.]

A

I

LONDON ORDERS OF 1517 FOR RESTRAINING VAGABONDS AND BEGGARS

Journal 11, 337 ff.

Te° Thome Exmewe [1] militis maioris.

Articles devysyd by the mayer and aldermen of the citie of london at the commaundement of the lordes of the kynges moste honorable Councell for thavoydyng and puttyng out of myghty Beggers and vacabundes out of the same.

First, it is certified by euery alderman the nombre and the names of euery persone abidynge wythin his warde beyng so impotent, aged, feble, or blynde, that they be nat able to gette their lyvynges by labour and worke, and also be in suche extreme pouerte that they may nat lyve but oonly by almes and charite of the people, whose names appere in the Guyldhall in the bylles of certificates of euery alderman more at large, whiche is and amounteth to the nombre of a M[l] and aboue.

Item, there is deuysyd as many tokens to be made as be certified poore almes persons in the seyd billes, that is to say a payer of beedes rounde with tharmes of london in the myddys, to be stryken with a stampe in metall of pure white tynne, and the tokens seuerally shalbe delyuered to euery alderman accordyng to the nombre of the seyd poore almes persones by hym certified to thentent that he shall delyuer to euery suche poore persone impotent, aged, and feble that can nat gette theyr lyvyng by labour or werke as is aboueseyd, and to none other, one of the seyd tokens by the seyd alderman to be sette vpon their ryght shulders of ther Gownes openly to be seene,

[1] Lord Mayor, 1517 to 1518.

which persones hauyng the seyd tokens vpon theym shalbe sufferd to begge and aske almes of the people within the citie and the suburbes of the same.

Item, if it happen any of the seyd poore people hauyng the seyd tokens to decesse that then the Constable or bedell by the commaundement of the alderman of the warde and parysshe, where the seyd poore persone was admitted and had his token delyuered shall cause the seyd token to be brought to the seyd alderman, and wyth hym to remayne tyll the tyme that some other like poore impotent, feeble, blynde, or aged persone by the same alderman be admytted to the same token.

Item, that none other persone as vagabunde or myghty begger nor any other be suffred to begge within the seyd Citie, but only suche seyd persones as haue the seyd tokens vpon theym as is aforeseyd.

Item, yf any suche vagabund or myghty begger come into the seyd citie, that then the lawes in suche cases ordeigned and prouyded be duely executyd vpon them accordyng to the statute therof made in the tyme of kyng henry the vijth without any favour or forberyng of the hole punysshment therof.

Item, it is farther aduysed that certayne persones, that is to saye, henry barker, Carpenter, pryncipall, with other ij persones vnder hym, shalbe assigned to survey aswell the seyd beggers and poore folke hauyng the seyd tokens as other vagabunds and myghty beggers repayryng to the Citie, that they from tyme to tyme geve notice and knolege to the seyd alderman Constable and bedell of euery suche vagabund and myghty begger commyng into the Citie to thentent that they may be avoyded out of the same and to go to ther countreis ther as they were borne or to the place where as they last made ther abode by the space of iij yeres, accordyng to the statute in that case ordeigned and prouyded.

Item, that the seyd persones hauyng their tokens do their laufull endeuour to expelle and kepe out the seyd vagabundes and myghty beggers out of the Citie by exclamacions, expulcions and puttyng out of thym, and yf they be nat able of theym selfes so to do, Then they to resorte to the seyd surueyours, Constable, bedell, and to the alderman if nede shal requyre, and of theym to haue helpe and assistence in that behalf vpon the payne of lesyng and forfeytyng of ther seyd tokens.

Item, it is ferther ordred that the seyd people hauyng the seyd tokens be of good behauoure in askyng their almes of the people, and if he or they be denyed of almes of any persone outher by his word or Countenaunce of his hand, That then the seyd poore persone or persones so askyng almes to cease of any farther crauyng of the seyd persone so denyeng, and to departe from hym for that tyme, and thys from tyme to tyme as often as it shall so happen, vpon the payne of lesyng and forfeytyng of ther seyd tokens, endeuour them selfe diligently to obserue and performe all thother premysses afore reherced for and concernyng the seyd auoydaunce of the seyd vagabundes and myghty beggers vpon the payne aforeseyd.

Prouyded alwayes that all such poore people as been visited with the greate pokkes outwardly apperyng or with other greate sores or maladyes tedyous lothsom or abhorible to be loked vpon and seen to the great anoyaunce of the people, be nat suffred to begge and aske almes in churchus and other open places but that they be sent to thospytallys suche nombre as the seyd hospytallys may or ought to logge accordyng to ther Foundacion ther to tary and abide vpon thalmes and charitie of the worshipfull and substanciall persones of the Citie and suburbes of the same for whose releif and comforte ther shalbe a proctour admytted for euery such hospitall hauyng as well one of the seyd tokens vpon hym as a token of the seyd hospitall to gather and receyue the almes of the people within the seyd Citie and Suburbes of the same.

Item, that a proclamacion be made of the premysses.

2

PROCLAMATION OF HENRY VIII AGAINST VAGABONDS

Bod. Arch. F. C. 10. (2).

Mense Iunii Anno regni metuendissimi domini nostri regis Henrici octaui, xxij.

A Proclamation made and diuysed by the kyngis highnes, with the aduise of his most honorable Counsaile, for punissh-inge of vacabundes and sturdy beggars.

The kynge our moste dradde soueraigne lorde, hauynge always in his moste blessed remembrance, as well the cure and charge of his dignite royall, as also the present astate of this his realme, and his subiectes of the same, considereth, that in all places thorowe out this his realme of Englande, vacabundes and beggars, haue of longe tyme encreased and daily dothe encrease in great and excessiue nombres, by the occasyon of ydelnes, mother and roote of all vices: whereby haue insurged and spronge, and dayly insurgeth and springeth contynuall theftes, mourdres, and other sundry haynous offences and great enormities to the high displeasure of god, the inquietation and damage of his true and faithfull subiectes, and to the disturbance of the hoole common weale of this his sayd realme: And where as many and sundry good lawes, statutes, and ordinaunces haue ben before this tyme deuised and made, as well by his hyghnes as also by diuers his moste noble progenitours kynges of Englande, for the moste necessary and due reformation of the premysses: yet that not withstandynge, the sayde nombres of vacabundes and beggars, be not seen in any parte, to be mynyshed but dayly to be augmented and encreased in to great rowtes and companyes. Whiche his grace euidently perceyueth to happen, for as moche as his sayde lawes, statutes, and ordinances be not from tyme to tyme put in effectuell execution, accordynge to his gracis expectacion, pleasure, and commandement: His highnes therfore wyllynge to declare to all his subiectes, his moste godly and vertuous purpose, and perseuerance in the persecution, correction and reformation of that moste damnable vyce of ydelnes, chiefe subuerter and confounder of commune weales, Eftsones wylleth and straytely commandeth all Iustices of the peas, maires, sheryffes, constables, bursholders, tethynge men, and other his mynysters, as they wyll auoyde his hygh indignation and displeasure, that if they or any of them, shall after two dayes nexte ensuynge after this proclamation publisshed, happen to fynde any vacabunde or myghty beggar (be it man or woman) out of the hundred where he or she was borne, or out of the towne or place, where he or she last dwelled in, and continued by the space of thre yeres nexte before, and that vpon knowledge of the sayde proclamation, he or she hath not demaunded a Byllet, to conuey them selfe to the sayde hundred or dwellynge place, and so be in theyr iourney thetherwarde, within the sayd two daies, that than the sayde Iustices and minysters and euery of them, shall cause the sayde vacabundes and beggars and euery of them, to be stripped naked, from the priuey partes of theyr bodies vpwarde (men and women of great age or seke, and women with childe onely excepte) and beinge so naked, to be bounden, and sharpely beaten and skourged. And after that they be so beaten in fourme afore said, that there be deliuered to them and euery of them so whypped or skourged, a sedule or byllet, the forme whereof appereth in the ende of this present proclamation: And that the sayde sedule or byllet be signed with the hande of the Iustice of peas, mayre, sheriffe, constable, bursholder, tethinge man, or other minister, by whose commandement the sayd vacabunde or beggar was whipped or skourged. And in case that any of them can not write, than the same byllet to be signed, by one of the best and most substantiall inhabitantes nexte adioynynge. And if it happen the person beaten in forme aforesaid, to be eftsones founden in the sayd place, as a vacabunde or beggar, that than he or she to be taken and eftsones beaten and skourged as is afore said: And so from tyme to tyme, and as often as they shall happen to be taken out of the place to them lymitted, for theyr abode by the statute. More ouer, if any of the sayd vagabundes or myghty beggars, whipped in forme aforsayd, do after the sayd whippinge, make their abode in any place longer than a dyner tyme, or the space of one night, vntyll they be come to the sayd place of their habitacion appoynted (beinge not veryly seke or hurte) that than they shalbe eftsones whypped, and ordered as is before written. Semblably if any vagabunde or mighty beggar beinge taken, wyll affirme that he was late whypped, and can not shewe forthe a cedule or byllet signed, as before is mencioned, he shall, not withstandynge his said affirmacion, be stripped naked and seen by the Iustice, or some of the ministers before named. And if it may euidently appere vnto them by the tokens on his body, that he hath ben al redy skourged or beaten, they shall than suffer hym to depart without other harme, with a byllet signed by them, mencionynge where, and at what tyme he was beaten. And if they fynde no tokens or signes of skourgynge or beatinge on his body, than they to se hym to be whypped or skourged, and further ordered as is before written. And more ouer, the kyngis highnes commandeth al Iustices of the peace, mayres, sheriffes, constables, bursholders, tethyngmen, and other his sayd ministers, that al vayne pitie and other excuses layde aparte, they endeuour them selfes with all their power, study, and diligence, to put this his sayd ordinance in effectuell execucion, without any delay. And also that they endeuour them selfes to kepe theyr watches and serches, accordynge to the lawes and statutes of this realme, and accordynge to the instructions before this tyme made and diuised by his highnes and his honorable counsayle, and by his grace to them sent, to be put in due execution: As they wyll answere to his highnes at theyr vttermoste peryls.

God saue the kynge.

The fourme and tenore of the sedule or byllet aboue mencioned.

A. B. taken at C. in the countie of D. as a vagabunde, without a cedule or token of skourginge, and therfore whypped at C. aforesaid, the day of the moneth of the yere of the reigne of our soueraigne lorde kynge Henry the eyght, in the presence of T. E. constable and other of the inhabitantes of the same towne.

Tho. Bertheletus regius impressor excusit. Cum priuilegio.

3

JOHN BAYKER'S LETTER TO HENRY VIII

S. P. Henry VIII, 141, fos. 134-5. *Calendar, Letters and Papers of Henry VIII*, xiii (ii). 1229.

For as myche as youre grace att all tyms haythe beyne redy to tayke intollerabyll payns not only for the settynge forthe off gods honor but allso for the common and publyq weall off youre Reallm I can do no lesse wythe dyschayrge off my contyens towarde god and my obedyence observyd wyche by the commandement off gode I ow vnto youre pryncly maiesty but I muste neydes opeyn and dysclosse syche thyngs as I thowght dyshonerous vnto your grace and tedyus and discomfortaybyll vnto the commonweall off your peopll: yett lesse that I shoullde be tedyus or trobylsome vnto youre grace or hyndrance off youre moste godly stydys I have drawne forthe and wrytyn heyre the thyng that at syche tyme as your grace shall thynke convenyent ye may loke apon yt: fyrst wer that youre moste gratyus nobyll and exelent maiesty haythe ordynyd and set forthe many tyms god and holsome statutes and lawes for the condynge punyshment off all vagabonds and valyent beggers that ys to say that none of thayme shall ryne frome towne to towne or place to place withoute a lawfull lysynys or cause but that they and all syche shall be taykyne and after your moste gratyus lawes to be punysshyd yett never the lesse I cannot perceave but the multytude of thayme dothe dayly encreace more and more: for werre that your grace and your grace hys predycesers haythe gyvyn and put forthe in fye farm lordshype to your rewlers and gentylmen of your Realme wome your grace puts in tryst to the entent that they shoulde hayde and defend youre pure subiects and commons in all ryght and iustyce: but alass I thynke you[r] pure friends had never more neyd to complayne vnto youre grace in any matter then they have in thys wyche yff yt pleasse your grace to perdon me your subiect I shall shortly shew: Now werapon that I am so bold to trobyll or dysquyet your grace hys maieste your grace shall vnderstand that I am a powre Artyfycer or craftesman, wyche haythe travyled and gone thorowe the most payrt of your Reallme to gett and erne my lyvynge. I have beyne in the most payrte off the cytys and greyt townes in england; I have allso gone thorowe many lytyll townes and vylygys: but alasse yt dyd pety my hert, to se in evyry place so many monyments wer that howsess and habytatyons hayth beyne and nowe nothynge but bayr walls standynge. Wyche thyng me thynk is very dyshonerous vnto your hyghynys and not that only but by the occatyon theroff myche inconvenience doth encreasse amenge your peopll: yt causythe men to lye by the hye way syde and thayre one[1] to robe and vnto another yt causythe allso myche morder and fornycatyon to be wythe in your Reallme; for yf so wer that every man myght have in townes and vylagys but one lythyll howsse or cotage to inhabyt and but a lytyl garden grownde wythe all thay wolde so order yt wythe thayr labor that thay woldeernethayr lyvynge: so showlde thayr noplace be untylde nor wythe oute inhabyters so that in townes or vylagys thay shoulde be allway in a reydynes att your grace hys call and comandement. Now yf yt please your grace to haerre wat ys the cause off syche decay and ruyne wythe in your Reallme your grace shall vnderstande that in evyry place wer that your gratyus maiesty hathe gyvyn in fey farme and Lord-sshype to any gentyllman or syche as be your grace hys fye farmers, that beynge your grace hys fye farmers showlde lett thayme agayne vnto your powre subiects to inhabyt and tyll, that they payinge thayre rent trewly to thayr landeslordys myghte have a suffytyent and compleyte lyvynge by thayr labor but alass how far be thes fey farmers or rewlers wyde in thys poynte, for yf so be that any of thes fye farmers have eny tenement or farme in thayr hands, yf a power man come vnto one of thayme desyrynge hym to be good vnto hym in thys tenement or farm that he myght have yt to inhabyt payinge the rent for yt as yt hathe beyne before tyme, he answeres and saythe yf that thow wylt have thys tenement of me thow must pay me so myche mony at thy commynge in for a fyne: so that he rasythe that thynge wyche never was at no fyne before to a greyt some of mony and the rent to be payd yerly besyde: the power [man] then seynge thayr ys no remedy but other to have yt or to be destytute of an habyta-tyon sells all that he haythe from wyffe and chyldryn to pay the fyne theroff. Then the landes lorde persavynge the howsse

[1] i. e. thereon.

in decay wyl not repayr yt tenendhabyll althoff the tenende payd never so myche for his fyne: so that the tenande comyth to a decayd thynge: then the landes lorde perceavyng yt the howsse ys redy to fall downe dothe call the tenand into the court. And thayr commands hym to beyllde vp hys howse ayenst a certayn day in payne of forfeytyinge a certayne sume of mony: then the power man because he payd so greyt a some of mony for the fyne of yt ys not abyll to beylde yt vp so shertlye; then the seconde tyme ys he callyd in agayne to the courte and thayr commandyd in payne off forfeytynge hys tenement to byellde yt so that the power man beynge not abyll to repayr yt dothe forfet yt agayne vnto the lorde: then because yt ys so far in decay and the fyne so greyt wythe all no man ys desyrous to tayke yt so that the howsse commythe downe shortlye after: yet saythe the landes lorde: the landes shall rayse me as myche rent as they dyd before wen the howsse was styndynge. O good lorde how myche dothe thes men regayrde more thayr owne peculyer and proper vantage then your grace hys honor, or havynge respect wer that your peopll showlde inhabyt that so lats your grac hys habytatyons decay: ys yt not as ryght that they showlde forfet vnto your grace wo ys lorde and governer over all as the pour tenands vnto thayme: you[r] grace may se how herdeherttyd they be vnto thayr tenands [that][1] thay rayther let fall then beylde: ys yt not a petyfull cays: to come in to a lytyll vylage or towne wer that thayre haythe beyne twentye or thyrty howses and now are halfe off thayme nothynge but bayre walls standing: ys yt not a petyfull cays to se one man have yt in hys hands wyche dyd suffyse ij or iij men wen the habytatyons were standynge. No dowte thys thynge ys the cause of myche [in]convenience[2] wythe in your reallm.

I thynke thayr were never moo peoplle and fewer habytatyons wyche thynge I wolde wysshe and desyer that your grace wolde se a reformatyon in: but in as myche that I have taykyn in hande to dysquiet your gratyus maiesty as concernynge thys complaynt I wold desyer your moste gratyus pardon: and that your grace wold accept the love and zeylle that I have to your hyghnys and to your most gratyus hayr and prince that I wolde not se that hys grace showlde enter into a decayd lande.

By your poure and faythfull subiect Ihon bayker in the cownte of Wylshier and lordship of Castyll cowme.

[*Superscribed.*] Iohn Baykers Devyse to redresse a comonwealth.

[1] MS. 'yet', evidently written by mistake for y^t = that.

[2] MS. torn at margin.

4

PROCLAMATION OF HENRY VIII AGAINST THE STEWS

Society of Antiquaries, London, *Proclamations*, ii. 164: 13 April, 1546.

A PROCLAMATION to avoyd the abhominable place called the *Stewes.*

Rex Maiori et vice-comitibus Ciuitatis London. Salutem. Vobis mandamus, etc.

The Kings most Excellent Maiestie, considering, howe by tolleracion of such dissolute and miserable persons, as putting awaie the feare of almightie God, and shame of the world, haue byne suffered to dwell besides London and elles where in Common open places, called the Stewes, and there without punishment or Correccion, exercise their abhominable and detestable synne, there hath of late encreased and growne such enormities, as not only provoke, iustly the anger and wrath of almightie God, but alsoe engender such Corrupcion amoung the people as tendeth to the intollerable annoyance of the Common wealth, and where not only the youth is provoked, inticed, and allowed to execute the fleshly lust, but alsoe by such assemblies of euill disposed persons haunted and accustomed as daily devise and Conspire howe to spoyle and robb the true labouring and well disposed men; For thes Consideracions, hath by the aduice of his Counsell thought requisite, vtterly to extinct such abhominable Licence and Cleerely to take awaye all occasion of the same; Wherefore his Maiestie straightlie chargeth and Commaundeth that all such persons as haue accustomed most abhominably to abuse their bodies, contrary to Gods lawe and honestie in any such Common places called the stewes, in or about the Cittie of London: Doe before the feaste of Easter next comyng depart from those Common places and resort incontinently to their naturall Countries with their bagges and baggages vpon paine of ymprisonment, and further to be punished at the Kings maiesties will and pleasure; Furthermore his maiestie straightlye chargeth and Comaundeth that all such Housholders as vnder the name of Baudes haue kept the notable and marked houses and knowne hosteries for the said euill disposed persons; That is to saie such housholders as doe inhabite the houses whited and painted with signes on the front for a token of the said houses shall avoyd with bagge and baggage before the feast of Easter next comyng, vpon paine of like punishment, at the Kings maiesties will and pleasure; Furthermore the Kings maiestie straightlye chargeth and Comaundeth that all such as dwell vpon the Banke, called the Stewes, neere London, and haue at any tyme before this proclamacion sold any manner victualls to such as haue resorted to their houses, doe before the said feast of Easter cease and leaue of their victualling and forbeare to retayne any Gest or strainger into their house, either to eate drinke or lodge after the feast of Easter next Comyng vntill they haue presented themselues before the Kings maiesties Counsell and there bound themselues with suertie in Recognizance not to suffer any such misorder in their house or Lodge any serving man, Prentice, or woman vnmarried, other then their hired servants, vpon the paine before specified; The Kings most excellent Maiestie alsoe Chargeth and Comaundeth that noe Owner or meane Tenaunt of any such whited howse or howses where the said lewd persons haue had resort, and vsed their most detestable life, doe from the said feast of Easter presume to lett any of the houses heretofore abused in the said mischeefe in the street called the Stewes aforesaid, to any person or persons before the same owner or meane Tenaunt intending to make lease as afore doe present the name or names of such as should hier the same to the Kings maiesties Counsell, and that before them the leasee hath putt in Bond and suertie not to suffer any of the said houses to be abused as hath byne in tymes past with the said abhominacion, vpon like paine as before is mencioned; Finallie, to thentent all resort should be eschued to the said place, The Kings maiestie straightlie chargeth and Comaundeth that from the feast of Easter next ensuing there shall noe Bearebating be vsed in that Rowe or in any place on that side the bridge called Londonbridge, whereby the accustomed assemblies may be in that place cleerely abolished and extinct, vpon like paine as well to them that keepe the Beares, and Dogges, which haue byn vsed to that purpose as to all such as will resort to see the same.

Et hoc sub periculo incumbenti nullatenus omittatur. Teste me ipso apud Westmonasterium xiij^{o} die Aprilis anno Tricesimo septimo regni Regis Henrici Octaui.

5

NAMES OF HARMAN'S ROGUES WHO ARE MENTIONED AS VAGABONDS IN OFFICIAL RECORDS

Apryce, Richard, upright man.
Rich. Aprisse, Johann his wife, and five children were whipped as vagabonds at Wotton, Oxon., April, 1572. *D. S. P. Eliz.*, vol. lxxxvi, no. 16 (9).

Barnard, James, upright man.
'James Barnard of burlyngton in ye North aged XXII yrs.' Punished as a vagabond in Surrey, September 12–13, 1571. *D. S. P. Eliz.*, lxxxi. 18 (3).

Basset, Thomas, upright man.
Thomas Basset punished at Burbach, in the Hundred of Sparkenhoe, Leicester, September, 1571. *D.S.P.Eliz.*, lxxxi. 24 (1).

Graye, John, upright man.
John Gray punished with a band of vagabonds on their way to Sturbridge Fair, Aug. or Sept. 1571. *D. S. P. Eliz.*, lxxxiii. 36 (5). (See p. 161 below.)

Harrys, John, rogue.
John Harris was whipped and branded in the ear as a vagabond in London, October 6, 1589. *Midds. Sess.*, p. 190.

Holmes, Ned., upright man.
Edward Holmes was whipped as a vagabond and branded in the ear, London, November 9, 1589. *Midds. Sess.*, p. 191.

Jones, John, upright man.
There is a record of a John Jones punished as a vagabond at Copthorne or Effingham in Surrey in 1571. *D. S. P. Eliz.*, lxxx. 44 (1).

Jones, William, upright man.
William Jones was stocked and whipped as a vagabond in Surrey in 1571. *D. S. P. Eliz.*, lxxx. 44 (1).

Mores, John, upright man.
John Morrys, stocked and whipped as a vagabond, Oxon., in 1571. *D. S. P. Eliz.*, lxxx. 57.

Myllar, John, upright man.
A John Mylner was stocked and whipped at Southcley, Notts., Aug. 1571; and he or another in the same county in September of that year. *D. S. P. Eliz.*, lxxx. 27 and lxxxi. 23.

Raynoles, John, rogue (Irysh man).
John Reynolds punished as a vagabond in Cambridgeshire,

1571. Caught with the band going to Sturbridge Fair. *D. S. P. Eliz.*, lxxxiii. 36 (5). (See p. 161 below.)

Robynson, Wm., upright man.
William Robinson convicted of being a vagabond, flogged and burnt on the right ear at Fulham, co. Midds., Oct. 15, 32 Eliz. (1589). *Midds. Sess.*

Smith, Thomas, rogue.
Thomas Smith convicted of being a vagabond and ordered to be flogged and burnt on the left ear, London, March 18, 1574. *Midds. Sess.*, p. 92.

Smyth, Harry, upright man.
Henrye Smythe, punished as a vagabond in Cambridge, among the band going to Sturbridge Fair, 1571. *D. S. P. Eliz.*, lxxxiii. 36 (5). (See p. 161 below.)

Thomas, Richard, palliard.
Richard Thomas of Wantage, Berks., was stocked as a vagabond at Dorchester, Oxon., November 1, 1571. *D. S. P. Eliz.*, lxxxiii. 2.

Thomas, William, palliard.
William Thomas was convicted as a vagabond, flogged and burnt on the left ear at Seynt Johns strete, co. Midds., Nov. 21, 1590. *Midds. Sess.*, p. 171.

Tomas, John, upright man.
John Thomas, whipped as a vagabond at Chelmsford, Aug. 20, 1571. *D. S. P. Eliz.*, lxxx. 24.

Williams (alias **Wyn**), **John,** upright man.
John Williams was punished as a vagabond in Northampton, September 12, 1571. *D. S. P. Eliz.*, lxxxi. 14.

Among these names a few are doubtless only accidental coincidences, but it seems fair to suppose that as many as ten or twelve belong to the vagabonds who visited Thomas Harman at his country house in Kent. It will be noticed that the places mentioned are nearly all in the middle and south of England.

There are twelve or thirteen more names in Harman's list which may coincide with entries in various records. In some cases Harman gives only the surname, thus making identification doubtful. In other instances men whose names exactly correspond are punished for highway robberies, for house-breaking, or for brawls in the suburbs of London—all crimes of which a vagabond might be guilty without departing far from his profession. But it has seemed best in this list not to include more doubtful examples.

6

PRIVY COUNCIL TO LONDON ALDERMEN

20 June, 1569. *Journal* XIX, fo. 171 verso—172.

After our verey hartie commendacions, where aboute the begynnynge of March laste, wee in the quenes Maiesties behalfe directed our Letters to you for the inquisicion of the multitude of vacabondes and such as comonlye are called Roges, and for the punyshment and ordre of them accordinge to the lawes of the realme, and therefore allso by our letters requyred you to make certificat vnto us, whereas vntill this tyme wee haue harde nothinge and therefore wee do chardge youe with that fault and do require youe forwith to aduertise vs what haith byn the cause thereof, whiche when wee shall heare wee will thereof consider, and procede against suche as shalbe found faultie therin as the cause shall require, for surelie wee doe not meane to overpasse so great an oversight, wherin besides your sellfes, wee fynde not many throughoute the whole realme that haue so notoriouslie offended. Nevertheles trustinge that for the contents of our letters some execucion hath byn, though the same be not to vs certefied, wee haue founde necessarie, and so haith her Maiestie commaunded vs to haue theise thinges folowinge to be duelie executed. First youe shall secretlie accorde by way of distribucion of your sellfes with the helpe of other inferior officers whom youe maie well trust, to cause a straight serch and good stronge watche to be begon on sondaie at night abowte ix of the clocke, which shall be the tenth of July, in every parishe and warde of that Citie and the suburbes of the same within youre rule and iurisdiccion and to continewe the same all that night, vntill foure of the clocke in the after none of the nexte daie, and in that search and watch to apprehend all vacabonds, sturdy beggers comonlie called Roges, or Egiptians, and all other idle vagarant personnes havinge no masters nor any certaintie howe or wherby to lyve, and theime cause to be imprisoned in stockes and suche like, and accordinge to the qualities of there faultes to procede againste theyme, as by the lawes ys ordered, and that with convenient severytye, so as thei may bee by punyshment forced to labor for theire lyvinge. And, as it is likly that youe haue in your former orders already remytted them whom youe haue not thought mete to retaine in work to departe to theire natyve countries, so are youe to take good heed howe to aduoid the abuses of youre pasportes, by the which when the names only of the places to which thei are directed ar speciallie namyd, the said lewed persones craftelie [do] spende theire tyme in passage, idellye, do stray fare oute of theire righte waies, and doo in some places coullor theire goinge to the bathes for recouery of theire counterfeit sycknes, and therfore in the pasportes would be also named speciall townes beinge in theire right waies, by which thei shuld be chardged in theire pasportes to passe so as yf thei shall be founde oute of those highe waies thei may be newely and more sharplie punyshed, and in this cause allso the pasportes woolde be so discreatlie sealed, subscribed, and written, as thei shuld not easilie counterfait the same, which, as it ys reported, some of theime can readely doo, and do carry aboute with theim certaine counterfait seales of corporat townes and suche like to serve theire purposes in that behalfe; for the which before they shalbe dimissed due searche woulde be made. And after this searche made, which is intended to be made generall at one tyme throughe the whole Realme, wee thincke yt good for more suertie to the totall rowtinge owte of this mischiefe that youe do agrey emongst your sellfes to make at the least monnethlie the like serch in that Citie vntill the firste of November or longer as youe shall see cause. And we requyre you for avoidinge of further reproofe to returne vs breefly the certificat of this that shall be doone by your firste searche.

Wee cannot allso but consideringe that in the search hereof dyverse vagrant personnes will be founde who will counterfait them selfes as impotent beggars, and that after triall thereof, and punyshment made in such caases, it wilbe necessarye to provide charitablie for suche as shalbe indede founde vnfaidnedlie impotent by age, sycknes, or otherwise, to get theire lyvinge by laboure, and for those wee earnestlie, and in the name of God, as wee ar all commaunded, requyre and chardge youe all and euery of youe, to consider dilgentlie howe suche of theime as dwell within youre iurisdiccion, may be releyved in every parishe by the good order that is devised by a late acte of parliament, and that thei be not suffred to wander or lye abroad as comonley thei doo, in the streites and highe waies, for lack of sustentacion. And for the due and charitable execucon of that statute, wee thincke it good that the Bisshope or other ordinaries of the Diocesse, be moved by you in owr name to directe commaundement to the Curates or ministers in all churches to exhort the parisshoners to gyu[e] there comen almes at there churches and to procure remedy against suche as haue welth and will not contribut at the churches vppon exhortacion and admonicion, and thervnto wee require you to gyve your aydes and assistance in every parishe where your dwellinge is, and by your good example incorage others to this charitable good dede.

Wee do furder requyre you at this your meetinge for this searche to conferre howe the statutes that are prouided for avoydinge of all vnlawfull games and speciallie of bowlinge (a disorder verey muche vsed at this daye throughoute the realme) and for the maintenance of Archery, maye be speedelye and rowndlie executed in all pointes throughoute youre rule and iurisdiccion, the great comon misusing hereof doth so abound, as wee cannot but presently, gyue you warninge thereof, and wee meane in deede to herken hereafter howe this oure admoniccion ys regarded of youe on all your behallfes. And in this behalfe also we cannot but admonishe you to be ware and carcumspecte what licences youe gyue to persones to kepe commen sommer gammes, for wee here of some great abuses therin in sundrie parts of the Realme, both that thei are over generall, and lewdnes and vngodlynes commytted by the confluence of nombers of evill disposed people, for lacke of the presence of some wise, honest and godlie iustices and officers, whereof as we shall be furder informed so will we provide remedy.

You shall do well also to cause the ordinary watchmen in all your parishes to be well warned that by no lewde practises of evill disposed personnes passinge by theime in the nyghte by pretence of watche woordes or suchelike lewed devises, any levye or raysinge of people be made, as in some corners of the realme hathe bynne latelie attempted, thoughe well stayed by the wyser men. As for other thinges wee meane not by any particuler chardge to admonishe you of any more, but wishe you to contynue in your carefulness of youre offices, to see the peace duelykepte, and the disturbers thereof by woordes, tales, newes, spreadinge of vnlawfull bookes and writinges or by deedes to be at the firste with speed stayed and sharplie punyshed. And so fare you well. From Grenewich the xxth of June 1569.

your lovynge Frendes

Bacon, Cancellarius

Norffolk	W. North
W. Howard	R. Leycester
F. Knollys	W. Cecill
[R. Sadleir (?)]	Wa. Mildmay.

[The letter of the same date in Cotton MS. Titus B II, fo. 278, ordering watches and searches in Yorkshire, which is quoted in Strype's *Annals*, is practically a duplicate of this.]

7

ARTICLES AGREED UPON BY JUSTICES IN DEVON FOR SUPPRESSING ROGUES AND VAGABONDS, NOV. 5, 1569

Bodleian MS. Rawl. B. 285. 11 verso—12.

Quinto Nouembris, 1569

Articles agreed vppon by the Iustices of peace in the Cowntie of Devon at the Chapter House in excester touchinge the Suppression of sedicious rumors and the punishemente of vacabondes and Rogues.

Firste that everye fortenighte betwene this and christmas Sessions there be stronge nighte watche, and serche in everie parishe, and tythinge in the same cowntie, and a stronge warde and serche the daye followinge, videlicit, the nynetene daye of November at nighte, iij° Decembris, xvij Decembris, et vltimo Decembris, in whiche watche and serche greate diligence to be vsed for the apprehendinge of all vacabondes, rogues, suspects, and breders of sedicious rumors, that shall in any place remayne and lurke in honeste barnes, woodes, hedges, or brakes, and to make strayte serche, whether they haue any letters or billes vppon them, and the same beinge founde together with certificate of the reste of their doinges in the serches, watches, and wardes, to be broughte before the nexte Iustice of the peace to be sene, vewed, and examyned by the said Iustice.

Item that none do lodge or keape lodginge for comon travelours but suche as haue bene heretofore or shall hereafter be assigned and appoyncted therevnto by the iustices of the peace of that division, and that those that do lodge common travaylours, shall with the officer of the towne, or two of the beste of the towne or villadge examyn all suche as they lodge of their names, dwellinge places, and whether they be bownded, and thoccasion of their travayle or passage. And findinge any suche suspicious by spreadinge of any slaunders or sedicious rumors or otherwise, to staye him and cause the constable or tythinge-man to bringe him before the nexte Iustice of the peace.

Item that the Rogues beinge alien or borne owte of this Realme taken in any serche [be] punyshed and conveyed from constable to constable vnto the nexte porte towne next adioyninge to the realme wheare he dwellethe or was borne. And that yf the inhabitaunts of the porte towne will not or do not receyve and transporte them, accordinge to the statute, that then foure of the said porte be bownden by the nexte Iustices of the peace to appere at the nexte Session.

Item that two Iustices of the peace at the leaste of everye of the thre divisions of the Iustices of the peace do assemble the xixth daye after this assemblye, and so the xixth after that assemblye at excester to certifie the privie cowncell of the state of this sheire accordinge to ther laste honors letters in that behalfe to them directed.

Item yf any matters of greate importaunce happen in anye of the thre divisions that then the same division do certifie with all spede the same to the privie cowncell.

W. Exon
Robertus Dennys
P. Edgecombe
William Strodevicer
Richardus Duke
Gregorye Doddes
Iohannes Wyddon
Roberte Earye
Iohannes Seintleger
Iohannes Fulforde
Iohannes Moore
Richardus Fortescue
Iohn Coplestonne
Thomas Domrishe
Iohn Parker
Richarde Renell.

8

LETTER FROM PRIVY COUNCIL TO SHREWSBURY ORDERING WATCHES AND SEARCHES FOR ROGUES, 1571

From Shrewsbury Corporation Muniments, No. 2,621, Petitions to the Bailiffs, &c. Printed in Transactions Shropshire Arch. and Nat. Hist. Soc., 1908, 3rd Series, vol. viii, Misc. p. ix. The document is here printed from a careful transcription made for me in 1907 by the Rev. C. H. Drinkwater.

After our hartie comendacions The grete benefitte towards the goode order of the comen wealthe which came this laste yere throughe your diligence in serching out and ponishing Vagabonds and sturdye beggars, according to the goode and holsome lawes of the Realme, and the disorders and inconveniences which hath rysen sith this laste wynter, and from thense hetherto a forbearing hath byn in executing the said lawes dothe cawse us by the Quenes Majesties comaundment ones agayne to call vpon you and to chardge you most straightly in this three next monethes, that ys Awgust, September, and October to cawse and see to be made throughe out all the hole shere as well in places exempte as all other, a most straighte watche and serche from the xxth of Auguste vij of the clock in the nighte vntill the next daye iij^{s} at the afternone, and that namely by Constables and ij^{o} iiij^{or} or more of the most substauncyall parisheners of eche paryshe, accordinge to the bignes of the paryshe to apprehend all Roges, Vagabonds, Sturdie beggars, masterles mene, and all persones otherwise suspected. All which so taken you shall cawse to be ponished by stockinge and sharpe and severe whippinge according to the lawes effectually: and that without redempcion or favor according to their deserts. And after ponishement due done to them to be conveyed from Constable to Constable tyll they do come to their place of birth or laste abode with in three yeres according to the Statute. The like watche, serch, and ponishment to be done to the same persones, if any shalbe founde the xijth of September and October at vij of the night vntill the next daye of the same moneth at three of the clock at the afternone. And from thense eche xvth or xxth dayes as you shall agree within your selfes most for the comodytye and quiet of your shere and the hole realme, not omittinge yf betwixt the tyme of the serches or after any such Vagaraunte persones be founde, that they be ponished accordinge to the lawes and statutes of the Realme. For there ys no greater disorder nor no greater root of theftes murders pickinge stealinge debate and sedicion then ys in these Vagabonds and that riseth of them. And therfore yt is her Highnes most godlye and zelouse plesure to have this evill repressed and redressed, wherin ye ought not to deceave her Majesties trust which ys reposed in you chefly by her highnes therto. And we praye you from tyme to tyme certifie vs of your doings herin from eche quarter and devisyon so as youe the Shirref shall cawse the same to be sent to vs wherof we praye you not to fayle, as ye tender her majesties pleasure and wyll answere to the contrary. So faire you well from Hamptone Courte the xxxth of July 1571.

Here follows a list of eleven bands of watchers and searchers with their captains, about 125 persons in all.

9

CHARACTERISTIC CERTIFICATES OF THE PUNISHMENT OF VAGABONDS, 1571

A

1571. *D. S. P. Eliz.*, lxxx. 45.

Ewellme.

Right worshippfull, these are to certyfye your worshippes that accordinge vnto your commaundement in your precepte directed vnto vs the xviijth of this Auguste 1571, concerninge the generall watche to be kept the xxth daye of the sayde monethe for all vagabundes and suspecte persons, we have warned every pettye Constable within our lymyts, and commaunded them to cause two, three, or foure of the Inhabytauntes of their townshippes or villages after the quantyty of the same to kepe watche from seven of the clocke of the aforesaide xxth daye vntyll three in the after noone of the next day ensuinge. And what soever vacabundes or suspecte persons as might happen or chaunce to come in their wallke within the foresaide tyme of their watche, to aprehend and brynge them before vs to have theym examyned and punyshed accordinge to the Statute. Therfore such masterles persons and vagarants as have ben taken in the sayde watche and brought vnto vs synce vntyll this present tyme, we have caused to be punyshed accordinge to the Statute, and have geven every one of them warrant vnder the Seale of our Lymyts to be conveyde from Constable to Constable vntyll they might com vnto the place where theye were borne or last dwelled by the space of three yeres, lymytinge vnto every one of them certayne dayes wherein we thought they might convenyentlye be convayde vnto the end of their iorneye, whose names we have here subscribed in this our certyfycate vnto your worshippes, the daye wherin they were taken, and the places whether we have directed them to be convayde, yeven vnder the Seale of our Lymyts this xxvth of this present moneth Auguste In the xiijth yere of the raigne of our Soveraig[n]e Ladye Elyzabeth by the grace of god Quene of England, Fraunce and Ireland, deffender of the fayth etc.

your woorshippes at comaundement,

Roger Quatermayne and Steeven Smyth high Constables of the hallff hundred of Ewellme.

Thomas Blese taken at haseleye the xxj[th] day of August, punyshed as a vacabounde and sent toward Kynnlett in the County of Salope where he said he dwelled last by the space of tenne yeres with Sir George Blunte, Knight.

Thomas Harrwood taken at Turnors Courte the xxiij[th] of this August, punyshed as a roge and sent toward oxeford where he said he abode last by the space of xix yeres.

Rychard meademan taken at Turnors Court the xxiij[th] of this August punyshed as a vacabounde and convayde toward Wantydge in the Countye of Berks where he sayd he last dwelled by the space of xiiij yeres.

Ioane Freeman taken the aforesaid xxiij[th] of August and punyshed accordinge to the S[t]atute and directed toward Chyllton in the county of Bucks where she said shee was borne and had her moste abyding.

Dorchester Hundred } Watche was orderly kepte in the said hundred and all things was founde well.

Olmer Doncaster.
Nichalas Higges.

Pirton Hundred } Watche was orderly kept in the said hundred and all things was founde well.

Robt. Ewstace.
Iohn Quatermayne.

B

1571. *D. S. P. Eliz.*, lxxxi. 25 (1).

Eccleshall, Stafford.

A certyfycate made to Sir Walter Aston Knyght and Sheriffe of the Countye of Staff. Towchinge the watches and searches for vagaboundes and Beggers as Foloweth. *Viz.*

Disesimo Die August.

Imprimis in Eccleshall home

In the constablewicks of {
Muccleston
Asheleye
Weare and Aston
Staundon
Cold Norton

No vagaboundes nor beggers Founde in these places.

Duodecimo Die Septembris.

Iohn Smyth—A yonge man and servaunte to one Robert Compton taken the xiij[th] Daye of September by the watchemen of Muccleston, and brought before me to Eccleshall by the Constable there, for suspicion, who had but one Letter writen by George Higgens of Salopp, to his maister. But for that there was no matter of suspicion in the sayed Letter, he was dymyssed.

Edward Greaves with Agnes his wiffe } Beinge of thage of xliij yeares, Taken at Asheleye, and brought to Eccleshall where they were punyshed accordinge to Lawe, and afterward send by pasporte to Bowsell strete in the parishe of Barkeswell within the county of Warc. where theye were borne.

Feales Buknall with one child } Being of thage of xlj yeares, and Taken in Asheley afforesayd was brought to Eccleshall and there punyshed as afforesayed, And afterward send by pasporte to Caps Madeley within the county of Salopp where she sayed she was Borne.

Eliz. Kingston widowe, with one child. } Beinge of thage of l yeares taken by the watchemen of wootton within Eccleshall home, was Brought to Eccleshall, and punyshed as affore, was send by pasporte to Newporte where she sayth she was borne.

Ione Smythe with one child } Beinge of thage of l yeares, was Taken in wootton afforesayd, and punished as afforesayed, was send by pasporte to the newcastle vnder Lyne where she was Borne.

Fowlk Conway } Taken by the Constables of Eccleshall, was Brought before me, but havynge a passeport was Send with the same to the next Constable homeward.

Margeret Billington } A pore woman, taken by the Constable of Staundon, was brought to Eccleshall. But send backe agayne and dymyssed for that she had taken harvest work in hand.

Thomas, Coveyt & Lich [1]

[1] i. e. Thomas Bentham, Bishop of Coventry and Lichfield.

C

1571. *D.S.P.*, *Eliz.*, lxxxiii. 36 (5).

Several Hundreds in Cambridgeshire.

Cambridge Shyre The Certifycate of the names of Rogues and Vagabondes taken and punyshed in severall townes within the hundreds of Wetherley and Thryplowe, Arnyngford and Stowe in the countye of Cambridge in two pryvie watches kepte the xx[th] daye of August and the xij[th] of September last past accordinge to the tenor of the letters of her Maiesties most honorable counsell, dyrected vnto the Iustices of the peax of the seid Shyre. Made and subscribed vnder the handes of the Justices within the same hundreds, as Foloweth—

Rychard Gryffith
Hughe Iennam and
Elizabeth his wyffe
Rychard Durman
Iohn Martyn and
Iohane his wyffe
Iames Westfelde and
Ioyce his wyffe
Elisabeth Anngell
Iohn Reynolde
Iames Thomas
Iohn Marshall
Martyn Norrys
Mathewe robynsone and
Elsabeth his wyffe
Gefferye smythe
Robt. Pasye and
Elsabeth his wyff
Wylliam Meakes
Richard Lewys
Richard Mortley
Iohn Arys and
Martha his wyffe
Launslytt Grene
Ellen Lyster
George Symson
Edwarde Reynolde
Elisabeth Bownde
William Tompson and
Iane his wyffe
Iames Bell
Iohn Ladlye
Iohn Davye
Alys Blumsted
Margareth Lownys
henrye smythe
Alyce Okeley
Thomas Carter
Richard Mylward
Robt. fyssher
Alyce Wicke
Margerie marvell
Margareth Lawe
Thomas Larnes
Iohn graye and
Margareth his wyffe
Iane Larde

The nomber whereof were so greate at that present by reason of the confluence to and from Sturbridge fayer.

(signed) John Boldwell
—ent.[1]
Ch. Chiley (?)

[1] First part of signature illegible.

10

TABLE OF SEARCHES, 1571–2

This table shows the number of rogues punished according to the official returns which *happen to be preserved.* There is every reason to believe that the number of searches and the number of vagabonds caught were many times what is represented here.

County.	20 Aug. 1571.		12 Sept. 1571.		12 Oct. 1571.		11 Nov. 1571.		Mch. Apr. 1572.	
	no. H.	no. V.	no. H.	no. V.	no. H.	no. V.	no. H.	no. V.	no. H.	no. V.
Cheshire . .	'divers' watches		'a few' V's. caught							
Hereford . .			1	a few						
Gloucester .	16	107	2	a few						
Notts. . . .	6	68	?	8						
Stafford . .	4 (?)	5	4 (?)	19						
Worcester .	'a few'									
Leicester . .	4	10	4	14						
Northampton	4	11	1	8	3 (?)	23			9	30
Oxford . . .	10 (?)	26	4	19	3	4	3	8	15	60
Bucks. . . .									6	20
Midds. . . .									'several'	
Lincoln . .									'watch kept'	
Essex . . .	6	50	1	2						
Cambridge .	1	4	5	51	2	2				
Hunts. . .	1	4	2	11						
Kent . . .	2	22								
Surrey . . .	15	59	12	13	3	20			9	11
	Total (about)	366	Total	145+	Total	49	Total	8	Total	121+

Total for 1571 . . . . 568+

11

AN ORDER FOR A SEARCH FOR FALSE DICE IN LONDON, 1598

Rep. 24, fo. 349 ff. Dec. 30, 41 Eliz. (1598).

Mr. Cornewallys serche for false dyce.

Forasmuch as great abuse hath bene commytted and daily is Commytted by the making of false dice and dyce of advantage, and by reason thereof by playne Cosenage and deceipt manie of her Majesties subiects stripped of their goodes and patrimony the discovery whereof is not easily discerned, but by those that be skilfull in those kinde of wares. And for somuch also as searche Correccion and punishment of all sorts of wares deceiptfully made and sett to sale within the City of London doth appertayne to the Lord Maior of the City of London as chiefe and principall warden of all misteries and Companies and to the maisters and wardens of the Companyes to which such wares are incident and belonging aswell by Charters graunted by her most excellent Maiestie and her most noble progenitors in that behalf as by Lawful prescripcion and vsage tyme owt of mynde vsed and accustomed. To thend that a speedy reformacion of theis abuses may be had and yett neverthelesse nothing attempted or done that ether shold tend to the infringing or impeaching of the libertyes of the Citty or of anye the worshipfull Companies within the same and especially to the Companie of Haberdashers who (as they alleadge) haue accustomed to haue the vtterance and searchin[g] of those wares: It is therefore ordred by the right honourable the Lord Maior and Courte of Aldermen with the Consent of Thomas Cornewallys Esquire her Maiesties groomeporter who hath charge and Commaundement from her most excellent Maiestie by letters Patents vnder the great seale of England to cause speedy reformacion of theis abuses to be had that two or three discreet Cittizens and freemen to be chosen by the Lord Maior and some one officer of the Lord Maior ayding and assisting them by the appointement of the Lord Maior shalbe appointed from tyme to tyme at their will and pleasure during the terme of her Maiesties graunte to the said Groomeporter made, to searche for all dyce vntruly and deceiptfully made and suche as shalbe so founde from tyme [to tyme] to seaze and deface and to thende that the dyce which be searched and allowed for square and good maye be discerned from other dyce deceiptfully made and receaue such allowance as appertayneth, The said searcher or searchers shall haue power from the said Groomeporter to seale euery bayle of the said dice so searched and founde and allowed for good with such seale as for that purpose by the said Groomeporter or his Deputie is or shalbe appointed: For the sealing whereof no fee nor profitt shalbe exacted or taken directly or indyrectly exceading or aboue the value of one halfe penny at the most for every baille so sealed and every baile to conteyne nyne paire of dyce: And which searcher or searchers at all tyme and tymes Conveynent shalbe readie to searche and seale all dyce truly made whereby no defalt shall any waie growe nor anye inhauncement to the price above the some of one halfe penny vpon every Baylle. And that from and after the first daie of Marche next commyng noe dyce shalbe offred to sale or bought within the Citty of London or liberties of the same which haue not bene or shalbe first so searched sealed and allowed as aforesaid vppon payne of forfeyture of the same and of such further punishment as to the Lord Maior shall seeme fitt and Convenyent; And this order during the tyme aboue Limytted from henceforth to be duly observed vpon perill that shall ensewe, Provided allweyes that if any thinge above sett downe shall at any tyme hereafter appeare inconvenyent to the then Lord Maior and Courte of Aldermen for the tyme being Or any preiudiciall to the Liberties of this Cittie or of any the Companies of the same, That then this present Order may be revoked and adnihilated at the pleasure of the Lord Maior and Courte of Aldermen for the tyme being, any thing in this Order to the Contrary notwithstanding.

12

A LETTER FROM THE LORD MAYOR AND ALDERMEN ABOUT CORRUPT BROKERS IN LONDON, 1601

Remembrancia, ii. 213 (fo. 63 verso).

To the Queenes Attorney generall[1]

After our verie hartie Commendacions. Whereas there is a bill preferred to the Parliament for the reformacions of abuses practized by brokers in and aboute this Cittie which bill hath beene twice reade in the vpper house and soe referred to Committyes 23nt for as muche as the Committies did not meete at the time appointed there hath bene nothinge at all done therein. Whereby soe necessarie a matter is like to fall to the ground: vnlesse yt be renued againe by some extraordinarie helpe. And therefore we thought good to be verey earnest suiters vnto yow being (as we vnderstand) one of the Committies for that busines for your honorable furtherance therein: as a matter of speciall Consequence for the discouerie of diuers Fellonies which the Brokers seeke by all possible meanes to abett by sellinge the stolen goods vnto duchmen, Scotts and French Brokers: Whoe secretlie convey the same beyonde the seas to the great hurte and preiudice of her Maiesties subiects. Soe much the rather for that those Brokers are nowe of late growen soe manie and soe dispersed into priveledged and exempt

[1] Sir Edward Coke.

places in and nere vnto this Cittie of verie purpose to auoide the entry into the Register of suche parcells of goods as they buy or take to pawne: By meanes whereof manie times suche goods as are stollen are neuer found althoughe they Come to the hands of the same Brokers, which by these meanes woulde easelie be preuented. And therefore once againe we verey seriously recommend yt to your grave consideracion and Committ you to the proteccion of the Almightie. Lond: i December 1601.

Your verey assured lovinge Freinds.

13

FORM OF LICENCE FOR GAMING-HOUSE IN THE TIME OF JAMES I

This form is made from three very much defaced indentures preserved in the records of the Court of Chancery in the Public Record Office.[1] Only a small part of any one is legible and the transcription following was possible only because the three follow the same form, differing only in the names. No. 1 is an indenture between Thomas Cornwallis, Groom-porter, and John Yardley; 2, between Thomas Cornwallis and William Judith; 3, between Thomas Cornwallis and Francis Stowe. A number in parenthesis above the line indicates that the portion following has been taken from that indenture. The transcription has some interest as showing that such licences existed and as suggesting what they were like, but, of course, it makes no pretence to complete accuracy.

(1) THIS INDENTURE Tripartite made the Thirtieth daie of Ianuary anno (3) and in the yer of our sover[aign] Lord Iames, by the grace of God King of England, Fraunce and Ireland, defendor of the faith, the (1) fifteenth, and of Scotland (2) the one and fiftieth . . . . (3) Sir Thomas Cornwallis, Knight, Groome porter to . . . (1) most excellent Maiestie of the one partie (2) And William Iudith Cittizen and cloth worker of London of the (3) other partie WITNESSETH that where our said Soveraigne Lord the Kinges Maiestie (1) that now is, in and by his highnes Letters Patents under the great (3) seale of england bearing date at Westminster the two and twentieth day of Ianuary (?) the Fourteenth yeare (2) of his Highnes Reigne hath giuen full power, licence and authoritie to the said Sir Thomas Cornwallis (1) to license such persons (2) as he shall (?) . . . . keepe Bowlinge allies, Tennys Courts and Plaie at Bowles, Cards and Dice for honest Recreation of Persons of (3) abilitie and credit . . . (2) the citties of London . . . . . . two miles

[1] Petty Bag, Certificates various, Bundle i.

distance of the same. As in and by the said Letters Patents more plainlie appeareth NOW THE SAID Sir (?) Thomas Cornwallis . . . . . of the good and honest behavior of the said William Iudith Hath by force of the said Letters Patents (1) Licensed and authorized and by these presents . . . (2) said William Iudith duringe the Terme of foure[1] yeere from the daie of the date hereof to keepe, haue and (1) reteine . . . . [at his house], ? . . . . (2) lyuinge and beeinge in Coleman streete in the parish of St. Stephen in London, Plaie and gameing at all convenient (1) tyme and tymes . . . . (3) and tables and at no other game or play (2) and the said William Iudith doth covenante promis and graunte to and wth the said Sir Thomas Cornwallis (1) his executors, administrators and assignes by thes Presents (2). . . the saide William Iudith shall and will soe foresee and provide That noe Plaie or game whatsoeuer shallbee used in his aforesaid howse . . . (1) upon anie Saboath daie or in the tyme of Divyne Service or (3) Sermon on any holyday or . . . . . after nyne of the clock And that the said (2) [William Iudith] (3) shall and will soe foresee and provide that noe apprentices (1) suspected or suspicious person or persons shall use any kinde of Plaie or Bettinge (3) in the said bowling alley, yard or house aforesaid nor to the uttermost of his power will use or suffer to be used (2) any sinister Practise, Cosoning, fraude or (3) [deceiptful] play or otherwise whereby any of his Maiesties liege (2) Subiects maie be defrauded or deceaved during the said Terme of one yeere AND the said William Iudith (3) doth further covenant promise . . . (2) the said Sir Thomas Cornwallis, his executors, administrators and assignes by thes Presents that he the said William Iudith (2) [will not] assyne or doe . . . . (1) away his present Licence, Placard and authoritie to anie persone or persons (2) without . . . with agrement and consent of the sayd [Sir Thomas] ? cornwallis indorsed under his hand on the Back side of the (1) indenture (2) AND ALSOE the said Willm Iudith promises and agreeth by thes presents . . . . [to allow] . . . . the said Sir Thomas Cornwallis his deputies and assignes duringe the said foure yere to enter and resort (1) into the said house of the said (2) [William Iudith] (3) there to search for (1) finde and trie out (2) abuses without the Lett or interruption of him the said William Iudith (1) his executors, administrators or assignes AND that the said (2) Willm Iudith (1). . his executors, administrators

[1] The MS. has been erased here and the word four written in; the same is true at the next occurrence of four below. The singular *yere* in each case and the expression *terme of one yere* below indicate that the licence was made for one year and then altered to four.

or assignes . . . (2) or any other clayming by, from, or under him . . . (2) And that the said Willm Iudith his executors administrators or assignes . . . (3) shall not doe any act or thing contrary to the intent and true meaning of (1) the said letters Patents . . . (2) PROVIDED allwaies that if the said William Iudith (1) his executors administrators or assignes shall not performe and fulfill the Condicion of our obligacion beringe the date hereof the said (2) William Iudith (3) standeth bounden to . . . of London gent in the (1) some of Thirty pounds of lawfull money of England (and) (2) that then and from henceforth (1) the present license and (3) authoritie to be utterly voide and of no effect (1) [PROVIDED allwais that the said shal not keep Plaie in his house from the daie of December next cominge untill the daie of January next followinge][1] IN WITTNES whereof the said parties to this presente Indenture . . . (3) haue sett their bondes and seales the day and year first aboue mentioned.

(signed) (2) Tho. Cornwaleys [Willm Iudith].

14

HEXT'S LETTER

British Museum, MS. Lansdowne, 81, Nos. 62 and 64. (Reprinted in Strype, *Annals*, 1824, vol. iv, pp. 404–13, Nos. 212–14.)

The four documents in MS. Lans. 81, Nos. 61–4, bear upon the same subject and seem to have been kept by Burghley together. No. 61 is an enclosure in Hext's letter, the calendar of various assizes in Somerset in the year 1596 (see page 73 above), in support of his contention that the laws are badly executed, that not one felon in ten suffers the legal penalty for his crime, with the result that the number of criminals grows daily larger. No. 63 is a plan, drawn up apparently by Recorder Fletewood and dated April 12, 1586, for a more efficient method of apprehending rogues and thieves in London, by a system of registration ward by ward throughout the city. The other two papers, which explain themselves, are as follows.

[1] This proviso is found in (1) but not in the others. It seems intended by the Groom-porter to avoid competition with the public gaming held at his house during Christmas time.

No. 6 (fos. 161–2)

Right honorable and my very good Lord,

Havynge longe observed the rapynes and thefts Comytted within this Countye wher I serve, and fyndynge they multyplye daylye to the vtter impoverysshinge of the poore husbondman that beareth the greatest burthen of all services, And knowyng your most honorable Care of the preservacon of the peace of this land, do thynck yt my bounden dewtye to present vnto your honorable and grave consideracion these Calenders inclosed of the prisoners executed and delyvered this yere past in this Countye of Somerset, wherin your Lordship may behold clxxxiij most wycked and desperate persons to be inlarged. And of these very fewe come to anye good, for none wyll receave them ynto servyce, And yn treuth worke they will not, nether canne they withowt most extreame paynes by reason their zinowes are so benumed and styff throwghe Idlenesse as theyr lyms beynge putt to any hard labor will greve them above measure, So as they will rather hazard ther lyves then work. And this I knowe to be trewe, for att suche tyme as our howses of Correccion weare vp (which are putt downe in most parts in Ingland the more pyttye) I sent dyvers wandrynge suspycyous persons to the howse of Correccion, and all in generall wold beseche me with bytter teares to send them rather to the gayle, and denyinge yt them, some confessed felonyes vnto me by which they hazarded ther lyves, to thend they wold not be sent to the howse of Correccion where they shold be ynforced to worke. Butt my good Lord these are not all the theves and Robbers that are abroad in thys Countye for I knowe yt yn the experyens of my service heare, that the fyveth person that comytteth a felonye ys not browght to this tryall, for they are growen so exceadynge Cunnynge by ther often beynge in the gayle as the most part are never taken, yf they be and come ynto the hands of the symple man that hathe lost hys goods, he ys many tymes content to take hys goods and lett them slypp, because he will not be bound to give evidens at the assises to hys troble and chardge, others are delyvered to simple Constables and tythingmen that sometymes wylfullye other tymes negligently suffer them to escape, others are brawght before some Iustice that eyther wanteth experyence to examyn a Cunnynge thief, or wyll not take the paynes that owght to be taken yn siftynge him vppon every circumstance and presumpsyon and that donne see that the partye Robbed give full evidence, and yf he find an Ignoramus found by the graund

Iurye, and knowe by the thexamynacion he hath taken, that yt ys in defalte of good evidence, then he owght to informe the Iudge that the party Robbed may be called and ynioyned by the Court to frame a newe byll and give better evidence. And then owght the Iustyce to be present att the tryall of his prisoner that he may informe both Iudge and Iury what he found by examynacion and lykewise see that the partye robbed give that evidence to the petytt Iury that he canne. In which default of Iustice manye wicked theves escape, for most comonly the simple Cuntryman and woman, lokynge no farther then ynto the losse of ther owne goods, are of opynyon that they wold not procure a mans death for all the goods yn the world, others vppon promyse to have ther goods agayne, wyll gyve faynt evidens yf they be not stryctly loked ynto by the Iustyce, And these that thus escape ynfect great numbers, ymboldenynge them by ther escapes, some havynge ther books by intreatye of the Iustices them selves that cannot reade a word, others havinge byn burnt in the hand more tymes then ones for after a moneth or too ther wilbe no signe in the worlde, And they will change both name and habytt and comonly go ynto other sheeres so as no man shall knowe them, And the greatest parte are nowe growen to thes petytt felonyes for which they may have ther booke, by which they are imboldened to this great wickednesse, And happye weare yt for England yf Clergy weare taken awaye in case of felonye. For god ys my wytnesse I do with grief protest yn the dewtye of a subiecte, I do not see howe yt ys possible for the poore Cuntryman to beare the burthens dewly layde vppon hym, and the rapynes of the Infynytt numbers of the wicked wandrynge Idell people of the land, So as men are dryven to watch ther sheepefolds, ther pastures, ther woods, their Cornfylds all things growyng too too comon. Others there be (and I feare me imboldened by the wandrynge people) that styck not to say boldlye they must not starve, they will not starve, And this yere there assembled lxxx in a Companye and tooke a whole Carte loade of Cheese from one dryvynge yt to a fayre and dispersed yt amongest them, for which some of them have indured longe imprisonment and fyne by the Iudgment of the good Lord Chief Iustice att our last Crismas Sessions, which may grow dangerous by the ayde of suche numbers as are abroade especyally in this tyme of dearthe, who no dowpt anymate them to all contempte bothe of noble men and gentlemen contynially Bussynge into there eares that the ritche men have gotten all into ther hands and will starve the poore. And I maye Iustlye saye that the Infynyte numbers of the

Idle wandrynge people and robbers of the land are the chefest cause of the dearthe, for thowghe they labor not, and yet they spend dobly as myche as the laborer dothe, for they lye Idlely in the ale howses daye and nyght eatinge and drynkynge excessively. And within these iij monethes I tooke a thief that was executed this last assises that confessed vnto me that he and too more laye in an Alehouse three weeks in which tyme they eate xx^ti^ fatt sheepe wherof they stole every night on, besydes they breake many a poore mans plowghe by stealing an Oxe or too from him and not beinge able to buy more leaseth a great parte of his tyllage that yere, others leese ther shepe owt of ther folds by which ther grounds are not so frutefull as otherwyse they wold be. And such numbers beynge growen to this Idle and thevyshe lief ther ar scant sufficyent to do the ordynary tyllage of the land, for I know that some having had ther husbandmen sent for souldiers they have lost a great parte of ther tyllage that yere and others are not to be gotten by reason so manye are abroad practysinge all kind of villanye. And when these lewde people are comytted to the gayle, the poore Cuntry that ys robbed by them, are inforced there to feede them which they greve att, And this yere ther hathe bynne disbursed to the releefe of the prisoners in the gayle above lxxiij^{l}, And yet they are alowed but vi^{d} a man weekely. And yf they weare not delyvered att every quarter Sessions, so myche more mony wold not serve, nor too suche gayles wold not hold them, but yf this monye myght be ymployed to buylde some howses adioynynge to the gayle for them to worke yn And every prisoner comytted for anye cause and not able to releve him self compelled to worke, And as manye of them as are delyvered vppon ther trialls, eyther by acquitall of the graund Iury or petytt Iurye, burnynge yn the hand, or whyppynge, presently transferred thence to the howses of Correccion to be kept in worke except some present will take any into servyce, I dare presume to saye the xth felonye will not be Comytted that nowe ys. And yf some lyke course myght be taken with the wandrynge people they wold easely be brawght to ther places of aboade, And beinge abroade they all in general are receavers of all stolen things that are portable, as namely the Tynker in his Budgett the pedler in his hamper the glasseman in his baskett, and the lewde proctors which carye the broad Seale and Grene seale yn ther baggs Covers infynytt numbers of felonyes yn suche sort as the tenth felony cometh not to light for he hath hys receaver at hand in every alehowse in every Bushe, And these last rable are very Norseryes of roages. And of wandryng souldiers ther are more abroade then ever weare notwithstanding her Maiesties most gracyous proclamation lately sett forth for the suppressinge of them, which hathe not donne that good yt wold, yf yt had bynne vsed as yt owght, for the Iustices in every shere owght to have assembled them selves vppon yt, and vppon dewe consideracion had of her Maiesties most gracyous pleasure therin aquaynted all inferior officers with yt, and so taken some stryct course for the apprehending of them, but the proclamacions beinge sent to the Shiryffs, they delyver them over to the Baylyffs to be proclaymed in the marketts ther a fewe ignorant persons heares a thinge redd which they have lyttle to do with and lesse regard And the xth Iustyce knoweth not yet that ever ther was any such proclamacion. Your good Lordship may perceave by this Counterfect passe that I send you inclosed that the lewde yonge men of England ar devoted to this wicked course of lief, for the man that traveled by color of yt, ys inheritor to xl[l] land after his father and hys name ys Lymeryck hys father a gentleman and dwelleth att northlache in the County of Gloucester. I kept him in prison to monethes and examyned him often and yet still confirmed the trewth of his pasporte with most execrable othes, whervppon I sent ynto Cornwall wher he sayde hys mother dwelt and by that meanes discoverynge him, he confessed all by which your Lordship may see yt ys most hard to discover any by examinacion all beinge resolved never to confesse anye thinge, assuringe them selves, that none will send too or three C myles to discover them for a whippinge matter which they regard nothinge, for all that weare whipped heare vppon my apprehension ar all abroade, And otherwyse will yt never be withowt a more severe course the libertye of ther wycked lyef ys so sweete vnto them. I may Iustlye saye that the able men that are abroade sekynge the spoyle and confusion of the land ar able yf they weare reduced to good subieccion to give the greatest enymye her Maiestie hath a stronge battell, And as they ar nowe they are so myche strength vnto the enymye, besides the generacion that daylye spryngeth from them ys lyke to be most wicked. The corn that ys wastfullye spent and consumed in Alehouses by the lewde wandring people will fynde the greatest parte of the poore, for yt ys most certeyne yf they light vppon an Alehowse that hath stronge ale they will not departe vntill they have druncke him drye, And yt falleth owt by experyens that the alehowses of this land consumeth the greatest parte of the barly, for vppon a surveighe taken of the Alehowses onely of the towne of wells leavinge owt the Tavernes and Inns yt appeared by ther owne confessions that they spent this last yere twelve thowsand busshells of Barly malt, which wold have afforded to every markett of this shere x busshells weekely, and wold have satisfied a great parte of the poore, a great parte wherof ys consumed by these wandring people, who being reduced to Conformytye, Corne no dowpt wilbe myche more plentyfull, By this your good Lordship maye informe your self of the state of the whole realme which I feare me ys in as ill case or worse then owrs for we are wounderfully ayded by the best lord Chief Iustice that ever was and the good Baron Mr. Ewens, and our Iustices of Assise very reverent good men and most carefull in ther callynge, But the greatest fault ys in the inferior mynyster[s] of Iustice, who shold vse more ernest indevor to brynge them to the seate of Iudgment and Iustice, wherin yf every Iustice of peace in England dyd in every of ther devisions quarterly meete and before ther metyng cause a diligent serche to be made for the apprehendinge of all roages and vagrant suspicious persons, And to brynge them before them where they shold receave the Iudgment of the lawe, and the sturdyest of them that are most daungerous Comytted to the howse of Correccion or gayle and at this meetynge inquyre of the defaults of Alehowses which harbor them, of Constables and Tythingmen that suffer them to wander, and of inhabitants that releve them contrary to the lawe, and inflyct punyshment accordinge to the statute a roage cold hardlye escape. Experience teacheth that thexecucion of that godlye lawe vppon that wycked secte of Roages the Egipsions had clene cutt them of, but they seynge the libertye of others do begynne to sprynge vp agayne and ther are in this Cuntry of them. But vppon the perill of my lief I avowe yt, they weare never so daungerous as the wandryng Souldiers and other stout roages of England, for they went visibly in on company and weare not above xxx or xl of them in a shere, but of these sort of wandringe Idell people there ar three or fower hundred in a shere, and thowgh they go by too and three in a Companye, yet all or the most parte yn a shere do meete eyther att feare or markett or in some Alehowse once a weeke, And yn a great haye howse in a remote place ther dyd resort weekely xl sometymes lx, where they dyd roast all kynde of good meat. The inhabitants beinge wounderfully greved by ther rapynes made Complaynte at our last Ester Sessions: after my Lord Chief Iustice departure precepts weare made to the Tythings adioynynge for the apprehendinge of them: they made aunswere they weare so stronge they durst not adventure of them, whervppon precepts weare made to the

Counstables of the hundred but fewe apprehended, for they have intellygens of all things intended agaynst them, for ther be of them that wilbe present at every assise, Sessions, and assembly of Iustices and will so clothe them selves for that tyme as anye shold deame him to be an honest husbondman, So as nothinge ys spoken, donne, or intended to be donne but they knowe yt. I know this to be trew by the confession of some. And they growe the more daungerous in that they fynde they have bread that feare in Iustices and other inferior officers that no man dares to call them into questyon, And at a late Sessions, a tall man a verye sturdy and auncyent traveller was Comytted by a Iustice and browght to the Sessions and had Iudgment to be whipped, he presently att the barre in the face and hearynge of the whole benche, sware a great othe that yf he weare whipped yt shold be the dearest whipping to some that ever was, yt strake suche a feare in him that Comytted him as he prayed he myght [be] deferred vntill the assises wher he was delyvered without anye whipping or other harme, And the Iustice glad he had so pacyfyed his wrath. And they lawghe in ther sleves att the lenyty of the lawe and the tymorousnesse of thexecutyoners of yt. And if [yt] please your honor for the good of your Cuntry to Comaund a view of the Callenders of all the gayles in England, you shall behold a lamentable estate, wherby your good Lordship may informe yourself and receave nothing from me which I humbly crave, fearinge least yt shold be conceaved amysse by some: but knowinge the danger that may growe by these wycked people to my dread and most deare soveraygnes most peaceable government, I will not leave yt unadvertysed thowghe I shold hazard my lyef by yt. And so most humbly crave pardon for this my boldnesse with your honorable acceptaunce of my most bounden dewty and love, from my poore howse att Netherham in Somersetshire this xxv[th] of September

your good Lordships in all humblenesse to be Comaunded

Edw. Hext.

No. 64 (fos. 169–70)

(Reproduced as Plate III in this book.)

This pasport confessed to be Counterfeicted by Raphe Bower a Scolemaster dwellyng att Pe[n]reth in Cumberland.

To all and singuler Iustices of the pease, Mayors, Baylifes, Constables; and all other her Maiesties officers, Minesters and lovinge subiectes; aswell within Liberties as withoute: Knowe that I (Thomas Scroope) Knighte, Lorde Scroope of Bolton;

Lorde warden of the middle marshe of Englande, a fore and agaynste Skottlande; and Capptayne of her Maiesties Cittye, and Castill of Carlile; gevethe ye and everye one, to whom this maye or shall concerne, that this bearer Iohn Maneringe, latelie arived in Skottlande, and came before me, bringinge Iuste proofe, by his Conduckte from the lorde warden of Skottlande, the cause of his arivall in that lande and countrye; These ar therefore to certifie you of a truthe, that the saide Iohn with other of his companye, (throughe tempeste of fowle wether) wer driven a shore vppon the northe parte of Skottlande; where by they wer by the north-lande-men Cawled the Skottyshe-Ireshe robbed and spoilede of theire Barke and all therin. Wherein the saide Iohn, loste of his owne parte the valewe of three-skore poundes with the better, besides beinge g[r]evouslie wounded in the theighe with a darte, and in the arme with an arrowe, vppon the gra[p]pelynge of theire shippe. These are therefore vppon the dewe consideration of this his losse his hurts and greate necessatie; not onlie to requeste you quietlie to permitt him to passe vnto wornyll in Cornwall to his mother and other of his Frindes there, but also in her Maiesties name requier you to se him releeved and holpen acco[r]dynge vnto her Maiesties moste godlye and gratious lawes in this case providede; And for that I am Credablye informed he is a gentleman of good parentage I doe in regarde of pietie and Christian charitie, allowe him fower monethes to passe vnto the a fore said towne of wornyll by reason of his hurte and grefe; not able to goe farr in a daye, yeaven vnder my hande and seale att Carlile this xxvth of marche in the xxxviijth yeare of her Maiesties most prosperous Reighne.

Tho. Scroope.

Cumberland. Allowed to passe this Countye xxxth of Marche by me Richard Lowther.

Westmorland. Allowed to passe this countye behavinge him selfe well and honestelie by me Iames Bellingam.

Yorke Shire. Accordynge vnto the tenore within written by me Allowed to passe Timothy Whittyngam.

Stafford. Allowed to passe this Countye xxth Apprill behavinge himselfe honestly Tho. Cresley.

Woster Shire. Seene and Alowed to passe this Countye the xxxth of Aprill by me Edward Horwell.

Gloster. Allowed to pass this countye accordynge to the tenor within written. Ed. Wynter.

B

PLAGIARISM IN ELIZABETHAN PAMPHLETS

The explanation of the use of the false die called the langret was copied by one hack-writer after another in the same words for at least sixty years. The following passages trace it from the reign of Edward VI to that of James I.

I

From the *Manifest Detection*, 1552, Sig. B_8 verso—C_1 verso (Percy Society reprint, xxix, p. 23 ff.).

M. . . . Then bringeth he forth a gret box with dice, and first teacheth him to know a langret.

R. a gods name what stuf is it? I haue often hard men talk of false dice, but I neuer yet heard so dainty a name giuen them.

M. so much the soner may ye be deceued, but suffer me a while and breke not my talk, and I shal paint you anon a proper kind of pouling, lo here saith the cheator to this yong Nouisse, a well fauored die that semeth good and square: yet is the forhed longer on the cater and tray, then any other way, and therefore holdeth the name of a langret, such be also called bard cater tres, bicause commonly the longer end will of his owne sway draw downwards, and turne vp to the eye sice sinke, deuis or ace, the principal vse of them is at Nouem quinque. So long as a paier of bard quater tres be walking on the bord so long can ye cast neither .v. nor .ix. onles it be by a great mischance that the roughnes of the bord, or some other stay, force them to stay and run against their kind. For without quater trey, ye wot that, v. nor .x.[1] can neuer fall.

R. By this reason he that hath the first dice is like alwaies to strip, and robbe all the table aboute?

M. Trew it is, wer ther not another help, and for the purpose an od man is at hand, called a flat cater tre, and none other numbre.

II

This was copied almost exactly by the anonymous pamphlet called *Mihil Mumchance*, 1597, Sig. B_4 verso.

Then drawing from his bosome a great bagge of Dyce, first the Cheator teacheth him to knowe a *Langret* which is a Dye that simple men hath seldome or neuer heard off, but often seene to theyr cost: Nowe quoth the Cheator to this young

[1] The x here is evidently a printer's mistake for ix.

Nouice, here is a well fauored Dye, that séemeth good and square, yet is it forged longer vppon the *Cater* and *Trea* than any other way, and therefore it holdeth the name of *Langret*: Such be also called *Bard Catertreas*, because commonly the longer end will of his owne sway drawe downewards, and turne vp to the eye, *Sice*, *Sinke*, *Dewce*, or *Ace*, the principall vse of them is at *Nouum*: For so long as a payre of *Bard Catertreas* be walking on the Boord, so long can ye not cast neither fiue nor nine, vnlesse it be by great chance that the roughnes of the table or some other stop force them to stay and runne against theyr kinde, for without *Catertrea*, ye know that fiue or nine can neuer come.

But then some will question, that by this reason hée that hath the first Dyce is like alwayes to strip and rob all the Table about: To whom I thus answere, that their must be a helpe, and for that purpose there must be ready at hand an odde Dye called a flat *Catertrea*, and no other number, etc.

The dicing lore in *Mihil Mumchance* was borrowed by Thomas Dekker in *Belman of London* (1608) and by Samuel Rid in his *Art of Iugling* (1612); in each case there is only a slight variation in the wording, as the following extracts will show.

III

THOMAS DEKKER: *The Belman of London*, 1608, Sig. E_3 verso (B.M. copy).

To set down all the *Legierdemaine* of this handy craft, would peraduenture instruct some ill minded persons in that villanie, which is published onely to haue others shunne it: I will therefore shew you a few of their iugling trickes, (that are *Graduates* in the Art) and by the shape of them iudge the rest, for all are alike.

A *Langret* is a *Die*, which simple men haue seldome heard of, and happily neuer séen (but to their cost). It is (to the eye of him that is but a *Nouice*) a good and square die, yet is it cut longer vpon the *Cater* and *Trea*, then vpon any other point, and is for that cause called a *Langret*: these *Langrets* are also called *Bard Cater Treas*, because in the running, the longer end will commonly (of his owne sway) draw downewards, and turne either *Sice*, *Sinke*, *Deuce*, or *Ace* vpwards on the boord; the principall vse of them is at *Nouum*. For so long as a paire of *Bard Cater Treas*, be walking, so long can you cast neither 5. nor 9, vnles it be by great chance, that the roughnes of the Table, or some other stoppe force them to stay, and to runne against their kind ; for without *Cater Trea*, 5, or 9, you know can neuer come.

Here some may imagine, that by this meanes, he that hath the first Dice in his hand, may strip all that play at the Table of their money ; but this must be their helpe. An odde Die called a *Flat Cater Trea*, (and no other number) is to be ready at hand, etc.

IV

SAMUEL RID : *The Art of Iugling*, 1612, Sig. C_4.

I dare not (as I could) shew the lewde Iugling that cheators practise, least it minister some offence, to the well disposed, to the simple hurt and losse, and to the wicked occasion of euill doing. But by the way, I will a little speake of dice, and the vse of them, as caueats, rather to let you take heede of their cosonings, then to giue you light to follow their doings : *Non ad imitandum sed ad euitandum.*

First, you must know a Langret, which is a die that simple men haue sildom heard of, but often seene to their cost, and this is a well fauoured die, and seemeth good and square, yet is it forged longer, vppon the Cater, and Trea, then any other way : And therefore it is called a Langret. Such be also cal'd bard Cater treas, because commonly, the longer end will of his owne sway drawe downewards, and turn vp to the eie, Sice, Sincke, Deuce or Ace. The principall vse of them is at *Nouum*, for so longe as a paire of Bard cater treas be walking on the bourd, so longe can ye not cast fiue, nor nine, vnles it be by greate chance, that the roughnes of the table, or some other stoppe force them to stay, and runne against their kinde: for without Cater or trea, ye know that fiue or nine can neuer come.

But you will say by this reason, he that hath the first dice, is like alwaies to stripp and rob all the table about. To helpe this, there must be for that purpose, an odde Die, called a flat Cater trea ready at hand, and no other number, etc.

INDEX

(In this index the general heads of the analytical Table of Contents are not repeated.)

Abraham Men, 27, 36.
Actors, *see* Players.
Ale-houses, 111; Sir Thomas Middleton on, 74; Hext on, 171–2.
Allen, T., haberdasher, Darcy's suit against, 108.
Alley, William, Bishop of Exeter, 156.
Andrews, Thomas, Privy Council to, 64.
Anglers, 27, 30–1. *See also* Courbing Law.
Anngell, Elisabeth, vagabond, 161.
Anthony Now-now, minstrel, 47–9.
Apryce, Richard, upright man, 150.
Archery, laws in favour of, 104; Privy Council on, 154.
Arden of Feversham, 76.
Argenter, Lucas, licensed to beg for ransom of his family, 23.
Armingford Hundred (Arnyngford), Cambridgeshire, vagabonds in, 161.
Arys, John, and Martha his wife, vagabonds, 161.
Asheleye, Stafford, vagabonds in, 159–60.
Aston, Sir Walter, Sheriff, 159.
Autem Morts, 27.
Autolycus, 31–3, 43.
Awdeley, John, his *Fraternitye of Vacabondes*, 117–18; mentioned, 114, 116, 119, 122; quoted on rogue customs, 19, 20, 27, 28, 36, 41.
Aylmer, John, Bishop of London, 24.

Babington's conspiracy, watch for members of, 67.
Bacon, Sir Nicholas, 154.
Ballad singers, *see* Minstrels.
Barclay, Alexander, *Shyp of Folys*, 115–17.
Barker, Henry, surveyor of the beggars in London, 61, 141.
Barnacle (in Conny-catching), 87–9.
Barnard (in Barnard's Law), 89.
Barnard's Law, 86, 89.
Barnard, James, upright man, 150.
Barnes of Bishop's Stafford, ballad-singing sons of, 45, 49, 96.
Basset, Thomas, upright man, 150.
Bat-fowling, 89.
Bawds, 74; proclamation of Henry VIII against, 148–9.
Bawdy-baskets, 27.
Bayker, John, his letter on causes of vagabondage, 11–12, 145–7.
Bear-baiting, 149.
Bearwards, 21, 68.
Beaumont and Fletcher, *Beggars Bush*, quoted, 30.
Bedingfield, Thomas, his patent for importing playing cards, 108; his request for a monopoly of all gaming houses in London, 109.
Beggars, surveyor of, 61–2, 141; badges for, 140–1; permits for, *see* Licences. *See also* Rogues, Vagabonds, and Poor Relief.
Bell, James, vagabond, 161.
Bellingam, James, endorsement on passport, 174.
Benhurst, robberies in hundred of, 100.
Bentham, Thomas, Bishop of Lichfield and Coventry, 160.
Billington, Margaret, vagabond, 160.
Bird of Holborn, dice-maker, 90, 107, 121.
Black Art, 86, 97.
Black Death of 1349, effect on economic conditions of sixteenth century, 7–10.
Blese, Thomas, vagabond, 159.
Blumstead, Alys, vagabond, 161.
Blunt, Nicholas, *see* Gennings.
Blunte, Sir George, 159.
Boldwell, John, 161.
Boorde, Andrew, his *Introduction of Knowledge*, quoted, 35.
Borrow, George, *Zincali*, 18.
Bower, Raphe, schoolmaster, 173.
Bowes, Raphe, his patents for importing playing cards, 108.
Bowling, Privy Council on, 154; alleys for, 94, 106. *See also* Vincent's Law.
Bownde, Elizabeth, vagabond, 161.

Branding, *see* Punishments.
Brandt, Sebastian, *Narrenschiff*, 115.
Bridewell, 67, 70.
Brinklow, Henry, 10; his *Complaynt of Roderyck Mors*, 12, 15.
Bristle dice, 92.
Brokers, 74, 97–8, 164–5.
Buckinghamshire, searches for vagabonds in, 64, 162.
Buknall, Feales, and child, vagabonds, 160.
Burbach, Leicester, vagabonds in, 150.
Burghley, Lord (William Cecil), 154; his letter to Walsingham, 67; letters from Fletewood to, 82, 95; letter from Hext to, 73, 167–74.
Burnet, Gilbert, *History of Reformation*, quoted, 13–14, 16, 35, 54, 64.
Burton, Robert, on date of Harman's *Caueat*, 123; on Dekker's thefts from Harman, 131; rogue lore in the *Anatomy of Melancholy*, 131.
Butler, Thomas, licensed to beg, 24.

Cambridgeshire, searches for vagabonds in, 161–2.
Cant language of rogues, Preface, 18, 77, 122.
Cardan, Jerome, on the number of rogues hanged in reign of Henry VIII, 5.
Cards, *see* Playing-Cards.
Carter, Thomas, vagabond, 161.
Cecil, Sir William, *see* Lord Burghley.
Celestina, 115.
Certificates of punishments of rogues and vagabonds, 65, 67, 72, 152–3, 156–62. *See also* Punishments, *and* Watches *and* Searches.
Chambers, E. K., *Mediaeval Stage*, on minstrels, 45.
Chandler, F. W., *Literature of Roguery*, Preface, 115, 118–19; his *Romances of Roguery*, 115.
Charity in sixteenth century, 16, 22.
Cheating Law, 86, 89–93.
Chelmsford, vagabonds in, 151.
Cheshire, searches for vagabonds in, 162.
Chester, ordinances against vagabonds, 60.
Chettle, Henry, *Kind-Harts Dreame*, on ballad-singing, 48–9; mentioned, 136.
Cheyney, Edward P., *Social Changes in England in the Sixteenth Century*, quoted, 7, 12.
Chiley, Ch., 161.
Clapperdudgeons, *see* Palliards.
Clerc, Gilbert, Keeper of Plays in Calais, 105.
Cloyer, 96.
Cock Lorell, 116, 117, 135; *Cocke Lorelles Bote*, 116, 117.
Coke, Sir Edward, Attorney-General, letter to, 164–5.
Cokes, Bartholomew, 78.
Cold Norton, Stafford, vagabonds in, 159.
Compton, Robert, 160.
Coningsby, Sir Richard, his patent for playing-cards, 108–9.
Conjurers, *see* Jugglers.
Conny (in Conny-catching), 86–9.
Conny-catchers, difficulty of legislating against, 103.
Conny-catching, meaning of the word, 1; methods, 86; Conny-catching Law, 86–9.
Conway, Fowlk, vagabond, 160.
Copland, Robert, *Hye Way to the Spyttel Hous*, 116–17, 131.
Coplestone, John, Justice, 156.
Copthorne, Surrey, vagabonds in, 150.
Cornwallis, Thomas, Groom-porter, his patents for protection of gaming, 104, 105–7, 109; licence for gaming-house, 165–7; search for false dice, 162–4.
Cotton MSS., quoted, 4, 64, 65, 101–2, 154.
Counterfeit Cranks, 27, 33–5, 118.
Courbing Law, 30–1, 86, 97.
Cousin (in sense of Conny), 89.
Cozeners, punishments for, 111–13.
Cresley, Thomas, endorsement on passport, 174.
Croft, Sir James, letter to, on number of vagabonds apprehended in 1569, 65–6; appealed to about bowling alleys in London, 106.
Crossbiting Law, 86, 97.
Crowley, Robert, 10; his *Informacion and Peticion*, on cruelty of landlords, 10–11; on uncharitableness of English clergy, 16; his *Way to Wealth* and *Last Trump*, on merchants buying land, 13.
Cunningham, William, *Growth of English Industry and Commerce*, 14.
Cunny-catcher, Cuthbert, *see Defence of Conny-catching*.
Cut-purses, *see* Pickpockets.

Dalton, Michael, *Countrey Iustice*, 26.
Damporte, Nicholas, Keeper of Plays in Calais, 105.
Darcy, Edward, patent for playing-cards, 108; Darcy *v.* Allen, 108.
Davye, John, vagabond, 161.

Decoy (game at cards), 88.
Defence of Conny-catching, 128; mentioned, 127; quoted, 79.
Dekker, Thomas, 77, 133, 137–8.
Belman of London, 129–31; plagiarisms from *Manifest Detection* via *Mihil Mumchance*, 176–7; mentioned, 123, 127, 129–36; quoted on rogue customs, 91, 99.
Dead Tearme, 84–5.
Guls Horne-booke, quoted, 78–9, 81; mentioned, 115, 133, 137.
Iests to make you Merie, 115, 132, 136.
Lanthorne and Candle-light, 131–3; mentioned, 127, 134–6; quoted, 18, 19, 40.
Newes from Hell, 132.
O per se O, 132, 133; quoted, 36–7, 41.
Shoemaker's Holiday, 133.
Villanies Discovered, 132–3.
Dells, 27.
Deloney, Thomas, *Gentle Craft*, on Anthony Now-now, 47–8.
Demanders for Glimmer, 27, 40.
Dennys, Robertus, Justice, 156.
Devon, articles for suppressing rogues in, 155–6.
Dice, false, art of cheating with, 89–93; kinds of, 90–3; efforts of City to restrain making of, 107; orders for search for, 162–4.
Dickenson, John, *Greene in Conceipte*, 136.
Discourse of Common Weal, quoted, 12–14.
Divorce, gipsy ceremony for, 20.
Doddes, Gregorye, Justice, 156.
Dogberry, 67.
Dommerers, 27, 35, 38–9.
Domrishe, Thomas, Justice, 156.
Doncaster, Olmer, 159.
Donyngton, Robert, Keeper of Plays in Calais, 105.
Dorchester, Oxon., certificates from hundred of, 151, 159.
Doxies, 27.
Duke, Richardus, Justice, 156.
Durman, Rychard, vagabond, 161.

Earye, Roberte, Justice, 156.
Eccleshall, Stafford, certificate from, 159–60.
Economic literature of sixteenth century, 10–14.
Edgecombe, P., Justice, 156.
Edward VI, Cardan's horoscope for, 5; *Discourse about the Reformation of many Abuses*, 13–14.
Effingham, Surrey, vagabonds in, 150.
Elizabeth, Queen, Letters patent for Wales, 25.
Ellis, James, pickpocket, 120.
Enclosures as cause of vagabondage, 5–7, 9, 12–14. *See also* Sheep-farming.
Essex, searches for vagabonds in, 162.
Eulenspiegel cycle of jest-books, 115.
Evanes, Robert ap Thomas ap, proctor, 25.
Evelyn, John, *Diary*, 105.
Ewelme, certificate from, 158–9.
Ewstace, Robert, 159.
Exmewe, Thomas, Lord Mayor, 140.

Falconers (cozening authors), 131.
Farmer, John S., and Henley, W. E., *Slang and its Analogues*, Preface.
Fencers, 68.
Fennor, William, *Compters Commonwealth*, 83, 129.
Feudal system, decay of, as a cause of vagabondage, 7–15.
Fiddlers, *see* Minstrels.
Figging Law, 86, 89. *See also* Pickpockets.
Fish, Simon, 10.
Fitzherbert, Sir Anthony, *Boke of Surueyeng*, on enclosures, 13.
Fletewood, William, Recorder of London, letters to Burghley, 82–3, 95; relationship to Whetstone, 137; scheme for apprehending rogues, 167.
Foists, *see* Pickpockets.
Fool-taking, 89.
Fortescue, Richardus, Justice, 156.
Fortune-tellers, 21.
Fragmenta Antiqua (in British Museum), licences to beg from, 23, 25.
Fraters, *see* Proctors.
Freeman, Joane, vagabond, 159.
Froude, J. A., on Cardan's and Harrison's 72,000 rogues, 5.
Fulforde, Johannes, Justice, 156.
Fulham, co. Middlesex, vagabonds in, 151.
Fullams, 92.
Fyssher, Robert, vagabond, 161.

Gallants, *see* Gulls.
Gamesters, 68.
Gaming, fondness of Elizabethans for, 104, 113; laws against, 104; Privy Council on, 154.
Gaming-houses, 79; licensing of, 103, 105–6, 165–7; Bedingfield's request for monopoly of, 109.
Gennings, Nicholas, *alias* Blunt, upright man and counterfeit crank, 33–5.

Gilpin, Bernard, sermon quoted, 11.
Gipsies, relation to English rogues, 17-20; their language and rogues' cant, 18; Hext on, 172.
Gloucester, searches for vagabonds in, 162.
Gordon, J. W., *Monopolies by Patents*, quoted, 108.
Gosson, Stephen, *Schoole of Abuse*, 137.
Gourds (false dice), 92.
Graye, John, upright man, 150; and Margareth his wife, 161.
Greaves, Edward, and Agnes his wife, vagabonds, 160.
Greene, Robert, 114, 118, 126, 134, 137; his plagiarisms from the *Manifest Detection*, 120, 125-6; use of his name in titles, 136.
 Conny-catching pamphlets, 1, 78, 121, 123-6, 128; *Notable Discouery of Coosnage*, 123-4; cribbings from *Manifest Detection*, 125-6; mentioned, 119, 130; quoted on rogue customs, 86, 88-90, 97; *Second Part of Conny-catching*, 124; mentioned, 119, 123, 125, 128, 130, 134; quoted on rogue customs, 39, 86, 94-5, 97; *Thirde and Last Part of Conny-catching*, 124; mentioned, 119, 125, 130, 134; quoted on rogue customs, 31, 89, 96-8; *Disputation*, 119, 124; *Black Bookes Messenger*, 124; mentioned, 120, 125, 134; quoted, 31.
 Neuer too late, 26.
 Greenes Vision, 124.
Greenes Newes both from Heauen and Hell, 136.
Grene, Launslytt, vagabond, 161.
Groom-porter, right to hold gaming-tables at Christmas, 105.
Groundworke of Conny-catching, 127-8, 129, 134.
Gryffith, Rychard, vagabond, 161.
Gulls, 78-9, 121.

Halliwell, J. O., edition of *Manifest Detection*, 120.
Hamilton, A. H. A., *Quarter Sessions*, 110.
Hanging, *see* Punishments.
Harington, Sir John, *Nugae Antiquae*, quoted, 93, 105.
Harleian MSS., quoted, 24, 92.
Harman, Thomas, 75-6; mentioned, 114, 118, 130, 132, 135.
 Caueat for Commen Cursetors, 122-3; evidence supporting its accuracy, 122, 150-1; date of, 122-3; mentioned, 1, 119, 121, 125, 128; quoted on rogue customs, 1-2, 19, 22-3, 26-31, 33, 36, 38-42.
Harrison, William, *Description of England*, on size of vagabond class, 4-5; on punishment of vagabonds, 67; on highway robberies, 100.
Harrwood, Thomas, vagabond, 159.
Harrys, John, rogue, 150.
Hazlitt, W. C., *Handbook*, quoted, 129.
Hereford, searches for vagabonds in, 162.
Herford, C. H., *Literary Relations of England and Germany*, &c., quoted, 115.
Hext, Edward, letter to Burghley on punishment of vagabonds, 73, 167-74; on gipsies, 19, 172.
Higgens, George, 160.
Higges, Nichalas, 159.
High Law (highway robbery), 86, 98-101.
Holmes, Ned, upright man, 150.
Hookers or Anglers, 27, 30-1. *See also* Courbing Law.
Horse thieves, *see* Priggers of Prancers.
Horwell, Edward, endorsement on passport, 174.
Hotten, J. C., translation of *Liber Vagatorum*, 119.
Houses, John Bayker on decay of, 146-7.
Houses of Correction, *see* Punishments.
Howard of Effingham, Lord, 154.
Hundred Mery Talys, 115.
Hunt, M. L., *Thomas Dekker*, 129.
Huntingdonshire, searches for vagabonds in, 162.
Hurtado de Mendoza, Diego, *La Vida de Lazarillo de Tormes*, 115.
Hutton, Luke, *Blacke Dogge of Newgate*, 129.
Hyberdyne, Parson, his sermon in praise of thieves and thieving, 101-2.

Initiation of rogues, 28-30.

Jarckmen, 27, 41.
Jennam, Hughe, and Elizabeth his wife, vagabonds, 161.
Jest-books, debt to German, 115; rogue stories in, 136.
Jones, John, upright man, 150.
Jones, William, upright man, 150.
Jonson, Ben, 137; *Alchemist*, 105; *Bartholomew Fair*, 78; *Masque of Metamorphosed Gipsies*, 19.
Judith, William, gaming-house keeper, 165-7.
Jugglers, 49-52, 68.
Jusserand, J. J., *English Wayfaring Life*, 3, 21, 53.

Kemp, Will, *Kemps Nine Daies Wonder*, quoted, 111.
Kent, searches for vagabonds in, 162.
King's Bench prison, false dice made in, 83, 90, 121.
Kingston, Elizabeth, and child, vagabonds, 160.
Kirkman, Francis, and Richard Head, *English Rogue*, 127.
Knollys, Sir Francis, 154.
Kynchin Coes, 27, 33.
Kynchin Morts, 27, 33.

Ladlye, John, vagabond, 161.
Landlords, John Bayker and others on, 10–12, 146.
Langrets, 91–2, 175–7.
Language of rogues, Preface, 18, 77.
Lansdowne MSS., quoted, 73, 83, 95, 109, 167–74.
Larde, Jane, vagabond, 161.
Larnes, Thomas, vagabond, 161.
Lawe, Margareth, vagabond, 161.
'Laws' (methods of cheating), 85–6.
Laws, *see* Statutes of the Realm.
Leicester, Town of, punishment of vagabonds in, 60–1, 70; search for playing-cards in, 108; records of, quoted, 33, 61, 70, 108, 112.
Leicester, County of, search for vagabonds in, 150, 162.
Leicester, the Earl of, 154.
Lemon, Robert, *Catalogue of Broadsides*, 24.
Leonard, E. M., *Early History of English Poor Relief*, quoted, 58.
Lewknor, Groom-porter, 105.
Lewys, Richard, vagabond, 161.
Liber Vagatorum, 119.
Licences to beg, kinds of, 23–6; early use of, 56, 58–9; counterfeits of, 38, 40–2, 69, 173–4. *See also* Passports.
Lifting Law, 86, 97.
Lilly, Joseph, *Collection of Black Letter Ballads*, 105.
Lincolnshire, search for vagabonds in, 162.
Lisieux, Bishop of, Cardan's authority for the 72,000 rogues, 5.
Liveries and Maintenance, *see* Retainers.
Lodge, Thomas, *Wits Miserie*, 55, 137.
London, ale-houses in, 74; authorities object to royal protection of unlawful games, 104, 106; brokers in, 74; jails as sanctuaries for rogues and dice-makers, 83–4, 90, 121; number of beggars in, 4, 61, 74, 140; orders for suppressing rogues and vagabonds, 61, 70, 140–2; ordinaries in, 78–81; Privy Council to Aldermen and Lord Mayor of, 64–5; sanctuaries of, 82; setting vagabonds to work in, 68; surveyor of beggars in, 61–2; term time in, 84–5; treatment of vagabonds in before 1530, 61–2; from 1550 to 1570, 67–8; after 1570, 150–1.
Places in, Alsatia, 82; Bishop's gate, 95; Cheapside, 52, 61; Counter prisons, 83–4; High Holborn, 82; Islington, 82; King's Bench prison, 83, 90, 121; Kent Street, 73, 95; Marshalsea, 83, 90, 121; Newington, 73, 82; Pickthatch, 83; St. Giles, 82; St. John's Street, 82, 151; St. Paul's, 52, 78, 80, 84–5, 96, 109, 111, 121; Savoy, 82; Smart's Key, 95; Southwark, 82; Westminster, 82–3, 96; Whitefriars, 82.
Records of, quoted, *Journals*, 41, 61–2, 64–5, 70, 113, 140–2, 152–4; *Remembrancia*, 4, 23, 74, 94, 106, 164–5; *Repertories*, 24, 26, 34–5, 40, 60–1, 63, 70, 107, 162–4; Wardmote Presentments, 111.
Look on Me, London, 137.
Lownys, Margareth, vagabond, 161.
Lowther, Richard, endorsement on passport, 174.
Luther, Martin, edition of *Liber Vagatorum*, 119.
Lyster, Ellen, vagabond, 161.

McDonald, Edward D., on plagiarisms in *Greenes Ghost*, 134.
Machiuells Dogge, quoted, 88.
Machyn, Henry, *Diary*, quoted, 83, 120.
Maitland, William, *History of London*, 95.
Maneringe, John, *alias* Lymeryck, vagabond, 171, 173–4.
Manifest Detection, 120–1; attributed to Gilbert Walker, 120; plagiarisms from, 120, 125–7, 129–30, 136, 175–7; mentioned, 114, 119, 122; quoted on rogue customs, 83, 88, 90–3, 96–7.
Mankynd, 22.
Marshall, John, vagabond, 161.
Marshalsea, false dice made in, 83, 90, 121.
Martyn, John, and Johane his wife, vagabonds, 161.
Marvell, Margerie, vagabond, 161.
Meademen, Rychard, vagabond, 159.
Meakes, Wylliam, vagabond, 161.
Middlesex, searches for vagabonds in, 150–1, 162; Sessions' Rolls of, quoted, 70–1, 99, 101, 110–11, 150–1.

Middleton, Sir Thomas, Lord Mayor, on beggars in the city, 74.
Middleton, Thomas, *Black Book*, quoted, 81; rogue characters in his plays, 76.
Mihil Mumchance, 129; mentioned, 91, 96, 127, 130, 134, 136; plagiarisms from *Manifest Detection*, 129, 175–6.
Mildmay, Sir Walter, 154.
Minstrels, 43–9, 68.
Monasteries, as a cause of begging and vagabondage, 15–17.
Moone, Thomas, licensed to beg for losses by fire, 23–4.
Moore, Johannes, Justice, 156.
More, Sir Thomas, *Utopia*, on enclosures and sheep-farming, 6.
Mores, John, upright man, 150.
Morris dance, 18.
Mortley, Richard, vagabond, 161.
Morts, 27.
Muccleston, Stafford, vagabonds in, 159–60.
Mumchance-at-cards, 88.
Myllar, John, upright man, 150.
Mylward, Richard, vagabond, 161.
Mynshul, Geffray, *Essayes and Characters of a Prison and Prisoners*, 83, 132–3.

Nash, Thomas, 138; *Vnfortunate Traueller*, 115, 137; *Pierce Pennilesse*, 137.
Nips, *see* Pickpockets.
Norfolk, Duke of, 154.
Norman, Thomas, licensed to beg, 24.
Norrys, Martyn, vagabond, 161.
Northampton (county), searches for vagabonds in, 151, 162.
Northampton, the Marquis of, 154.
Nottingham, vagabonds in, 61, 150; searches in, 162; records of, quoted, 25, 61.
Now-a-dayes, on retainers becoming thieves, 15.

Oeconomy of the Fleet, quoted, 83–4.
Okeley, Alyce, vagabond, 161.
Ordinaries, gaming in, 79–81.
Ordinary, quoted, 105.
Oxford, Register of University of, list of begging scholars, 24.
Oxfordshire, searches for vagabonds in, 150–1, 158–9, 162.

Palliards (or Clapperdudgeons), 27, 35–7, 118, 151.
Pamphleteers, character of, 76, 131.
Parker, John, Justice, 156.
Passports, 60, 64–6, 143–5, 158, 160; abuse of, 152–3; counterfeiting of, 40, 73, 153, 173–4; form for, 145. *See also* Licences to Beg.
Pasye, Robert, and Elizabeth his wife, vagabonds, 161.
Patents for protection of gaming, 103–9.
Patrico, 19–20, 27.
Pedlars, 21, 27, 42, 68, 170.
Peeles Jests, 115, 136.
Pepys, Samuel, *Diary*, quoted, 105.
Pickering, Laurence, pickpocket, 95.
Pickpockets, 77, 94–7; corporation of, 94–6, 109–10; devices for attracting a crowd, 49, 96; haunts of, 96; laws against, 109–11; Nips and Foists, distinction between, 96; punishment in Theatre, 110–11; training required for, 95–6. *See also* Figging Law.
Pillory, *see* Punishments.
Pirton Hundred, certificate from, 159.
Players, 21–2, 68.
Playing-Cards, cheating with, *see* Conny-catching Law; patents for importing, 107–9.
Pollard, A. W., on vagabond players, 21–2.
Poor relief, development in methods of, 3–4, 53; early ideas of, 56, 62; methods after 1535, 57, 59, 72–4, 153–4.
Popham, Chief Justice, 108.
Popish spies, 54–5.
Priggers of Prancers and Prigging Law, 27, 39–40, 86, 97.
Privy Council, letters from, ordering watches and searches for vagabonds, 4, 65, 152–4, 156–7; other measures against vagabonds, 41, 57–8, 60, 63–8, 72, 74, 100–1, 109.
Acts of Privy Council, quoted, 54, 64.
Proclamations: against cozeners, 112–13; false pursuivants, 41–2; playing-cards, 108; Popish agitators, 55; Stews, 111, 148–9; tale-tellers, 53, 63; traffic in St. Paul's, 111; vagabonds, 60, 74, 142–5; vagrant soldiers, 72.
Enforcement of, 171.
Proctors, 24–5, 27, 40, 62, 68, 142, 170.
Provost-marshals, 71–2.
Punishments for rogues and vagabonds, changes in, during the sixteenth century, 56–7; certificates of, 65, 67, 72, 152–3, 156–61; laxness of, 73, 168–73.
Varieties of: branding, 63, 69–71, 150–1, 169; death, 56, 59, 63, 69–70; drumming out of the city, 61; ears cut off, 56, 58, 62; imprisonment, 56, 61; marking with a yellow

V, 61; pillory, 39, 54, 58, 111-12; servitude or slavery, 63, 69-70; stocks, 56, 58, 61, 66, 150-1, 157; tying to post on stage, 110-11; whipping, 54, 56, 58, 66-7, 69-71, 75, 143-4, 150-1, 157; work, 54, 59, 63, 68-70, 73-5.
Puttenham, George, 126.

Quatermayne, John, 159.
Quatermayne, Roger, constable, 158.

Ratsey, Gamaliell, highwayman, *Life and Death of*, 99-100, 127.
Rawlinson MSS., quoted, 155-6.
Raynoles, John, rogue, 150-1.
Renell, Richarde, Justice, 156.
Retainers as source of vagabondage, 5, 14-15.
Reynolde, Edwarde, vagabond, 161.
Reynolde, John, vagabond, 161.
Richard, Thomas, palliard, 151.
Richardson the burneman of Leicester, 70.
Rid, Samuel, *Art of Iugling*, 135-6; mentioned, 127, 129; plagiarisms from *Manifest Detection* via *Mihil Mumchance*, 177; quoted on rogue customs, 42.
Martin Mark-all, Beadle of Bridewell, 134-6; authorship of, 135-6; mentioned, 133.
Robin Hood Ballads, cribbings from, 99-100, 127.
Robynson, William, upright man, 151.
Robynsone, Mathewe, and Elsabeth his wife, vagabonds, 161.
Rogue characters in Elizabethan literature, 76.
Rogue life, historical evidence for, 77-8.
Rogue pamphlets, craze for, 2, 77-8, 126-7; literary value of, 137-9; spirit of, 101-2.
Rogues, Harman's, found also in records, 150-1; 'rogues' (in canting sense), 27, 31-3, 118, 150-1.
Rogues and Vagabonds of Shakespere's Youth, quoted, 102. *See also* Awdeley, Harman, and *Groundworke of Conny-catching*.
Rolls of Parliament, on serfs becoming vagabonds, 8.
Romany, relation to rogues' cant, 18.
Rose, Miles, counterfeit crank, 34-5.
Rowlands, Samuel, 133-6; plagiarisms, 77.
Greenes Ghost Haunting Conie-catchers, 134; mentioned, 127, 129-30, 133-4, 136; quoted on rogue customs, 31, 89, 96.
Martin Mark-all, *see* Rid, Samuel.
Roystering boy, 76, 97.
Rufflers, 27-8.
Russell, Lord, Privy Council to, 64.
Rutland, Lord, Privy Council to, 64.
Rutter (in Barnard's Law), 89.
Rymer, Thomas, *Foedera*, quoted, 105.

Sacking Law, 86, 97.
Sadler, Sir Ralph, 154.
Sailors, as vagabonds, 69, 71.
Sanctuaries, 82-3.
Satirical works, rogues mentioned in, 137.
Scholars of universities, begging, 69.
Scogin's Jests, 115.
Scot, Reginald, *Discouerie of Witchcraft*, on jugglers, 50-2; on cards, 88-9; on dice, 90; mentioned, 76, 114, 127, 136.
Scott, Sir Walter, *Fortunes of Nigel*, 82-3.
Scroope, Lord, name forged to passport, 173-4.
Seals, counterfeit, how made, 41.
Seebohm, Frederic, on Black Death, 7.
Seintleger, Johannes, Justice, 156.
Setter (in Conny-catching), 86-7, 89.
Setter, Hodge, dicer, 90, 121.
Shadwell, Thomas, *Squire of Alsatia*, 82.
Shakespeare, William, *Henry IV*, 100; *Henry VI*, 38; *Lear*, 36; *Macbeth*, 76; *Merry Wives*, 40, 76, 103; *Taming of the Shrew*, 42; *Winter's Tale*, 21, 32, 43.
Shakysberie, Robert, counterfeit crank, 34-5.
Shallow, Justice, 67.
Sheale, Richard, minstrel, 45-7, 100.
Sheep-farming as cause of vagabondage, 6-7, 9. *See also* Enclosures.
Shrewsbury, letter from Privy Council to, 65, 156-7.
Shrewsbury, Elizabeth, Countess of, 22.
Sidney, Sir Philip, *Apologie*, 44, 126.
Simpson, Richard, *School of Shakespeare*, 111.
Simson, Walter, *History of the Gipsies*, 20.
Skelton's Jests, 115.
Slavery, *see* Punishments.
Smart, B. C., and Crofton, H. T., *Dialect of the English Gipsies*, 18.
Smith, Thomas, rogue, 151.
Smyth, Harry, upright man, 151, 161.
Smyth, John, servant, 160.
Smyth, Steeven, constable, 158.
Smythe, Gefferye, vagabond, 161.
Smythe, Ione, and child, vagabonds, 160.

Snappage, 96.
Soldiers, vagrant, 69, 71; Hext on, 170–1.
South Clay, Notts., vagabonds in, 150.
Spencer, Sir John, Lord Mayor, on poor in city, 73.
Stafford, searches for vagabonds in, 162.
State Papers, quoted: S.P. Henry VIII, 60, 145–7; D.S.P. Eliz. 64, 66–7, 72, 109, 150–1, 158–61; Chancery records, 165–7; Patent rolls, 104–6, 108; Warrant book, 24.
Stationers' Company, Register of, quoted, 123, 136.
Statutes of the Realm, quoted: Statutes of Labourers, 8–9; 22 Henry VIII, c. 12 (vagabonds and poor), 16, 25, 58–9, 63; 27 Henry VIII, c. 25 (poor), 16, 59, 63; 33 Henry VIII, c. 10 (vagabonds), 60; 37 Henry VIII, c. 9 (usury), 79; I Edward VI, c. 3 (poor and vagabonds), 16, 63; 3 & 4 Edward VI, c. 16 (poor and vagabonds), 63; 2 & 3 Philip and Mary, c. 7 (selling of horses), 39; c. 9 (gaming), 105; 8 Eliz. c. 4 (pickpockets), 94–5, 109–10; 8 Eliz. c. 10 (gaming), 104; 14 Eliz. c. 5 (poor and vagabonds), 68–70; 18 Eliz. c. 3 (poor), 69–70; 31 Eliz. c. 12 (selling of horses), 39; 35 Eliz. cc. 3, 4 (vagrant soldiers), 71; 39 Eliz. c. 25 (highway robberies), 100; Poor Laws of 1597 and 1601, 17, 69, 72; 8 & 9 William III, c. 27, s. 15 (sanctuaries), 82.
Staundon, Stafford, vagabonds in, 159–60.
Stevenson, R. L., on Villon, 126.
Stews, Henry VIII's proclamation against, 148–9.
Stocks, *see* Punishments.
Stow Hundred, Cambridgeshire, vagabonds in, 161.
Stow, John, *Survey of London*, 84.
Stowe, Francis, gaming-house keeper, 165.
Strodevicer, William, Justice, 156.
Strutt, Joseph, *Sports and Pastimes*, 92, 109.
Strype, John, *Annals*, quoted, 4, 65–6, 154, 167; *Ecclesiastical Memorials*, quoted, 11, 24–5, 53–4.
Stubbes, Philip, *Anatomie of Abuses*, 137–8; on minstrels, 43–4.
Sturbridge Fair, vagabonds on way to, 150–1, 161.
Summer games, abuse of, 154.
Supplication of the Poore Commons, on rent raisings, 12; on uncharitableness of new clergy, 16.
Surrey, searches for vagabonds in, 150, 162.
Sussex, Earl of, Privy Council to, 64.
Swynerton, John, *alias* Vennet, gaming-house keeper, 105.
Symson, George, vagabond, 161.

Taker-up (in Barnard's Law), 89.
Tales and Quicke Answeres, 115.
Tale-tellers and spreaders of sedition, 52–5, 154.
Tarlton's Jests, 136.
Taverns, 111. *See also* Ale-houses.
Tenants, John Bayker on eviction of, 147.
Thieving, Parson Hyberdyne's sermon in praise of, 101–2.
Thomas, James, vagabond, 161.
Thomas, Richard, palliard, 151.
Thomas, William, palliard, 151.
Tinkers, 27, 42, 68, 170.
Toller, office of, 39.
Tomas, John, upright man, 151.
Tompson, William, and Jane his wife, vagabonds, 161.
Trevelyan, George Macaulay, *Age of Wycliffe*, quoted, 7–8.
Triplow Hundred, Cambridgeshire, vagabonds in, 161.
Turner, C. J. Ribton, *History of Vagrants and Vagrancy*, Preface, 102.

Upright men, 27–30, 117–18, 150–1.
Usury, 79.

Vagabonds, badges for, 61; boldness of, 169–73; customs in fourteenth and fifteenth centuries, 17, 21; legal definition of, 68–9; legal measures against, *see* Statutes, Punishments, Certificates, and Watches; menace to peace, 17, 53–4, 64; orders or ranks of, 27; ordinances for restraining, 140–2; passports for, *see* Passports and Licences.
Verser (in Conny-catching), 86–7, 89.
Versing Law, 86.
Viles, Edward, and F. J. Furnivall, *Rogues and Vagabonds of Shakespere's Youth*, 101–2, 122. *See also* Awdeley, Harman, and *Groundworke of Conny-catching*.
Villon, François, 126.
Vincent's Law, 86, 94.
Vinogradoff, P., *Villainage in England*, quoted, 7–8.
Vox Populi, Vox Dei, on merchants buying land, 13.

Walker, Gilbert, *see Manifest Detection.*
Walking Morts, 27.
Walsingham, Sir Francis, Lord Burghley to, 67.
Wantage, Berks., vagabond from, 151.
Watches and searches for vagabonds, 4, 64–7, 72, 152–62.
Weare and Aston, Stafford, vagabonds in, 159.
Webbe, William, 126.
Westfelde, James, and Joyce his wife, vagabonds, 161.
Wetherley Hundred, Cambridgeshire, vagabonds in, 161.
Whetstone, George, *Rocke of Regard*, 137; *Touchstone for the Time*, quoted, 79, 81, 99, mentioned, 137.
Whip-jacks, 27, 40.
Whipping, *see* Punishments.
Whittyngam, Timothy, endorsement on passport, 174.
Wicke, Alyce, vagabond, 161.
Wild rogues, 17, 27, 33.
Williams, John (*alias* Wyn), upright man, 151.
Wilson, F. P., on editions of *Belman of London*, 129.
Woodrofe, Sir Nicholas, Lord Mayor, on bowling alleys, 94, 106.
Wootton Hundred, Oxon., vagabonds in, 150.
Wootton, township, Stafford, vagabonds in, 160.
Worcester, searches for vagabonds in, 162.
Work-houses, *see* Punishments.
Wotton, keeper of school for pick-pockets, 95.
Wright, Thomas, *Queen Elizabeth and her Times*, quoted, 83, 95; *Songs and Ballads*, 47, 100.
Wright, Thomas, and Halliwell, J. O., *Reliquiae Antiquae*, 102.
Wyddon, Johannes, Justice, 156.
Wynstone, Joan, vagabond, and Thomas, her husband, 70.
Wynter, Ed., endorsement on passport, 174.

Yardley, John, gaming-house keeper, 165.
York, Archbishop of, Privy Council to, 64.
Yorkshire, *North Riding Records*, quoted, 110.

For Product Safety Concerns and Information please contact our EU representative GPSR@taylorandfrancis.com
Taylor & Francis Verlag GmbH, Kaufingerstraße 24, 80331 München, Germany

www.ingramcontent.com/pod-product-compliance
Lightning Source LLC
Chambersburg PA
CBHW071407100726
47908CB00004B/1090

* 9 7 8 1 1 3 8 0 1 0 8 3 3 *